THE BOOK OF
MURDER

THE BOOK OF
MURDER

Edited by

SEBASTIAN WOLFE

A LYLE STUART BOOK
Published by Carol Publishing Group

A Lyle Stuart Book
Published by Carol Publishing Group

Editorial Offices
600 Madison Avenue
New York, NY 10022

Sales & Distribution Offices
120 Enterprise Avenue
Secaucus, NJ 07094

Queries regarding rights and permissions should be addressed to: Carol Publishing Group,
600 Madison Avenue, New York, NY 10022.

First published in Great Britain by Xanadu Publications Ltd. This selection copyright © 1992 by Xanadu Publications Ltd. The copyright notice on pages 246-247 constitutes an extension of this page.

Manufactured in Great Britain.

Library of Congress Cataloging–in–Publication–Data

The Book of Murder/edited by Sebastian Wolfe.
    p.   cm.
    "A Lyle Stuart Book."
    ISBN 0-8184-0564-3
    1. Murder—United States—Case Studies. 2. Murder—
Great Britain—Case Studies. I. Wolfe, Sebastian.
HV6529.B66   1992   91-40045
364. 1'523—dc20   CIP

Contents

Foreword   vii

It Could Happen to Anyone . . .
    There's a Maniac Out There – *Kurt Vonnegut Jnr.*   3

Mind and Motive – Portrait of the Murderer
    Then It All Came Down – *Truman Capote*   15
    Dennis Nilsen – *Colin Wilson*   25
    Charlie Simpson's Apocalypse – *Joe Eszterhas*   38

Who Dunnit? – The Fascination of the Unsolved
    In The Grip of Murder – *Amanda Mitchison*   81
    The Devils of Nancy – *Patrick Marnham*   92
    Fiona Jones – *Brian Masters*   101

Rich, Famous – and Dead
    The Case of Claus Von Bulow – *Martin Amis*   111
    Brando: A Family Affair – *Clancy Sigal*   122
    Nightmare on Elm Drive – *Robert Rand*   131
    A 'Wronged' Woman's Fury – *Jay Robert Nash*   143

Farewell to the American Dream
    Some Dreamers of the Golden Dream – *Joan Didion*   171
    The Killings in Atlanta – *Martin Amis*   189

The Miscarriage of Justice
    Alice Crimmins – *Ann Jones*   203
    Edgar Smith – The Human Copperhead –
      Mary Higgins Clark   213
    Into a Thrilling Silence – *Christianna Brand*   224

Anyone Could do it . . .
    Perfect Murderers – *Pamela Smith*   239

Sources and Acknowledgements   246

Foreword

In his piece on the Menendez murders, Robert Rand mentions that they now feature in Graveline Tours of Hollywood, which 'for $30 will expose you to "100 years of death, sin and scandals." For three hours, camera-toting tourists ride in a long, black hearse for a visit to the dark side. The tour includes the house where Marilyn Monroe committed suicide and the hotel where John Belushi overdosed on cocaine and heroin.'

This book is itself a sort of Graveline tour of modern murder. It aims to show not only different varieties of murder – though it does do that – but also to demonstrate the different ways in which murder is thought and written about, from Martin Amis's cynical Englishman-abroad approach, via murder-as-news and first-person accounts by some of the best reporters of our times, to the more reflective approaches of Joan Didion and Christianna Brand.

It is a truism that murder fascinates. I hope that the multiple portrait of murder built up by this outstanding array of contributors (my thanks to them all) will prove to be more enlightening than some of the true-crime books currently on offer, and will contribute something to our understanding of this most interesting of subjects.

SEBASTIAN WOLFE
London, 1992

It Could Happen
to Anyone

KURT VONNEGUT JNR

There's a Maniac Out There

Jack the Ripper used to get compliments on the way he dissected the women he killed. 'It is stated that some anatomical skill seems to have been displayed in the way in which the lower part of the body was mutilated,' said the London *Times* of October 1, 1888.

Now Cape Cod has a mutilator. The pieces of four young women were found in February and March of this year – in shallow graves in Truro. Whoever did it was no artist with a knife. He chopped up the women with what the police guess was probably a brush hook or an ax.

It couldn't have taken too long to do.

At least two of the women, a schoolteacher and a college girl from Providence, Rhode Island, had been shot with a .22. Since the victims were cut into so many random chunks, only the murderer could make an informed guess as to what the actual causes of death might have been.

Stained rope was found at the foot of a tree near the graves. There was also rope around one of the victims' heads, and so on. The details are horrible and pitiful and sickening.

The police are sure they have the murderer. He is locked up now in the Barnstable County House of Correction – high on a hill, three blocks from here. He is a divorced Provincetown carpenter, a gentle, quiet six-footer – a twenty-four-year-old whose ex-wife, Avis, is prepared to testify that he is innocent. He married her after he got her pregnant – when she was only fourteen.

His name is Antone C. Costa. He is the father of three. 'He wanted a little girl,' says his wife. 'He was disappointed when the first child

3

was a boy. When the second was a boy he was really depressed. But when Nichole was born he was overjoyed. He adores Nichole.'

My nineteen-year-old daughter Edith knows Tony Costa. She met him during a crazy summer she spent on her own in Provincetown, knew him well enough to receive and decline an invitation he evidently extended to many girls: 'Come and see my marijuana patch.'

There really was a marijuana patch for girls to see, Tony claims, a modest one – two female plants not far from the graves.

Graffiti seen recently on the wall of a Truro Laundromat: 'Tony Costa digs girls.'

Sick joke told recently on Cape Cod: 'Tony Costa, with his mustache and long sideburns and granny glasses and dark turtleneck, walked into a Cadillac agency in Hyannis, and priced an El Dorado. "It'll cost you an arm and a leg," said the salesman. And Tony said, "It's a deal."'

An architect told me that joke. He laughed nervously afterward. And I sense that his giggling blankness in the face of horror is a reaction typical of most middle-class males on Cape Cod. The blankness is a failure to imagine why anybody would want to chop up four harmless girls.

Edmund Dinis, the district attorney who will personally present the Commonwealth's case against Costa, is troubled by this blankness too. 'In this instance,' he told us, 'we will not attempt to establish a motive. Who knows why anybody would do such a thing?'

Mr. Dinis was interested to hear that my daughter knew the accused. 'What does *she* say?' he asked. Dinis is a large, grave, earnest man who has never married. He is three years younger than I am, which makes him forty-four. He seemed bleakly open to any sort of information from young people which would allow him to understand this young people's crime.

'If Tony really is a murderer,' I said, 'it is a surprise to Edith. She never suspected it. Then again, she isn't very old. Up to now she has never suspected *that* much evil in anybody. She has always felt safe.'

'What did *she* say – exactly?' insisted Dinis. 'What were *her* words?'

'She said, and this was on the telephone from Iowa City, where she goes to school now: "If Tony is a murderer, then *anybody* could be a murderer." This was news to her.'

Mr. Dinis sat back, disappointed. What he had hoped to hear, I guess, was something enlightening about the culture of the hippies, who are so numerous in Provincetown – maybe talk about drugs.

I myself have spoken to a few young people about the Provincetown drug scene, have put this question to them: 'If the person who committed the Truro murders was high on something when he killed, what drug do you think he swallowed?' I remind them how crude the butchery was, how shallow the graves were, even though it would have been easy to dig deep tombs in the woodland floor, which was sand.

The answer, invariably: 'Speed.'

The Truro murders may not be speed murders, and Tony Costa may not have committed them – but he has had at least one really awful trip on speed. That was in San Francisco. He thought he was going to suffocate, and passed out. So he was admitted to the emergency room of a hospital.

I found out about that from Lester Allen, one of two Cape Codders I know who are writing books about the murders. Mr. Allen is a retired newspaperman who has seen seven executions – three of them in one night. They made him ill. He has been hired by the defense lawyers, two local men, to find out all he can that will help Tony's cause. Tony and his friends and relatives have talked to him copiously. He has 1,100 pages of transcribed conversations so far.

Nowhere in all those pages, he told me, is there the slightest hint of how or why the murders were done. Nobody can imagine.

After Tony was arrested, he was sent to Bridgewater State Hospital for observation. He was polite but uncommunicative. At one point, though, he asked to see the district attorney. He wanted to ask Mr. Dinis what he was doing about the murders on Cape Cod. He said this: 'There's a maniac loose out there.'

★   ★   ★

'Everybody closely related to the case has had some experience with drugs,' Lester Allen told me, 'except, of course, for the lawyers and police.' He finds the culture of the young in Provincetown so different from his own that he often sounds like an anthropologist far from home – among the Kwakiutls, say, or the Yukaghir.

Among the young, Hermann Hesse is thought to be a very great writer. Authority is despised because of its cruel stupidities in pot busts and slums and Vietnam. Pot and speed and LSD are easily available close to home – or *were*, anyway, until Tony got busted for murder. Participants in the culture commonly refer to themselves as 'freaks'.

Here is a question a Provincetown freak put to a straight person, a diffident attempt to find out how angry the straight community might be about the chopped-up women: 'Is this going to be bad for the freaks?'

Freaks are worth money to the businessman on the narrow streets of Provincetown. Thousands of tourists come in the summertime to gawk at them – and to gawk at all the shameless, happy homosexuals, and at the painters and the Portuguese fishermen too. I doubt that tourists seeing Tony around town last summer found him much of an entertainment. He was neat and clean – cleaner than almost anybody, in fact, since he took three showers a day.

Tony Costa has an ulcer, says Lester Allen.

When the bodies were found late last winter, tourists arrived off-season. Many brought kiddies and shovels and picnic lunches. They wanted to help *dig*. They were puzzled when park rangers and police and firemen found them disgusting.

Headline in the Cape Cod *Standard Times*, March 9, 1969: MORBID MAGNET DRAWS CROWDS TO TRURO GRAVES

Lester Allen assures me that an enterprising young businessman is now selling packaged sand from the grave sites for fifty cents a pound. Want some?

Here is who the pitiful victims were, in order of off-season death:

Sydney Monzon, eighteen, a local girl from Eastham, who disappeared around May 25, 1968. She was working for a Provincetown A&P, left her bike leaning against the store one day, was never seen again. Her sister thought she had gone to Europe with another girl. Bon voyage.

Susan Perry, seventeen, of Provincetown, who disappeared September 8 – after Labor Day. Her parents were divorced. Her father was a fisherman. Her parents never reported her missing, assumed that she had moved to another town. Bon voyage again. Hers was the first body found. It was identified by a ring – her mother's wedding band.

Patricia Walsh and Mary Ann Wysocki, both twenty-three, both of Providence, who came to Provincetown together on Friday, January 24 of this year – in Miss Walsh's pale-blue VW bug. They were on an off-season lark. If they knew Tony, they gave no sign of it when their landlady introduced them to him after they had checked into a rooming house for five dollars a night. Off-season rates are low.

Tony, divorced for about six months, was staying there too. He helped with their luggage. Who says chivalry is dead?

And Miss Walsh and Miss Wysocki vanished. Their empty car was spotted near the marijuana patch, then the car vanished too. Then bodies were found – not two, but four.

The missing car showed up in storage in Burlington, Vermont. It had been stored by Tony Costa, so they busted him for murder.

Evelyn Lawson, a Hyannis friend of mine, a columnist for the *Register*, a weekly paper, is also writing a book about the murders. With the help of Provincetown's Norman Mailer, she got a contract with World Publishing. New American Library made a lot of money with *The Boston Strangler*. Tony Curtis made a lot of money out of that one too.

The Strangler was another New England specialist in killing women, as opposed to men. Women are so easy to kill – so weak and friendly, so fond of new people and places, of dates. And what *symbols* they are.

Evelyn Lawson is a witchcraft buff. She is also a Provincetown expert, an exotic métier. The village at the fingertip of the Cape seems a passionate and foreign little port to most people farther up the arm. As almost everybody knows, Cape Cod *is* shaped like a human arm. Chatham is at the elbow, Falmouth and Cataumet and Buzzards Bay are in the armpit. I live atop the biceps. The murdered women were found at the wrist.

The 100 percent American Pilgrims anchored briefly off Provincetown, did some laundry, then hastened on to Plymouth. There are now Portuguese where they did their laundry, and New Yorkers, and God-knows-what-else up there. 'Many of the first settlers were pirates and mooncussers,' says Evelyn. 'Many were runaway witches who escaped from Salem.'

Here is what she wrote in her column after the district attorney held a sensational press conference about the bodies:

> As Dinis talked . . . I felt my skin prickle in dread and disgust. The place where the bodies had been found . . . was near an old cemetery, not far from a back dirt crossroad, the typical traditional site for the witches' Sabbath ceremonies. . . . Dinis indicated there was evidence of cannibalism.

Evelyn further on described Tony Costa's being taken off to jail, with his many friends watching.

> One of the long-haired men of this group [she wrote] got down on his knees in front of the prisoner and reached for and kissed his manacled hands, proclaiming loudly: 'Tony, we love you!'

The kissing of the manacled hands, incidentally, didn't really happen. Evelyn didn't see it, simply heard about it, as did I, from everywhere. It was such a typical thing for a freak to do, even if he didn't do it.

And the district attorney may have been stretching facts, too, when he mentioned cannibals. He also announced that some of the hearts were missing. The next day, the medical examiner, who should know, said the hearts were there.

The so-called news became so loud and gruesome that Costa's lawyers went to court about it, complained justly of publicity '. . . fraught with images of sexual perversions, mutilation, diabolic mischief and suggestions of occultism.' They asked a judge to stop the mouths of the prosecuting authorities. The judge complied.

So it is quiet now – except for a few tiny leaks.

★ ★ ★

You can meet people in bars sometimes who want to leak for money. Their brother-in-law knows a guard up at the jail who sees Costa every day – and so on. If I wanted to see the official color photographs of what was left of the women, I could probably get them from somebody – if I were willing to pay.

I might even be able to buy a piece of the rope Tony tied the girls up with – *after* the trial. Business is business, after all, and always has been. There is money to be made on the fringes of famous murders. For instance: *I* am being paid.

Murder is no novelty on Cape Cod – nor are multiple murders that reek of drugs. Back in the lemonade summer of good old 1901, a nurse named Jane Toppan murdered Alden P. Davis, his wife and his two daughters with morphine and atropine. This was in lovely Cataumet, about ten miles from here, where windmills sometimes still ground grain.

Leonard Wood, commander of the swashbuckling Rough Riders in the Spanish-American War, was vacationing there at the time. The President was McKinley, who was about to be shot. It might be argued that Jane Toppan was, in her own way, responding to the corporate greed and the militarism and the murderousness and corruption of her times. If so, she certainly responded in a great big way. She confessed not only to the Davis murders, but to twenty-seven others besides.

She died in a crazyhouse in 1938. That is surely where multiple murderers belong – in a crazyhouse.

Jane Toppan was an orphan who never could find out who her parents were. Tony Costa, on the other hand, knows all about his parents, and about shoals of other affectionate relatives. His father was a hero off New Guinea in the Second World War. He saved another sailor who was drowning. Then he banged his head on a coral outcrop and died. Tony has a newspaper clipping about this, proudly shows it around.

His father's life was insured for $10,000. Part of this treasure was put in trust for Tony by his mother, who remarried after a while. She still lives in Provincetown. When Tony was only thirteen, he was keeping books and handling business correspondence and making out the income tax for his stepfather, a mason.

How straight can you be?

Tony has an intelligence quotient of 121.

Tony and his ex-wife used to be Catholics. They aren't any-more. Avis said the other day, 'We both believe in reincarnation, psychedelia, and God in nature.'

She divorced him a year ago June, charging him with '. . . cruel and abusive treatment'. This is a customary accusation, even among timid souls, in divorce actions in the Commonwealth.

Reporters who talk to Provincetown freaks about Tony often hear him spoken of in the past tense – as though he were long gone, would never return. They resent the gory advance publicity.

They want one thing very much for Tony: a fair trial.

Is it possible that Tony was framed? In early 1968 he did one of the most suicidal things a young drug-dabbler can do: He told the local police that so-and-so was selling dope. So-and-So was busted. There was a certain amount of tribal justice in this: So-and-so was from out of town.

But who would chop up and bury four nice girls to frame one small canary?

Tony was a spoiled little boy, one hears. He was never punished for anything.

In his closet in the rooming house where he helped Patricia Walsh and Mary Ann Wysocki with their luggage, police found a coil of stained rope.

Young women in America will continue to look for love and excitement in places that are as dangerous as hell. I salute them for their optimism and their nerve.

I remember now my own daughter's summer in Provincetown, where she was supposedly studying painting with oils. After that summer, she told me and her mother about a young man who would inform her from time to time that he wanted to kill her – and would. She didn't bother the police with this. It was a joke, she supposed – like inviting somebody to come see a marijuana patch.

When Tony was arrested, I called her up in Iowa City, and I said, 'Edith – that guy who kept saying he was going to kill you: was his name Tony Costa?'

'No, no,' she said. 'Tony wouldn't say anything like that. Tony wasn't the one.'

Then I told her about Tony Costa's arrest.

Mind and Motive –
Portrait of the Murderer

TRUMAN CAPOTE

Then It All Came Down

Scene: A cell in a maximum-security cell block at San Quentin prison in California. The cell is furnished with a single cot, and its permanent occupant, Robert Beausoleil, and his visitor are required to sit on it in rather cramped positions. The cell is neat, uncluttered; a well-waxed guitar stands in one corner. But it is late on a winter afternoon, and in the air lingers a chill, even a hint of mist, as though fog from San Francisco Bay had infiltrated the prison itself.

Despite the chill, Beausoleil is shirtless, wearing only a pair of prison-issue denim trousers, and it is clear that he is satisfied with his appearance, his body particularly, which is lithe, feline, in well-toned shape considering that he has been incarcerated more than a decade. His chest and arms are a panorama of tattooed emblems: feisty dragons, coiled chrysanthemums, uncoiled serpents. He is thought by some to be exceptionally good-looking; he is, but in a rather hustlerish camp-macho style. Not surprisingly, he worked as an actor as a child and appeared in several Hollywood films; later, as a very young man, he was for a while the protégé of Kenneth Anger, the experimental film-maker (*Scorpio Rising*) and author (*Hollywood Babylon*); indeed, Anger cast him in the title role of *Lucifer Rising*, an unfinished film.

Robert Beausoleil, who is now thirty-one, is the real mystery figure of the Charles Manson cult; more to the point – and it's a point that has never been clearly brought forth in accounts of that tribe – he is the key to the mystery of the homicidal escapades of the so-called Manson family, notably the Sharon Tate–Lo Bianco murders.

It all began with the murder of Gary Hinman, a middle-aged professional musician who had befriended various members of the

Manson brethren and who, unfortunately for him, lived alone in a small isolated house in Topanga Canyon, Los Angeles County. Hinman had been tied up and tortured for several days (among other indignities, one of his ears had been severed) before his throat had been mercifully and lastingly slashed. When Hinman's body, bloated and abuzz with August flies, was discovered, police found bloody graffiti on the walls of his modest house ('Death to Pigs!') – graffiti similar to the sort soon to be found in the households of Miss Tate and Mr. and Mrs. Lo Bianco.

However, just a few days prior to the Tate–Lo Bianco slayings, Robert Beausoleil, caught driving a car that had been the property of the victim, was under arrest and in jail, accused of having murdered the helpless Mr. Hinman. It was then that Manson and his chums, in the hopes of freeing Beausoleil, conceived the notion of committing a series of homicides similar to the Hinman affair; if Beausoleil was still incarcerated at the time of these killings, then how could he be guilty of the Hinman atrocity? Or so the Manson brood reasoned. That is to say, it was out of devotion to 'Bobby' Beausoleil that Tex Watson and those cutthroat young ladies, Susan Atkins, Patricia Krenwinkel, Leslie Van Hooten, sallied forth on their satanic errands.

RB: Strange. Beausoleil. That's French. My name is French. It means Beautiful Sun. Fuck. Nobody sees much sun inside this resort. Listen to the foghorns. Like train whistles. Moan, moan. And they're worse in the summer. Maybe it must be there's more fog in summer than in winter. Weather. Fuck it, I'm not going anywhere. But just listen. Moan, moan. So what've you been up to today?

TC: Just around. Had a little talk with Sirhan.

RB (laughs): Sirhan *B.* Sirhan. I knew him when they had me up on the Row. He's a sick guy. He don't belong here. He ought to be in Atascadero. Want some gum? Yeah, well, you seem to know your way around here pretty good. I was watching you out on the yard. I was surprised the warden lets you walk around the yard by yourself. Somebody might cut you.

TC: Why?

RB: For the hell of it. But you've been here a lot, huh? Some of the guys were telling me.

TC: Maybe half a dozen times on different research projects.

RB: There's just one thing here I've never seen. But I'd like to see that little apple-green room. When they railroaded me on that Hinman deal and I got the death sentence, well, they had me up on the Row a good spell. Right up to when the court abolished the death penalty. So I used to wonder about the little green room.

TC: Actually, it's more like three rooms.

RB: I thought it was a little round room with a sort of glass-sealed igloo hut set in the center. With windows in the igloo so the witnesses standing outside can see the guys choking to death on that peach perfume.

TC: Yes, that's the gas-chamber room. But when the prisoner is brought down from Death Row he steps from the elevator directly into a 'holding' room that adjoins the witness room. There are two cells in this 'holding' room, two, in case it's a double execution. They're ordinary cells, just like this one, and the prisoner spends his last night there before his execution in the morning, reading, listening to the radio, playing cards with the guards. But the interesting thing I discovered was that there's a *third* room in this little suite. It's behind a closed door right next to the 'holding' cell. I just opened the door and walked in and none of the guards that were with me tried to stop me. And it was the most haunting room I've ever seen. Because you know what's in it? All the leftovers, all the paraphernalia that the different condemned men had had with them in the 'holding' cells. Books. Bibles and Western paperbacks and Erle Stanley Gardner, James Bond. Old brown newspapers. Some of them twenty years old. Unfinished crossword puzzles. Unfinished letters. Sweetheart snapshots. Dim, crumbling little Kodak children. Pathetic.

RB: You ever seen a guy gassed?

TC: Once. But he made it look like a lark. He was happy to go, he wanted to get it over with; he sat down in that chair like he was going to the dentist to have his teeth cleaned. But in Kansas, I saw two men hanged.

RB: Perry Smith? And what's his name – Dick Hickock? Well, once they hit the end of the rope, I guess they don't feel anything.

TC: So we're told. But after the drop, they go on living – fifteen, twenty minutes. Struggling. Gasping for breath, the body still battling for life. I couldn't help it, I vomited.

RB: Maybe you're not so cool, huh? You seem cool. So, did Sirhan beef about being kept in Special Security?

TC: Sort of. He's lonesome. He wants to mix with the other prisoners, join the general population.

RB: He don't know what's good for him. Outside, somebody'd snuff him for sure.

TC: Why?

RB: For the same reason he snuffed Kennedy. Recognition. Half the people who snuff people, that's what they want: recognition. Get their picture in the paper.

TC: That's not why you killed Gary Hinman.

RB: (Silence)

TC: That was because you and Manson wanted Hinman to give you money and his car, and when he wouldn't – well . . .

RB: (Silence)

TC: I was thinking. I know Sirhan, and I knew Robert Kennedy. I knew Lee Harvey Oswald, and I knew Jack Kennedy. The odds against that – one person knowing all four of those men – must be astounding.

RB: Oswald? You knew Oswald? Really?

TC: I met him in Moscow just after he defected. One night I was having dinner with a friend, an Italian newspaper correspondent, and when he came by to pick me up he asked me if I'd mind going with him first to talk to a young American defector, one Lee Harvey Oswald. Oswald was staying at the Metropole, an old Czarist hotel just off Kremlin Square. The Metropole has a big gloomy lobby full of shadows and dead palm trees. And there he was, sitting in the dark under a dead palm tree. Thin and pale, thin-lipped, starved-looking. He was wearing chinos and tennis shoes and a lumberjack shirt. And right away he was angry – he was grinding his teeth, and his eyes were jumping every which way. He was boiling over about everything: the American ambassador; the Russians – he was mad at them because they wouldn't let him stay in Moscow. We talked to him for about half an hour, and my Italian friend didn't think the guy was worth filing a story about. Just another paranoid hysteric; the Moscow woods were rampant with those. I never thought about him again, not until many years later. Not until after the assassination when I saw his picture flashed on television.

RB: Does that make you the only one that knew both of them, Oswald and Kennedy?

TC: No. There was an American girl, Priscilla Johnson. She worked for U.P. in Moscow. She knew Kennedy, and she met Oswald around the same time I did. But I can tell you something else almost as curious. About some of those people your friends murdered.

RB: (Silence)

TC: I knew them. At least, out of the five people killed in the Tate house that night, I knew four of them. I'd met Sharon Tate at the Cannes Film Festival. Jay Sebring cut my hair a couple of times. I'd had lunch once in San Francisco with Abigail Folger and her boyfriend, Frykowski. In other words, I'd known them independently of each other. And yet one night there they were, all gathered together in the same house waiting for your friends to arrive. Quite a coincidence.

RB (lights a cigarette; smiles): Know what I'd say? I'd say you're not such a lucky guy to know. Shit. Listen to that. Moan, moan. I'm cold. You cold?

TC: Why don't you put on your shirt?

RB: (Silence)

TC: It's odd about tattoos. I've talked to several hundred men convicted of homicide – multiple homicide, in most cases. The only common denominator I could find among them was tattoos. A good eighty percent of them were heavily tattooed. Richard Speck. York and Latham. Smith and Hickock.

RB: I'll put on my sweater.

TC: If you weren't here, if you could be anywhere you wanted to be, doing anything you wanted to do, where would you be and what would you be doing?

RB: Tripping. Out on my Honda chugging along the Coast road, the fast curves, the waves and the water, plenty of sun. Out of San Fran, headed Mendocino way, riding through the redwoods. I'd be making love. I'd be on the beach by a bonfire making love. I'd be making music and balling and sucking some great Acapulco weed and watching the sun go down. Throw some driftwood on the fire. Good gash, good hash, just tripping right along.

TC: You can get hash in here.

RB: And everything else. Any kind of dope – for a price. There are dudes in here on everything but roller skates.

TC: Is that what your life was like before you were arrested? Just tripping? Didn't you ever have a job?

RB: Once in a while. I played guitar in a couple of bars.

TC: I understand you were quite a cocksman. The ruler of a virtual seraglio. How many children have you fathered?

RB: (Silence – but shrugs, grins, smokes)

TC: I'm surprised you have a guitar. Some prisons don't allow it because the strings can be detached and used as weapons. A garrote. How long have you been playing?

RB: Oh, since I was a kid. I was one of those Hollywood kids. I was in a couple of movies. But my folks were against it. They're real straight people. Anyway, I never cared about the acting part. I just wanted to write music and play it and sing.

TC: But what about the film you made with Kenneth Anger – *Lucifer Rising?*

RB: Yeah.

TC: How did you get along with Anger?

RB: Okay.

TC: Then why does Kenneth Anger wear a picture locket on a chain around his neck? On one side of the locket there is a picture of you; on the other there is an image of a frog with an inscription: 'Bobby Beausoleil changed into a frog by Kenneth Anger'. A voodoo amulet, so to say. A curse he put on you because you're supposed to have ripped him off. Left in the middle of the night with his car – and a few other things.

RB (narrowed eyes): Did he tell you that?

TC: No, I've never met him. But I was told it by a number of other people.

RB (reaches for guitar, tunes it, strums it, sings): 'This is my song, this is my song, this is my dark song, my dark song . . .' Everybody always wants to know how I got together with Manson. It was through our music. He plays some, too. One night I was driving around with a bunch of my ladies. Well, we came to this old roadhouse, beer place, with a lot of cars outside. So we went inside, and there was Charlie with some of his ladies. We all got to talking, played some together; the next day Charlie came to see me in my van, and we all, his people and my people, ended up camping out together. Brothers and sisters. A family.

TC: Did you see Manson as a leader? Did you feel influenced by him right away?

RB: Hell, no. He had his people, I had mine. If anybody was influenced, it was him. By me.

TC: Yes, he was attracted to you. Infatuated. Or so he says. You seem to have had that effect on a lot of people, men and women.

RB: Whatever happens, happens. It's all good.

TC: Do you consider killing innocent people a good thing?

RB: Who said they were innocent?

TC: Well, we'll return to that. But for now, what is your own sense of morality? How do you differentiate between good and bad?

RB: Good and bad? It's *all* good. If it happens, it's got to be good. Otherwise, it wouldn't be *happening*. It's just the way life flows. Moves together. I move with it. I don't question it.

TC: In other words, you don't question the act of murder. You consider it 'good' because it 'happens'. Justifiable.

RB: I have my own justice. I live by my own law, you know. I don't respect the laws of this society. Because society doesn't respect its own laws. I make my own laws and live by them. I have my own sense of justice.

TC: And what is your sense of justice?

RB: I believe that what goes around comes around. What goes up comes down. That's how life flows, and I flow with it.

TC: You're not making much sense – at least to me. And I don't think you're stupid. Let's try again. In your opinion, it's all right that Manson sent Tex Watson and those girls into that house to slaughter total strangers, innocent people –

RB: I said, who says they were innocent? They burned people on dope deals. Sharon Tate and that gang. They picked up kids on the Strip and took them home and whipped them. Made movies of it. Ask the cops; they found the movies. Not that they'd tell you the truth.

TC: The truth is, the Lo Biancos and Sharon Tate and her friends were killed to protect you. Their deaths were directly linked to the Gary Hinman murder.

RB: I hear you. I hear where you're coming from.

TC: Those were all imitations of the Hinman murder – to prove that you couldn't have killed Hinman. And thereby get you out of jail.

RB: To get me out of jail. (He nods, smiles, sighs – complimented) None of that came out at any of the trials. The girls got on the stand and tried to really tell how it all came down, but nobody would listen. People couldn't believe anything except what the media said. The media had them programmed to believe it all happened because we were out to start a race war. That it was mean niggers going around hurting all these good white folk. Only – it was like you say. The media, they called us a 'family'. And it was the only true thing they said. We *were* a family. We were mother, father, brother, sister, daughter, son. If a member of our family was in jeopardy, we didn't abandon that person. And so for the love of a brother, a brother who was in jail on a murder rap, all those killings came down.

TC: And you don't regret that?

RB: No. If my brothers and sisters did it, then it's good. Everything in life is good. It all flows. It's all good. It's all music.

TC: When you were up on Death Row, if you'd been forced to flow down to the gas chamber and whiff the peaches, would you have given that your stamp of approval?

RB: If that's how it came down. Everything that happens is good.

TC: War. Starving children. Pain. Cruelty. Blindness. Prisons. Desperation. Indifference. All good?

RB: What's that look you're giving me?

TC: Nothing. I was noticing how your face changes. One moment, with just the slightest shift of angle, you look so boyish, entirely innocent, a charmer. And then – well, one can see you as a sort of Forty-second Street Lucifer. Have you ever seen *Night Must Fall*? An old movie with Robert Montgomery? No? Well, it's about an impish, innocent-looking delightful young man who travels about the English countryside charming old ladies, then cutting off their heads and carrying the heads around with him in leather hat-boxes.

RB: So what's that got to do with me?

TC: I was thinking – if it was ever remade, if someone Americanized it, turned the Montgomery character into a young drifter with hazel eyes and a smoky voice, you'd be very good in the part.

RB: Are you trying to say I'm a psychopath? I'm not a nut. If I have to use violence, I'll use it, but I don't believe in killing.

TC: Then I must be deaf. Am I mistaken, or didn't you just tell me that it didn't matter what atrocity one person committed against another, it was good, all good?

RB: (Silence)

TC: Tell me, Bobby, how do you view yourself?

RB: As a convict.

TC: But beyond that.

RB: As a man. A *white* man. And everything a white man stands for.

TC: Yes, one of the guards told me you were the ringleader of the Aryan Brotherhood.

RB (hostile): What do *you* know about the Brotherhood?

TC: That it's composed of a bunch of hard-nosed white guys. That it's a somewhat fascist-minded fraternity. That it started in California, and has spread throughout the American prison system, north, south, east and west. That the prison authorities consider it a dangerous, troublemaking cult.

RB: A man has to defend himself. We're outnumbered. You got no idea how rough it is. We're all more scared of each other than we are of the pigs in here. You got to be on your toes every second if you don't want a shiv in your back. The blacks and Chicanos, they got their own gangs. The Indians, too; or I should say the 'Native Americans' – that's how these redskins call themselves – what a laugh! Yessir, *rough*. With all the racial tensions, politics, dope, gambling, and sex. The blacks really go for the young white kids. They like to shove those big black dicks up those tight white asses.

TC: Have you ever thought what you would do with your life if and when you were paroled out of here?

RB: That's a tunnel I don't see no end to. They'll never let Charlie go.

TC: I hope you're right, and I think you are. But it's very likely that you'll be paroled some day. Perhaps sooner than you imagine. Then what?

RB (strums guitar): I'd like to record some of my music. Get it played on the air.

TC: That was Perry Smith's dream. And Charlie Manson's, too. Maybe you fellows have more in common than mere tattoos.

RB: Just between us, Charlie doesn't have a whole lot of talent. (Strumming chords) 'This is my song, my dark song, my dark son.' I got my first guitar when I was eleven; I found it in my grandma's attic and taught myself to play it, and I've been nuts about music ever since. My grandma was a sweet woman, and her attic was my favorite place. I liked to lie up there and listen to the rain. Or hide up there when my dad came looking for me with his belt. Shit. You hear that? Moan, moan. It's enough to drive you crazy.

TC: Listen to me, Bobby. And answer carefully. Suppose, when you get out of here, somebody came to you – let's say Charlie – and asked you to commit an act of violence, kill a man, would you do it?

RB (after lighting another cigarette, after smoking it half through): I might. It depends. I never meant to . . . to . . . hurt Gary Hinman. But one thing happened. And another. And then it all came down.

TC: And it was all good.

RB: It was all good.

COLIN WILSON

Dennis Nilsen

On the evening of 8 February 1983, a drains maintenance engineer named Michael Cattran was asked to call at 23 Cranley Gardens, in Muswell Hill, north London, to find out why tenants had been unable to flush their toilets since the previous Saturday. Although Muswell Hill is known as a highly respectable area of London – it was once too expensive for anyone but the upper middle classes – No. 23 proved to be a rather shabby house, divided into flats. A tenant showed Cattran the manhole cover that led to the drainage system. When he removed it, he staggered back and came close to vomiting; the smell was unmistakably decaying flesh. And when he had climbed down the rungs into the cistern, Cattran discovered what was blocking the drain: masses of rotting meat, much of it white, like chicken flesh. Convinced this was human flesh, Cattran rang his supervisor, who decided to come and inspect it in the morning. When they arrived the following day, the drain had been cleared. And a female tenant told them she had heard footsteps going up and down the stairs for much of the night. The footsteps seemed to go up to the top flat, which was rented by a 37-year-old civil servant named Dennis Nilsen.

Closer search revealed that the drain was still not quite clear; there was a piece of flesh, six inches square, and some bones that resembled fingers. Detective Chief Inspector Peter Jay, of Hornsey CID, was waiting in the hallway of the house that evening when Dennis Nilsen walked in from his day at the office – a Jobcentre in Kentish Town. He told Nilsen he wanted to talk to him about the drains. Nilsen invited the policeman into his flat, and Jay's face wrinkled as he smelt the odour of decaying flesh. He told Nilsen that they had found human remains in the drain, and asked what had happened to the rest of the body. 'It's in there, in two plastic bags,' said Nilsen, pointing to a wardrode.

In the police car, the Chief Inspector asked Nilsen whether the remains came from one body or two. Calmly, without emotion, Nilsen said: 'There have been fifteen or sixteen altogether.'

At the police station, Nilsen – a tall man with metal rimmed glasses – seemed eager to talk. (In fact, he proved to be something of a compulsive talker, and his talk overflowed into a series of school exercise books in which he later wrote his story for the use of Brian Masters, a young writer who contacted him in prison.) He told police that he had murdered three men in the Cranley Gardens house – into which he moved in the autumn of 1981 – and twelve or thirteen at his previous address, 195 Melrose Avenue, Cricklewood.

The plastic bags from the Muswell Hill flat contained two severed heads, and a skull from which the flesh had been stripped – forensic examination revealed that it had been boiled. The bathroom contained the whole lower half of a torso, from the waist down, intact. The rest was in bags in the wardrobe and in the tea chest. At Melrose Avenue, thirteen days and nights of digging revealed many human bones, as well as a cheque book and pieces of clothing.

The self-confessed mass murderer – he seemed to take a certain pride in being 'Britain's biggest mass murderer' – was a Scot, born at Fraserburgh on 23 November 1945. His mother, born Betty Whyte, married a Norwegian soldier named Olav Nilsen in 1942. It was not a happy marriage; Olav was seldom at home, and was drunk a great deal; they were divorced seven years after their marriage. In 1954, Mrs. Nilsen married again and became Betty Scott. Dennis grew up in the house of his grandmother and grandfather, and was immensely attached to his grandfather, Andrew Whyte, who became a father substitute. When Nilsen was seven, his grandfather died, and his mother took Dennis in to see the corpse. This seems to have been a traumatic experience; in his prison notes he declares 'My troubles started there.' The death of his grandfather was such a blow that it caused his own emotional death, according to Nilsen. Not long after this, someone killed the two pigeons he kept in an air raid shelter, another severe shock. His mother's remarriage when he was nine had the effect of making him even more of a loner.

With his mother's second marriage, the family moved to Strichen, not far from Fraserburgh, and Nilsen lived there until August 1961, when he enlisted in the army. As a child, he was quiet and withdrawn, and read a great deal; he also developed some artistic skill. He and his elder brother Olav – two years his senior – never got on together, but he seems to have been fond of his younger sister, Sylvia, and to have been on good terms with the daughters of his mother's second marriage. There was more than a touch of Scots puritanism in the home – for example, his mother insisted that the children should change their clothes in the privacy of the bedroom or bathroom; for the boys and girls to glimpse one another in a state of undress would have been thought indecent. Nilsen loved birds and animals, using them as an outlet for an emotional warmth that would otherwise have remained unexpressed. At school, he was well behaved and shy. Discipline seems to have appealed to him, and as soon as he was old enough, he joined the local army cadets, and was delighted with the uniform. He was still a few months under sixteen when he joined the army. Three years later, he became a cook. He was in Aden, then at Sharjah, on the Persian Gulf, then in Cyprus, then Berlin. He remained a loner, befriending animals, reading and writing poetry, avoiding close relationships. Photographs of the time show him as a good-looking young man with a sensitive mouth and an almost feminine lower lip, full and sensuous. He even considered marriage at one point, but was too shy to propose.

He spent twelve years in the army, until 1972. Then he went to London, and became a policeman. But it was not the kind of life he enjoyed. As an army cook he had been able to come and go much as he pleased, get drunk when he liked – which was fairly frequently – and feel part of an organisation. Being a policeman was altogether more restrictive. He was older than most of the other probationers, and inclined to talk down to them – Nilsen seems to have been an obsessive talker. There was an attitude of intolerance about homosexuals – although his colleagues were unaware of his leanings – which made him irritable. He enjoyed the uniform and the authority, but otherwise felt like a fish out of water. After only eleven months, he resigned from the force. The station at which he had spent much of his time – Kilburn – later became a search headquarters when the Cricklewood house was being investigated.

His next job was as a security guard, working for the Department of the Environment, mainly patrolling government buildings. That was also unsatisfactory. He became a clerical officer for the Manpower Services Commission, and his duties included interviewing job applicants. He was always immaculately dressed, and was regarded as an efficient officer. The Jobcentre was in Denmark Street, in Soho, close to Leicester Square, and he became aware of the immense number of down-and-outs and homosexuals who sleep rough in central London. It seems possible that this job was the disastrous turning point in Nilsen's life, the point at which temptation was placed under his nose.

In 1975, Nilsen was living in Teignmouth Road, Willesden, and there was a curious episode when a young man went to the police and alleged that Nilsen had attacked him in the flat there; Nilsen denied it, and no further action seems to have been taken.

It was while living in Teignmouth Road that Nilsen met a young man – ten years his junior – named David Gallichan, and when Gallichan said he was looking for a flat, suggested that they should share. Because Teignmouth Road was too small, the two of them looked for a larger place, and found the flat in Melrose Avenue, into which they moved in November 1975. Gallichan insists that there was no homosexual relation with Nilsen, and this is believable; many heterosexual young men were later to accept Nilsen's offer of a bed for the night, and he would make no advances, or accept a simple 'No' without resentment. Nilsen was certainly not a 'sex maniac' in the sense of a Dean Corll or John Gacy. The drive behind the later killings appears to have been a combination of loneliness and a morbid obsession with death.

The loneliness seems to have been assuaged by the relationship with Gallichan. It was, in many ways, a domestic situation. They shared the cooking; Gallichan did some gardening. They acquired a dog – a bitch called Bleep – and took her for walks on Sundays. They also took in a stray cat. Nilsen had a strong protective streak about stray animals, as well as about human waifs and strays. He was far more dominant than Gallichan, and was inclined to hold forth at length, usually on political subjects – his views were strongly left wing, and Mrs. Thatcher seems to have been one of his detestations. Gallichan found a job as a railway porter. For Nilsen, Christmas

1976 was unusual in that he celebrated the festivity like any normal householder, with a Christmas tree, a turkey and seasonal booze. If they had continued to live together, it seems fairly certain that Nilsen would never have become a killer. It seems clear that, whatever Gallichan's feelings, Nilsen was strongly attached to him, and the relationship provided him with a kind of emotional stability that he had always wanted.

So it came as a severe shock when, in May 1977, Gallichan announced that he was leaving. He had a craving to live in the country, and had been offered a job by an antique dealer. Nilsen was furious but, as usual, his fury showed itself as a cold and highly controlled rage. 'It was as though I had insulted him, and he wanted me to go immediately,' said Gallichan. Nilsen felt rejected, and it may have aroused neuroses that had been latent since childhood. For Nilsen, self-assertion and self-esteem, were immensely important. To be 'deserted' by someone he had always dominated seemed the ultimate insult. He became cold and dismissive. When he and Gallichan met for a drink six months after the separation, Gallichan offered his address, and Nilsen said he didn't want it.

It was after this that the killings began. Nilsen was drinking heavily – he had always spent much of his spare time in pubs. Towards the end of December 1978, he picked up a young Irish labourer in the Cricklewood Arms, and they went back to his flat and continued drinking. Nilsen wanted the young man to stay with him over the New Year, but apparently the Irishman had other plans. In the notes he later wrote for Brian Masters, Nilsen gives as his motive for this first killing that he was lonely and wanted to spare himself the pain of separation. In another 'confession', he also implies that he has no memory of the actual killing – that he woke in the morning 'and found I had a corpse on my hands'. Nilsen strangled him in his sleep with a tie. Then he undressed the body, and carefully washed it, a ritual he observed after all his killings.

What happened then? This may be something we shall never know. As incredible as it sounds, Nilsen kept the corpse in his flat from late December 1978 until August 1979. He placed it under the floorboards, now once more fully clothed. He denied that there were any acts of necrophily with the corpses, and in view of his frankness about other details of the murders, this could well be true. Eight months later, on 11 August 1979, he removed the body, which had been encased in two plastic bags, and noted that there was little decomposition. He built a large bonfire at the bottom of the garden (of which he now had exclusive use), took his unnamed victim down to it, and burned the corpse together with a quantity of rubber, to cover the smell.

Nilsen's first reaction to his discovery that he had committed murder was – according to his own account – panic; he was convinced that he would be arrested the same day. When no one called him to account, he found it almost unbelievable.

Three months after burning his first victim, Nilsen picked up a young Chinaman in the Salisbury pub, and took him back to his flat. Nilsen claims the Chinaman offered sex, but that he did not want it. The Chinaman offered to tie him up; Nilsen made a counter-offer, and was allowed to tie the Chinaman's legs with a tie. Then he placed another tie around the man's neck and tried to strangle him. The man broke free and threw a brass candlestick at his attacker. Then he rushed off and told the police what had happened. When the police arrived, Nilsen told them that the Chinaman was trying to 'rip him off', and, to his astonishment, they accepted his explanation. He had expected to be arrested.

The next murder victim was a 23-year-old Canadian called Kenneth James Ockenden, who had completed a technical training course and was taking a holiday before starting his career. He had been staying with an uncle and aunt in Carshalton after touring the Lake District. He was not a homosexual, and it was pure bad luck that he got into conversation with Nilsen in the Princess Louise in High Holborn around 3 December 1979. They went back to Nilsen's flat, ate ham, eggs and chips, and bought £20 worth of alcohol. Ockendon watched television, then listened to rock music on Nilsen's hi-fi system. Then he sat listening to music wearing earphones, watching television at the same time. This may have been what cost him his life; Nilsen liked to talk, and probably felt 'rejected'. 'I thought bloody good guest this . . .' And sometime after midnight, while Ockendon was still wearing the headphones, he strangled him with a flex. Ockendon was so drunk that he put up no struggle. And Nilsen was also so drunk that after the murder, he sat down, put on the headphones, and went on playing music for hours. When he tried to put the body under the floorboards the next day, rigor mortis had set in and it was impossible. He had to wait until the rigor had passed. Later, he dissected the body. Ockendon had large quantities of Canadian money in his moneybelt, but Nilsen tore this up. The rigorous Scottish upbringing would not have allowed him to steal.

The murder made Ockendon's family frantic; his parents came to England to search for him. It was only much later that Nilsen became aware of the misery his casual murders had caused.

In May 1980, Nilsen picked up a 16-year-old butcher named Martyn Duffey, and they went 'on the piss'. The next morning, says Nilsen, Duffey was dead on his floor. He put the body under the floorboards, beside Kenneth Ockendon. By now, he says, he was resigned to the notion that the killings would happen again. There are moments in the confessions when it sounds as if, like so many killers, Nilsen felt he was being taken over by a kind of Mr. Hyde personality.

Sometime between July and September 1980 – Nilsen is not sure of the date – a 26-year-old Scot named Billy Sutherland spent an evening drinking with Nilsen around West End pubs, and went back with him to Melrose Avenue. Sometime that night, he strangled Sutherland with his tie. After leaving the body around for two days, he placed it under the floorboards. Sutherland was in many ways typical of Nilsen's victims. He had been in trouble with the police in Scotland, and served time in jail. His girlfriend had given birth to a baby in 1977 and came to live with him in London. He was unable to find work, and she returned to Scotland. When Billy found work, he asked her to return to London and marry him, but she disliked the metropolis. When he stopped writing to her, she experienced a sad conviction that she would never see him again.

The next victim was a Mexican or Filipino, who was picked up in the Salisbury a few months after the last murder. Says Nilsen, 'I can't remember the details. It's academic. I must have put his body under the floorboards.' Nilsen kept chunks of the bodies in a wooden garden shed, enclosing them in a kind of makeshift tomb of bricks; he sprayed the inside of the shed daily with disinfectant.

Nilsen's accounts of the murders are repetitive, and make them sound almost mechanical. The next victim – soon after number five – was another Irishman, a building worker. 'My impression was that I strangled him.' Number seven was an undernourished down-and-out he picked up in a shop doorway on the corner of Charing Cross Road and Oxford Street. Nilsen took him home, gave him a meal, then watched him fall asleep. Nilsen then got drunk on Bacardi and 'experienced some kind of a high'. He got out a tie, went up behind the sleeping man, who was in an armchair, and strangled him; the man did not struggle. This man 'was so thin that I didn't want to look at him', so he was wrapped in plastic and burned on a bonfire in one piece. Nilsen burned many other decomposing fragments from the brick shed at the same time.

Nilsen could remember almost nothing of number eight, killed soon after the previous one ('this was a period of intense activity'). He later took the body from under the floorboards and cut it into three pieces, then put it back again; it was burned one year later.

Victim nine was picked up in the Golden Lion in Dean Street, a Scot of about 18 years of age, with short fair hair. 'I remember sitting on top of him and strangling him.'

Victim ten Nilsen refers to simply as 'this guy', a 'Billy Sutherland type'. He found him dead in the morning, and placed the corpse under the floorboards, to join two intact bodies and one dismembered body.

Victim eleven was a skinhead with a London accent, who boasted how tough he was. When he was in a drunken sleep in Nilsen's armchair, a substance like vomit dribbling from his mouth, Nilsen strangled him, then went to bed. The youth had many tattoos, including a line of dots around his neck with the inscription: 'Cut here.' Nilsen did just that when dismembering him. In May 1981, Nilsen had to have yet another body-burning session in the garden.

Victim twelve was picked up in September 1981. He was sitting with his back against the garden wall, and complained that he could not use his legs. Nilsen took him indoors and sent for an ambulance, which took the man to hospital. The next day, the man made the mistake of coming back. Nilsen cooked him a meal, and the man drank Bacardi, together with his pills. He became unconscious, and Nilsen strangled him. He claims that his motive was to save trouble: 'I didn't want to deal with ambulance men asking silly questions.'

The man's name was Malcolm Barlow, and he was the last victim to die at Melrose Avenue. Nilsen was a sitting tenant, and when offered an 'incentive payment' of £1,000 to leave the flat, he accepted, and had one final large bonfire to cover his tracks.

In October 1981, Nilsen moved into the upstairs flat in Cranley Gardens. Seven weeks later, on 25 November he met a homosexual student, Paul Nobbs, in the Golden Lion in Soho, and took him back to his flat. Nobbs remembers nothing until he woke up the next morning with a hangover. He went into University College Hospital for a check-up, and was told that the bruises on his throat indicated that someone had tried to strangle him. Nobbs decided not to take any action. Nilsen's own account is that as he was strangling Nobbs with a tie, he became aware of what he was doing, and tried to revive him by throwing a glass of water in his face.

The first victim to be killed in Muswell Hill was a man named John Howlett, and he gave Nilsen the hardest struggle of his murderous career. As Nilsen tried to strangle him, Howlett fought back hard; Nilsen had to strike his head against the headrest of the bed. He strangled him, then went to pacify the dog, which was barking; when he returned, Howlett was breathing again. Nilsen then drowned him in the bath. Then he placed the body in a cupboard, and went to work. Howlett had to be disposed of 'because a friend was coming to stay for a few days', so Nilsen hacked up the body in the bath and boiled chunks of it in a large pot (which has subsequently become an exhibit at Scotland Yard's Black Museum).

In May 1982, Nilsen picked up a homosexual revue artist named Carl Stottor, whose stage name was Khara Le Fox. Stottor was another 'one that got away'. Stottor met Nilsen in a pub called the Black Cap in Camden High Street, and returned to his flat. Nilsen offered him a number of very large whiskies, then gave him a sleeping bag, warning him that the zip was dangerous. In the early hours of the morning, Stottor woke up with the zip tightening around his throat. He asked, 'What are you doing?' and passed out. When he woke up he was in a bath of cold water, and Nilsen was pushing his head under. Then he woke again on the settee with the dog licking his face. Nilsen told him that he had almost choked on the 'dangerous zip', and that he had placed him in the cold bath to revive him. It seems clear that the killing urge had vanished before the murder was completed; Nilsen may well have anticipated something of the sort when he warned Stottor about the zip – providing himself with a kind of alibi. The next morning, Stottor went for a walk with Nilsen in the woods, and was suddenly struck a violent blow in the neck that knocked him to the ground. But Nilsen only jerked him to his feet and continued the walk. They parted with an agreement to meet again, but Stottor decided not to keep the appointment. He went to the police only after he read of Nilsen's arrest a year later.

Victim fourteen was a drunk Nilsen picked up in Shaftesbury Avenue. In the Cranley Gardens flat, the drunk fell asleep while he was eating an omelette. Nilsen claims to be unable to remember the actual killing. He removed the man's clothes and washed him in the bath; he left him there for two days. Then he dissected him, and boiled parts of the body, placing some of the bits in a tea chest, and others in a plastic sack. Other pieces he flushed down the toilet.

Victim fifteen – the last – was a drug addict whom Nilsen picked up in the George in Goslett Yard on 1 February 1983, eight days before his arrest. They sat in front of the television, while Nilsen drank whisky and lager and the man injected himself with drugs. Nilsen listened to the whole of the rock opera *Tommy*, then killed his guest – he claims to have no recollection of the murder, but later admitted to Brian Masters that he had.

For a few days, the body lay in the bedroom, with a blanket over it. Then Nilsen cut off the head and boiled it in the pot; while it was boiling, he went out with his dog to a pub. The next day, Saturday, tenants complained that the drains were blocked. Nilsen could easily have removed the blockage himself, and so avoided arrest; instead, he simply dismembered the body.

Mike Cattran, the Dyna-rod man, discovered the drain blocked with human flesh the following Tuesday. That night, Nilsen went out and tried to buy chicken to put down the drain, but could not get enough; so he simply removed the human flesh. Then, knowing that his arrest was imminent, he went and spent a perfectly normal day at work; no one noticed that he seemed in any way tense or distressed.

His trial began on 24 October 1983, in the same court where Peter Sutcliffe, the Yorkshire Ripper, had been tried two years earlier.

Nilsen was charged with six murders and two attempted murders, although he had confessed to fifteen murders and seven attempted ones. Nilsen gave the impression that he was thoroughly enjoying his 'moment of glory'. The defence pleaded diminished responsibility, and that the charge should be reduced to manslaughter. There was considerable discussion around the question: Mad or bad? Nilsen insisted that he was not mad, and this is the view that was eventually taken by the court. Nilsen's own theory was that he was a 'creative psychopath' who became a destructive psychopath under the influence of alcohol. At the root of his crimes, he said, was 'a sense of total social isolation and a desperate search for sexual identity'. Paul Nobbs and Carl Stottor both gave evidence against him, as did another 'one that got away', a Scots barman named Douglas Stewart, whom Nilsen had tried to kill at Melrose Avenue on 12 November 1980. After trying to strangle Stewart, and then threatening him with a carving knife, Nilsen had finally allowed him to go. Stewart went to the police, but Nilsen managed to convince them that he and Stewart had had a 'lovers' quarrel', and they decided not to pursue the matter.

The defence psychiatrist, Dr. James MacKeith, argued that Nilsen suffered from a severe personality disorder, due to lack of a father, the death of his grandfather, and loneliness. He also recounted how, at the age of ten, Nilsen had lost his footing when paddling in the sea and almost drowned. When he recovered consciousness, he was lying naked in the dunes with his wet clothes beside him and a sticky substance on his chest. He believed that he had been rescued by a nearby 16-year-old boy, who had then masturbated on him.

Later, according to Nilsen, he had acquired the habit of masturbating in front of a mirror with his body covered with talcum powder, to look like a corpse. He said that he powdered the bodies of his victims, and then looked at them – and himself – in the mirror. Another psychiatrist, Dr. Patrick Gallwey, said that Nilsen was suffering from the 'false self syndrome'.

On Friday 4 November 1983, Nilsen was found guilty of all murder charges by a jury vote of 10–2, and was sentenced to life imprisonment.

In prison, Nilsen met the gunman David Martin, for whom there had been a nationwide manhunt after the shooting of a policeman;

Martin was a bisexual transvestite, and Nilsen formed a powerful emotional attachment to him, although it is not clear how far Martin reciprocated. A girl who had sheltered Martin was charged with aiding and abetting him, and Nilsen is reported to have made an offer to reveal details of yet more murders if the police would stop their 'persecution' of the girl (who was subsequently sentenced to six months in jail). But it seems unlikely that the offer was genuine; Nilsen's painstakingly detailed confessions make it clear that he was not the kind of person to 'forget' several murders.

What general conclusions can be reached about Nilsen? The most obvious thing that emerges from accounts of those who knew him is his dominance; there can be no doubt that he belongs to the 'dominant five per cent'. Said one acquaintance: 'The only off-putting thing about him was his eyes. They can stare you out, and not many people can stare me out.' From his writings, it is also clear that he is a man with a fairly high IQ. Dominant and intelligent people urgently require some means by which they can express their dominance; they have an urge to be 'recognised', to be admired, to be accepted among equals. In this sense, Nilsen never seems to have met any equals. He undoubtedly put his finger on the root of his problem when he spoke of his 'total social isolation'. One of the notebooks he wrote for Brian Masters begins: 'I was always a loner.' A similar temperament seems to have led to the crimes of Ian Brady, the Moors murderer. And the loneliness leads to a sense of alienation and of contempt for other people – the kind that made Brady refer to them as 'insects'.

A powerful sex drive is also characteristic of most highly dominant individuals. When such a person lives in isolation, the result is likely to be a morbid build-up of sensuality that can explode into violence – like the Wisconsin necrophile Ed Gein who, in the late 1950s, dug up female corpses from graves, had sex with the bodies, and even made waistcoats from their skin. Nilsen's morbid obsession with corpses and death, combined with the sense of unreality that develops from isolation, would have been seen as a danger signal by any psychiatrist who could have interviewed him in the late 1970s.

An important determining factor was, of course, his homosexuality, and the fact that he was brought up in a small Scottish community where he had to conceal it. This is what may have caused him to enter the army at sixteen; it is certainly what made him leave his home to go to London when he came out of the army. Nilsen does not seems to have been exclusively homosexual; he told psychiatrists that he was excited by homosexual and 'normal' pornography, and that he had had sex with women as well as men. The early desire to marry shows that he recognised that one of his major problems was to find close contact with at least one other human being. He achieved this to some degree when living with Gallichan – only to experience an embittered sense of isolation and rejection when Gallichan left him to live with another man.

But the chief determining factor in the murders was undoubtedly the heavy drinking. It seems clear that drink acted as the catalyst that finally removed all inhibitions and allowed all his negative emotions – self-pity, resentment, irritation, contempt – to build up into an orgasm of violence.

The increasing casualness of the murders, and his increasing carelessness, suggest that his originally robust self-esteem was being undermined by self-contempt and a desire to 'make an end of it' by being caught. The same point emerges, in a less direct way, from an incident reported during his early days in custody. The prison chaplain is said to have suggested that Nilsen might like to come to chapel and ask forgiveness for his sins; Nilsen retorted: 'I'm a mass murderer, not a bloody hypocrite.' It is as if he had finally established some perverse sense of identity through this notion of being Britain's 'highest scoring' mass killer.

The final impression of Nilsen's life is of a man whose basic craving was to find himself, and who somehow drifted further and further away from this objective.

JOE ESZTERHAS

Charlie Simpson's Apocalypse

Right after the sun comes up, first thing folks do around Harrisonville, Missouri, is go up to the barn and see if the mare is still there. Horse-thieves drive around the gravel roads and brushy hills in tractor-trailers looking to rustle lazyboned nags. Then they grind them up into bags of meat jelly for the dogfood people. It's getting so that a man can't live in peace anywhere, not even on his own plot of land.

Harrisonville is 40 miles southeast of Kansas City along Interstate 71, just down the blacktop from the red-brick farmhouse where Harry S. Truman, haberdasher and President, was born. The little town is filled with weeping willows, alfalfa, Longhorn steer, and Black Whiteface cows. Life should be staid and bucolic, a slumbering leftover of what everyone who buys the $3.00 Wednesday-night Catfish Dinner at Scott's Bar B-Q calls Them Good Old Days. But it isn't like that anymore. There's always some botheration to afflict a man these days and if it isn't the horse-thieves or the velvetleaf that plagued the soybeans last year, then it's them vagrant tornadoes.

They call this lush area Twister Alley. Of all the woebegone acreage in America, Harrisonville and the fast-blink single-gas-station towns clustered about it – Peculiar, Lone Jack, Gunn City – attract more funnel clouds and 90 mph whirlwinds each hardluck year than anyplace else. The whirlwinds sweep down across greenbacked rows of wheat and corn, tottering power lines and flame onto dried haystacks – raising hell two or three times a season with the insurance rates and the little money a farming man has left after Uncle Sam takes his share. For some reason the land provokes these killer-storms and, out around a bonfire on a warm

38

spring night, a man can sit around with his Mail Pouch and wait for jagged strips of angry lightning to neon the wisteria and the hollyhock.

Except for the twisters, the horse-thieves and the velvetleaf, it is like any other tacky, jaundiced Southern town. It carries a weighty but atrophied Dixie tradition, having once been a proud link of the Confederacy, although it is not very far from the Kansas border-town where John Brown, saintly revolutionary murderer, launched his blood-bath a century ago. Its most famous citizen is a machinist named Jerry Binder, who won a ballyhooed $5000 suggestion award from Trans World Airlines for improving the turbine of the JT3D jet engine. Billy Quantrill's Civil War raiders once raped and ravaged here to historical acclaim and Harry 'Harricula' Truman, or just plan 'Harry S.' (as they say at Scott's Bar B-Q) visited here one Appreciation Day not long after he dropped the Aye-Tomic Bomb. Harry S. chewed saucy chicken wings on the courthouse steps and told the folks the White House was nothin' but a big white jail.

Harrisonville serves as Cass County's seat – population 4700 – and by 1980 will be only a few miles south of the exact demographic center of America. It will be at the very heart of the calcified Heartland, a patriotic footnote which pleases the town's flaccid watery-eyed mayor and dentist, Dr. M. O. Raine, to no end.

This spring the last snowfall was shoveled away on April Fool's Day and folks started getting ready for the summer: The Harrisonville Fire Department tested its six Civil Defense Air Raid-Tornado Warning sirens and even the 89-year-old Harrisonville Hotel, the oldest building in town, its roof damaged by generations of funnelclouds, got a homey face-lift. Its eroded brick was scraped and washed down. The Missouri Turkey Shoot Season was opening; the American Legion Building at 303 Pearl Street, a mausoleum of cigar butts, housed a nightly clap-happy gospel meeting – 'Do You Want to Be Saved?' – and the Peculiar Panthers knocked off the favored Harrisonville Wildcat basketball team 66–55. The Chamber of Commerce announced 'real-big, real-good' news – the long-delayed acquisition of a shiny new cherry-topped 1972 ambulance.

Less than a month later on a muggy thunderheaded warm day, Friday, April 21st, at 5.55 pm, the Civil Defense sirens let out a high-pitched scream that cut across the wheatfields for miles around. Folks hurried to their citizens' band radios to await emergency instructions.

They thought it was another goddamn tornado.

They couldn't understand the breathless disjointed words which G. M. Allen, town banker and the fire chief, garbled at his white-helmeted Civil Defense volunteers in the hamlets and hollows around town.

What in tarnation was G. M. talking about? 'Hippies . . . Killed two policemen . . . Dead . . . M-1 carbine . . . Blood all over the place . . . the Simpson boy . . . Come on into town . . . Bring your guns . . . There's more of 'em . . . Yo, a revolution.'

1 Charlie Simpson's mad-dog dance

On Friday, April, 21st:

Astronaut John W. Young leaped up off the moondust and exuberantly saluted the American flag. At North Carolina State University, a thousand kids danced around a hand-painted sign that said: NIXON'S MACHINE IS FALLING. In Lawrence, Kansas, 600 persons met in front of Strong Hall to plan an anti-war march.

At 5.55 pm on the town square in Harrisonville, Missouri, Charles Simpson, 24 years old, 6'3", 180 pounds, flowing shoulder-length gun-metal black hair, known to his friends as 'Ootney', leaped out of a red Volkswagen. He was an asthmatic who liked Henry David Thoreau and had eyes like razor slits. The car was driven by a friend, John Risner, 26, a pallid Navy veteran, the son of a former deputy sheriff, beer-bellied, wire-bearded, blue-jeaned, wearing a picaresque black felt English Derby hat. The car had a peace symbol on its windshield.

Charles Simpson jumped out of the car on Independence Avenue, less than a thousand feet across the street from the Allen Bank and Trust Company, a modernized plate-glass structure facing the courthouse. It was minutes away from closing. Simpson was a farmboy who grew up in the apple-knocker village of Holden, 24 miles away, the son of a totally disabled World War II combat veteran. He started walking south on Independence Avenue. He was wearing knee-popped bell-bottoms, a waist-length Army fatigue jacket, and yellowed dry-goods boots caked with mud and cowflop. He had high jutting cheekbones, a hooked and fist-kissed nose, a swarthy complexion, and uneven calcimine-white teeth. His eyes were coal-black and slanted. There was whipcord in his muscles but he looked a little funny when he suddenly crossed the street and started running.

As he loped across Independence onto Pearl Street, he reached under his patched Army jacket and took out an M-1 semi-automatic carbine with clip and over 140 rounds of ammunition. It was the same weapon which National Guardsmen used at Kent State University in 1970, killing four students and wounding nine. He had used the combat-regulation weapon in the fields around town with his friend Rise Risner, target-shooting overfed squirrels, moonlighting packrats, and non-returnable bottles of Budweiser beer.

On this Friday afternoon, as Charles Simpson reached for the M-1 under his fatigue jacket, he saw two brown-uniformed members of the Harrisonville Police Department – Donald Marler, 26, and Francis Wirt, 24, a Vietnam veteran, back from the war only four months, and a policeman less than a month. They were part of the department's foot-patrol, recently pressured by the town's businessmen to keep an ever-alert eye on the square. Both men were armed with holstered police-regulation .38s. Both men knew Simpson.

As Friday afternoon traffic backed up around the square – the shops were closing and each of the town square's four corners is red-lighted – Charles Simpson leaned into a crouch and aimed his semi-automatic carbine waist-high at the two policemen. They were less than 100 feet away. He fired a quick burst of bullets. The two policemen went down poleaxed. A lady 20 feet from the gunfire fainted and her car rammed into the Happiness-Is-Tastee-Freeze delivery truck in front of her.

Simpson ran toward the two policemen sprawled on the concrete. Both were moaning, bleeding badly, unable to return fire. He stood rigidly over both men, pointed the muzzle down over first one and then the other, and fired two more staccato bursts into their bodies at point-blank range. The bullets, made for warzones, ripped into and through the bodies. Patrolman Marler was hit twice in the chest, twice in the abdomen, and once in each hand. Wirt was shot twice in the abdomen and three times in the right arm. His elbow looked as if it had been fragged.

Simpson spinned, turning to the Allen Bank and Trust Company, and ran inside. He didn't say anything. He didn't aim the carbine at anyone. He pointed it willy-nilly toward a rear wall covered with advertising slogans – INVEST IN AMERICA, BUY U.S.SAVING BONDS – and fired again. Bullets ricocheted around the floor and walls, wounding two cashiers. Simpson turned again, ran outside, waving the rifle in front of him, and ran west on Pearl, heading toward the town's water tower – HI THERE! CLASS OF '69 – and the Cass County Sheriff's Office. He was a death-dealing whirligig. He had a shitfire grin on his face.

The sheriff's office is about a thousand feet west on Pearl Street from the Allen Bank. Across the street from it is the Capitol Cleaners, which hold a monopoly on the town's laundry trade, offers STARCH BARGAINS.

As Charles Simpson dashed from the bank to the sheriff's office down the narrow street, a 58-year-old man with boils on his neck named Orville T. Allen was getting out of his battered pick-up truck in front of the cleaners. He had operated a dry-cleaning store in nearby Garden City for 27 years and was there to pick up some part-time weekend laundry.

Charles Simpson saw Orville Allen across the street, a man in faded khaki pants he had never seen before, and aimed his carbine. The burst caught Allen in the chest. He dropped to the pavement, twisted on the ground, turned his bleeding chest to the sky, and clasped his hands in prayer. 'God,' he moaned. A trail of blood tricked across the street toward the sheriff's office.

Sheriff Bill Gough, 46, a hulking and slow-footed man, had just taken off his holstered .38 revolver and was sitting down reading that week's issue of the Democrat-Missourian. The paper had come out that noon and carried a front-page story about an 18-year-old Kansas kid the sheriff's deputies had arrested for possession of marijuana. Gough heard something rat-tat-tat outside his office as he scanned the paper, but he didn't think it was gunfire. He thought it was some fool beating a piece of tin with a stick. He went outside, unarmed, to see what all the commotion was about.

As he got outside, he saw Simpson coming toward him, the M-1 aimed head-high. He tried to duck but wasn't quite fast enough (although the savage reflex twist of his big body probably saved his life). He was hit in the right shoulder and the left leg but staggered inside his office. His wife, sitting at a desk, screamed. He knocked her to the floor, grabbed his revolver, and flung himself behind a desk with such force that his elbows were purple for weeks. Covered with his own blood, Sheriff Gough aimed the revolver at the door and waited for Simpson to open it. His hands shook. He was afraid he'd lose control and wildly pull the trigger before Simpson stuck his head inside.

But when he hit Gough in the Street, Simpson spinned around and, waving the gun wildly in the air, started trotting back toward the square. Allen's body lay a few feet away from him. Suddenly, in front of the Harrisonville Retirement Home, a dim gray-slab matchbox of a building across the street from Allen's bleeding body, he stopped. He bent down, put the carbine inside his mouth, sucked the barrel. He fired his last burst. He blew the top of his head off. His mad-dog dance was over.

He had fired more than 40 rounds. Four people were dead, three wounded. The town's shiny new Chamber of Commerce ambulance drove around the square and collected bodies. As the Civil Defense sirens screamed and G. M. Allen's volunteer firemen hosed down the bloodstains, gun-wielding deputies and policemen grabbed all the long-hairs around the square and took them to Bill Gough's jail.

2 The hippies, and G. M. Allen

All roads lead to the square, an editorial in J. W. Brown's shopping-news weekly, the Cass County Democrat-Missourian, once said with prophetic innocence. 'At least that's what it seems like to outsiders. The Square seems to us to be a big chunk out of the past, sitting in the middle of the present. The cobblestone streets, the old hotel and courthouse, are probably taken for granted by the townspeople.' Charles Ootney Simpson's fierce assault on the town square was the final escalation of a guerrilla war of raw nerves and icy glares. It was fought for control of a seemingly insignificant logistical area: courthouse steps, shrubbery encircling it, and sidewalks facing its entrances on Wall and Pearl Streets. To understand the fated intensity of this cornpone guerrilla war, one must understand the uniquely claustrophobic architecture of the square itself and its place in Harrisonville's rustic-schizoid tradition.

The courthouse anchors the square, surrounded on four sides by contrasting clapboard and imitation brick shops. It is the epicentre of a tight and walled-in rectangle decorated by butterflies and honeybees. The cobblestoned pavement on the four streets surrounding it – Wall to the south, Lexington to the east, Pearl to the north, Independence to the west – is chokingly narrow. It is less than 30 feet from the courthouse curb to any of the businesses on its sides. The streets were designed for horses and buggies, not delivery trucks. All the streets are one-way in a looping arc; you have to drive through Lexington and Pearl to get to Independence. Since the streets are so narrow, the shops on all sides – like South Side Prescriptions, Felix Hacker's Paint Supplies, Ballon's Dry Goods and Wright's Shoe Palace – are literally but steps away from whatever is happening around the courthouse. If someone sitting on the courthouse steps shouts an epithet – 'Off the pigs!' for example – the shout will echo dramatically, reverberating through the little stores where, in years past, only the cash registers made noise.

The courthouse was built in the first decade of the 20th century. It is red-brick, three stories tall, topped by a cupolaed belltower and a flagpole. The bells ring once a year – on the Fourth of July. The flagpole is bare; a new one splits the grass in front of the War Veterans statue and flies the flag 24 hours a day. The building sits atop a mound-like elevation exactly 16 steps above the neatly swept sidewalk. A black iron railing leads to the south side doors, which are flanked by four columnar greystone pillars. The elevation transforms the courthouse steps into a stage. If Old Lloyd Foster, for example, who ebulliently runs South Side Prescriptions, glances out his store window at the courthouse, he is looking up. The building is at the tip of his nose.

On the Wall Street Side of the courthouse there is a fixed metal sign that says: LEARN TO LEAD! ARMY NCO CANDIDATE SCHOOL. The same kind of sign on the Independence Street side in blue and red says: THE MARINE CORPS BUILDS MEN – 2735 B TROOP. Six feet of manicured grass and shrubbery surround the building on all sides. The clock atop the belltower is dead. It's been stuck for more than a decade. For some bizarre reason, the clock's hands paralyzed at different times – it is 2.20 to the south, 6.25 to the east, 1.20 to the west. The northern clock face has been removed – pigeons flutter there. A deeply carved inscription above the southern door says: A PUBLIC OFFICE IS A PUBLIC TRUST.

The courthouse steps and the town square have served for generations as a place of public lolling. Saturday-night hoedowns were celebrated there; its four streets were barricaded and strung with multi-colored lightbulbs. Three times a year there was a carnival. And gradually the town fathers – meaning the bankers, aldermen, and Chamber of Commerce officials (the mayor was always a yoyo) – accepted too that the courthouse steps and shrubbery served as a haven for grizzled lushes to gulp their pints of Missouri corn whiskey. Every small town has its drunks, but they always become harmless and somewhat valuable characters, walking examples to contrast with Godfearing lives. The old bullshit artists are happy enough just to be left alone. They exude alcohol and sour courtesy, never fuss anyone, and the judges and deputies avert their eyes and walk smugly past them to wood-paneled chambers where decanters of aged bourbon are kept out of sight.

In the late summer of 1971, the town drunks abandoned the courthouse steps and claimed they were being spooked out. The figures now lazing in the shade and dangling their legs were a bewildering new phenomenon and no one knew quite what to make of them. They were townie kids who had grown up around Cass County and played for the Harrisonville Wildcats, getting their first fifths of sourmash from tight-mouthed Old Lloyd Foster. But when Old Lloyd looked across at these homegrown kids now, they gave him a fright. They were different. They had changed. They were their own kids but . . . somehow they weren't their own kids anymore. They wore their hair long and untrimmed and grew chinbound moustaches and billowing beards. They wore all manners of beegum strawhats and cropduster clothes – always bluejeans and a lot of Army jackets, engineer's boots, and $2 teeny-shoes which Old Lloyd's son, Don, sold them at the Sears Country Catalog Store. They played riotous Frisbee in the middle of the street and collected wilted flowers in back of Vann's Florist Shop and decked themselves out with dead roses and carnations. They wore 'love crosses' around their necks from which Jesus' body had been blasphemously ripped away.

Some of the women who came in once a week to Connie's Beauty Salon said they called them filthy names and scratched their privates. Some of the policemen said they called them 'Pigs' face to face and were always talking about their godalmighty 'Civil Liberties'. Some of the businessmen claimed the one word they heard echoing around the square from morning 'til closing was a four-letter word they couldn't even repeat out aloud what with women and children in town. 'There was no doubt about it,' said 60-year old J. W. Brown, editor and publisher of the Democrat-Missourian, a flatulent pipe-smoking country gentleman. 'What we had here were our own hippies, settin' up there, raisin' hell, callin' our women names, drinkin' wine and smokin' some of that marijuana. I even heard they was right up there in the bushes havin' sexual intercourse. Yes sir, Sex-You-All intercourse. Now those old drunks who used to set up there, those old boys never did any of that.'

Sex-You-All debauchery 16 steps above ground level right at the nosetips of righteous town merchants is not what the new courthouse squatters had in mind. Not at all. They were there in the beginning because there was no other place to go. Where could you go in Harrisonville? – this small time place haunted by homilies, platitudes, and bushwah. Into Guido's Pizza Parlor? Well, maybe, but couldn't stay there too long. As time went by Win Allen, the kingpin, Rise Risner, Ootney Simpson, George Russell, Harry Miller and the Thompson Brothers hung around the square because it got to be an entertaining mock-serious game. They were liberating Harrisonville, Missouri, showing the Sho-Me State some puffed-up balls. They were fighting their revolution against people they had cowedly called 'Sir' all their teenage lives.

Beer-bellied Rise Risner and Gary Hale, a reedy and subdued James Taylor look-alike, went off to the Navy as cowlicked country boys and came back dazedly turned-on, rejecting everything around them. They were home but home sure as hell didn't feel like home.

Liberating Harrisonville meant a lot of mind-blowing. They soon found themselves romantic figures, idolized by some of the high school kids. They conducted hoohawing teach-ins in front of the

War-Vets statue as Legionnaires stood around on the sidewalk in their peaked caps and called it 'jackrollin' the blind'. They'd read selections from Abbie Hoffman, Timothy Leary and Bobby Seale in stentorian tones, lifting their voices to phrases like 'Off the pigs!' and 'Up against the wall, motherfucker!'

They had Dylan and Jimi Hendrix tapes in their cars and boomed 'Stone Free' and 'Lay Lady Lay' in the night. They smoked as much dope as was available and there was always more than enough. The Army had planted crops of hemp during World War II and five-foot high marijuana plants shadowed the wheatfields.

Snake-charmed, the high school kids started imitating them, of course, using words like 'motherfucker' and acting heavylidded in civics class just for the aggravation of it. The principal, an ex-Marine, freaked, naturally, and zeroed-in on the new villains at council meetings when the school budget was discussed and the vandalism dollar-damage was counted. Only the year before, the principal fired a matronly English teacher who made *Stranger in a Strange Land* required reading. The townspeople picked up the taboo; the lady was once seen going into a liquor store and the town's elders were soon saying she was fucking and sucking all the seniors in her classes.

So these plowboy hippies – who were convinced, perhaps from experience, that their elders still cornholed cows when they got horny – came to dominate the town's consciousness and its square. And of all the revolutionaries and sugartits cavorting around the square, two seemed the most frightening – the Simpson boy, who'd always rub his pecker when a woman went by, and The Nigger, one of the town's six blacks. Win Allen, 24, frail and bird-like, with bloodshot eyes and a habit of slurring his words, made no secret of the fact he was shanghaied into Uncle Sam's Army, went AWOL, and managed to con himself a dishonorable discharge. He was a Bad Nigger as opposed to his younger brother, Butch, 17, a walking bowling ball who played forward for the Harrisonville Wildcats scoring an average 15 points a game. Butch was a Good Nigger. But Win (short for Edwin) had an Afro popout hairdo and was always up there on the steps, holding hands with a white girl, talking about Love, and waving books like *The Fire Next Time* and *Do It!*

Every time one of Bill Davis' policemen or Bill Gough's deputies passed the square, Win Allen would cheerfully yell: 'Hey, here comes The Pigs.' He even spoke his special blackevil language, and pretty soon half the kids in the high school were using this garbled childrenese, not just ordinary hippie words the townspeople heard in television commercials but words they'd never heard before. Words like 'bro' and 'gritting down' (eating) and 'Crib' and 'P-ing down' (sexual intercourse) and 'bogosity' (anything he disagreed with). But the single phrase which all the kids were using was just gibberish for anything that Win liked. When Win liked something as much as he liked P-ing down, he said, 'Most ricky-tick.' 'Most ricky-tick' was being heard all over town. A high school senior even used it in an essay on 'The Prospect of Marriage.' The townspeople would go home at night, after having to endure the raucous courthouse shenanigans all day, and their own kids would say bogosity and gritting down and most ricky-tick.

Some action clearly had to be taken. G. M. Allen, fire-chief, got up at a special Chamber of Commerce meeting and said with hawkshaw eloquence: 'I'm an American, damn it, and I'm proud to be an American and I don't go for all this hangin' the flag upside-down stuff.'

G. M. Allen had another reason for urging civic action, a pocketbook reason. Rise Risner and Charles Simpson and Win Allen and the rest of that pestiferous crew had become an economic menace. Business was off all over town, from the Capot Department Store to alderman Luke Scavuzzo's grocery. Some of the people who shuffled in to make their monthly mortgage payments to G. M. Allen's bank told him they were afraid to come into town. The hippies. The hippies were scaring business away. Harrisonville just couldn't sit around and let itself get overrun, G. M. Allen said.

The aldermen agreed that action had become a matter of local survival, although one of them, sucking his teeth, pointed out alternatives – 'Don't stretch the blanket, now, G. M.' – explaining the financial setback. There was a nationwide economic crisis and wage-price freeze and 11 miles down Interstate 71 one of those deluxe glass and chromium shopping centers, calling itself Truman Corners, had just opened up. Maybe folks were shopping there.

'Maybe so,' G. M. Allen told the tooth-sucker, 'but they'd be leavin' their money here if it weren't for them hippies.' And the

Chamber of Commerce spring offensive, to recapture the town square for the old drunks, was under way.

3 *The battle of the town square*

Actually, the aldermen had two offensives to mount at the same time, and they were both G. M. Allen's hardnosed command: Operation Hippie and Operation Tornado.

To facilitate the war against tornadoes, G. M. Allen thought it would be a civic coup if the Fire-Fighters Association of Missouri – tornado-watchers of the entire state – held their annual convention in Harrisonville. The aldermen, perhaps contemplating the weekend revenue from 500 firefighters and their wives, gratefully applauded G. M.'s boosterism. G. M. lined the convention up for Friday, April 21st. There would be a tornado committee meeting Saturday morning and a brass-band parade Saturday afternoon. Doris' House of Charm announced it would offer a 'Fireladies' Shampoo Special' for its beehive-headed lady tourists. As a further step, G. M. ran off hundreds of emergency doomsday leaflets and distributed them in the stores around the square. His directive began: 'When a tornado is spotted in the Harrisonville area, six sirens around the *city* will sound a long *blast* for three minutes. Our air-raid emergency *bombing warning* differs from a storm warning by sounding an up-and-down warbling *blast* rather than a long continuing *blast*. BE ALERT, G. M. ALLEN, FIRE CHIEF.'

To facilitate the offensive against hippies, G. M. figured it was necessary that everyone in town understand the critical nature of the crisis. He arranged with the Kiwanis Club to import a 'drug addict expert'. The 'drug addict expert' was Robert Williams, the police chief from Grandview. Chief Williams, a man of profound second-hand insight, heard about drugs and hippies all the time from his police friends in Kansas City.

'It's approaching a crisis stage,' he told the Kiwanians. 'Police can't even eliminate the problem. We've got to wake up and take a hard stand. What we've got to do is stand up and inject some old-fashioned moral values before all our young fall victim to those older marauders who prey on them.' The Harrisonville Community Betterment Council appointed a Drug-Abuse Committee.

Late at night on March 23rd, G. M. Allen, a delegation of town
businessmen and members of the city council met with police
officials at G. M.'s Citizens National Bank on Wall Street. A list
of crimes the hippies were suspected of was compiled. Someone
broke into the courthouse one night by forcing open a window and
crept up three flights to the belltower. Nothing was damaged, or
stolen, but three marijuana cigarette butts were found on the floor.
Several merchants claimed to have received anonymous threatening
phone calls. The caller always used the word 'motherfucker' and
threatened 'torching'. In nearby Archie, a carload of the hippies –
Risner, Simpson, Win Allen – were seen driving through and that
same day bomb threats were reported at the Archie State Bank and
the Archie Elementary School. And they all knew, G. M. Allen
scowlingly said, about the obstruction of traffic in the square.

The mobilization meeting agreed on some immediate meas-
ures. The shrubbery around the courthouse would be trimmed
so there couldn't be anymore sexual intercourse going on up there.
Superwatted bright lights, the kind used in urban high-crime areas,
would be erected around the square. Chief Davis promised a new
foot patrol, two of his nine men acting as roving beatmen, walking
in circles around the square 12 hours a day. A list of city ordinances
– 'Ordinances, man,' Win Allen would say, 'dig?' – was drawn up
for city council approval.

'Vulgar, profane, or indecent' language in public was punishable
by a $500 fine or 60 days in the county jail or both. Picketing and
parades were illegal unless authorized by the city attorney or Chief
Davis. And the topper, a declaration of virtual martial law: any
assembly of three or more persons in the town square was declared
an illegal assembly punishable by a $1000 fine.

G. M. Allen, the little man with bifocals and Alfred E. Newman
haircut that stopped a full inch above his red-veined ears, was happy
as a clam. He had a responsibility as fire chief and Civil Defense
coordinator and he intended to live up to it. 'You listen to TV, it
used to be cowboys and Indians, now it's "Kill the Cops," ' he'd
say. He was a World War II combat veteran who'd raised four
decent law-abiding kids and, even though his youngest daughter
had gone to school with Risner and Win Allen and had liked them,
even though she was 'a little bit oversold on Civil Rights', G. M.

Allen was convinced that what they'd decided in his bank that night was for the betterment not only of Harrisonville but of America too. 'If they don't believe in America,' he told the meeting, 'they should get the hell out.'

Hours after the anti-hippie-frisbee-promiscuity meeting ended, a 30-pound slab of concrete was tossed through the $495 plate-glass window fronting G. M. Allen's bank. He sputtered down half a block to see J. W. Brown at the Democrat-Missourian and ordered a boldset black-bordered ad. He was petrified with emotion. The Citizens National Bank was offering a $500 reward for 'information leading to the arrest and conviction of the person or persons who maliciously broke our window.'

For Rise Risner, Gary Hale, Win Allen, and Ootney Simpson, the 'shit coming down from the black sky' was a routine part of 'life in the Hick City.'

During the second week of April, as the footpatrols made ten minute reconnaisance sorties around the square, Win Allen came up with what he told Charles Simpson was 'Dee-Vine Inspiration'. Saturday, the 22nd, would be a national day of protest against the War in Vietnam. Win Allen decided he was going to organize Harrisonville's own anti-war march, a ragamuffin parade of cow-dunged kids screaming anti-imperialist slogans right under the Harrisonville brownshirts' noses. On Wednesday, April 19th, Win Allen and Ootney Simpson, friendly, grinning and wary, marched to the office of the city attorney and asked for a parade permit. They were told they didn't need one. 'We want somethin' in writin', not jive,' Win said. 'Go ahead and march,' the ferret-faced attorney smiled. But he'd give them no paper.

Charles Simpson, who trusted his instincts, was sure it was a booby-trap. 'The fuckers'll just bust us,' he said.

But Win's dreams escalated: The march would protest not only the war but the new town ordinances. Win would carry a sign that said DOWN WITH NIXON'S WAR and Ootney would carry a sign that said DOWN WITH G. M. ALLEN'S WAR.

'It's gonna be most ricky-tick,' Allen said.

'Crazy fuckin' niggers,' Simpson laughed.

G. M. Allen heard about the anti-war march The Nigger and the hippies were planning and went to see Chief Davis about it. He

wasn't going to have his big weekend spoiled. The Fire-Fighters
Association of Missouri would be in town and each of the forty
departments was going to bring its fire engine. At two o'clock
Saturday afternoon, after they finished caucusing over the tornadoes,
all those beautiful firetrucks, their sirens blasting, would be driven
around the square.

All the firefighters would be in their starched parade outfits and
the sidewalks would be filled with farmers who'd come into town
to see the firetrucks and would spend a few dollars while they
were there. It would be the biggest thing on the square since the
horseshoe-pitching contests they used to hold. G. M. Allen was
damned if he was going to let those spitshined firetrucks be set
upon by an army of crablice – hometown purvoids spewing filth,
contumely and treason.

The day after the haggling session with the city attorney was spent
coordinating Saturday's anti-war march. Win Allen and Ootney
Simpson discussed logistics with Rise, Gary Hale and the others –
and just about everyone agreed that it was a trap, the march certain
to end inside Sheriff Gough's roach-crawling jail. But no one cared.
They were high on their own daydreams. They'd march anyway.
Fuck it! The theatrical aspects were simply too tempting, too
ricky-tick to worry about the whip and thud of the brownshirts' new
Japanese billyclubs. They would march up Wall Street, gathering at
Guido's Pizza Place minutes before the firefighters' cortège was to
assemble near the Missouri Farm Association silo. The square would
be decked with bunting and the farmers would be tip-toeing around
the sidewalks waiting for the sirens when, led by Win Allen, led by
a nigger, the outlaws would shamble into that red-white-blue arena,
blowing minds, ruining everything, filling the square with clenched
fists and that eyeteeth-rattling cry: 'ONE TWO THREE FOUR WE
DON'T WANT YOUR FUCKIN' WAR!'

Word went out Thursday to the timid and sheepish 'Teeny Bros'
at the high school that all those interested in coming to jail for the
war should come down to the square after school and Win or Rise
or Ootney would give them the lowdown. A lot of kids showed up
because the Teeny Bros themselves were in the process of launching a
guerrilla action of their own, a pep-rally protest against Bar B-Q Ham

on Cheese Bun, Chicken Fried Steak-w-cream-gravy, and Cheese-burger Noodle Loaf. The Teeny Bros were actually threatening to take to the streets carrying big signs that said, NO MORE BAR B-Q HAM and waving the signs in front of the struck-dumb principal's office.

The Teeny Bros drifted into town that afternoon, keeping a paranoid eye out for the footpatrols, and organized themselves into action groups. The freshmen and sophomores – 'The Snots' – would all paint signs. The Snots were more than anxious to paint words like NO MORE WAR and demonstrate their militance. As the day wore on and the footpatrols told Chief Davis there seemed to be a pow-wow of outlaws in town, some of the outlaws got bored and went home while other part-time badmen slouched by, having heard about Win's Dee-Vine Inspiration from some squiggly-excited Teeny Bro. Charles Simpson went home around 4 o'clock to his Holden farm-house, reluctantly, going along with Win's fantasy, noting the ironies offered by the prospect of the two parades. The firefighters would be cheered because they drove shiny engines; the outlaws would go to jail because they dreamed of a warless world. 'Fuck it, they'll just bust us,' Ootney told Win Allen again. 'The whole shit just turns my teeth sour.' Ootney was tired. He was going home and he was going to mowdown some squirrels with his itty-bitty machine gun.

Harry Miller was one of the hangers-on who slouched by – about an hour after Ootney left to do battle with his doomed squirrels. Harry Miller drove into the square, nodding respectfully at the brownshirts, and then catfooted over to Rise and Win and some of the others. Everything looked cool; Win was chasing dragonflies.

Harry Miller is 24 years old and his jeans are too tight because there is a gut bulging at his belt. His face is puffy and there is a Brando-like sluggishness, a hovering petulance, about him. He doesn't rattle very easily and he looks like he can take care of himself – a veteran of bicep-building Army infantry training. He looks like a young Bill Haley. His hair is parted in the middle and shoved to the sides but his hair isn't long enough and sometimes a few hairs dangle into the forehead forming perfect curleycues.

It was near 5.30. The air was stuffed with heat and they were thirsty. Win and Rise and Gary Hale and Harry Miller and George Russell and John Thompson, their smart-cracking court-jester, walked across the street to Lloyd Foster's drug store. One of the

Teeny Bros whose mother had given him allowance money that day was sent inside to spend it on a carton of Pepsi-Cola.

'Here we are,' Harry Miller says, 'standin' not exactly under the drugs store's roof but out in front, near the Sears store, which Old Lloyd's boy, Don, runs. So we're waitin' for this kid to bring us some belly-wash. We are standin' right beside a mailbox which is public property. OK, out of nowhere, Don Foster drives up. Man, I seen that car comin', you could tell he was gonna do somethin', it was in his eyes, like he already knew he was gonna do this. OK, when he comes over there, there were already police parked on the other side of the square so we couldn't see 'em. Don Foster pulls up and he immediately jumps out and storms up. He's a big guy, wears nice cowboy boots, got sideburns, carries a pencil behind his ear, walks around wantin' everybody to cut down trees.

'So he storms up and he starts sayin', "Get away from my store." He says to Win, "Get your black ass out of here." So he starts violently throwin' shit and John Thompson says, "Listen, man, we pay taxes, I'm not gettin' out of here." So the Foster dude says, "Oh, you wanna fight, I'll fight you." So he pushes John with both hands, just pushes John and knocks him back. John weighs about 40 pounds less than the dude and most of his weight is stuck up on top of his head in his hair. Well, right then I caught a sense, I knew exactly what was gonna happen. OK, so then the old man, Old Lloyd, comes runnin' out and starts throwin' some bogus shit. I don't know what he was sayin', just yellin' and screamin'. Somehow Don Foster got a hold of John again and pushed him again.

'So I got in between them. I says to Foster, "Man, leave us alone, you're tryin' to fight us, you wanna get us throwed in jail, just leave our asses alone, we're not goin' to jail for you." And he says: "You get out of the way or I'll smack your ass, buddy." So I got out of the way and they got off by theirselves again and started pilin' at it. So his father, Old Lloyd, says: "By Gawd, I'm gonna call the police." So he walks back to his store, takes about four steps, doesn't even get to his phone, turns back out again watchin' them hassle, and here comes the police already turnin' the corner of the courthouse, boogeyin' from the courthouse. OK, after they turn the courthouse, it is like 50 feet before the first one gets to the fight – here's John and this Don Foster on the ground.

'The Foster dude is on top smackin' John beside the head. John's on the bottom gettin' ahold of him by the neck and ear. So here's Sgt. Jim Harris, the police officer, the other two pigs are behind him. OK, so Harris is 500 feet away, his club in the air, runnin' right at him. Here's John at the bottom with Foster on top of him. So Harris twists around and leans down so he can hit John even with Foster on top of him. He hits John in the shoulder and across the side of the face. Foster jumped off and the other two policemen picked up Foster's jacket for him. Foster got his jacket and walked up beside his old man and Old Lloyd starts pointin' at us, sayin' "Him and him and him" and points to Win and says: "The Nigger, The Nigger, The Nigger!" over and over again. So the pigs put us all under arrest for disturbin' the peace and start walkin' us over to the jail in the sheriff's office. Eight of us: Rise and Win and Gary Hale and John Thompson and George Russell and some of the others.

'On the way over there, one of the pigs decides he's gonna have a little fun with Win, so he sticks Win in the spine with his nightstick as hard as he can. When Win turns around the pig yells: "The Nigger's resistin' arrest." When we get to the jail we says, "We wanna file a complaint against the Foster dude for pushin' John," 'cause I mean, if they're gonna play that game on you, you might as well play it back on them. Chief Davis is there and the sheriff is there and Sgt. Jim Harris is there and they all said they didn't have the authority for us to file a complaint.

'So we had to just scream, say, *"Goddamnit, I want a damn report! I wanna file a complaint!"* I mean we had to scream for 15, 20 minutes. Finally they brought the city attorney down and he gives us two sheets of paper with nothin' on it except the top says MUNICIPAL COURT and some bogus printed stuff. But all they had us do was sign our names on it and that couldn't – man, when you file a complaint there's somethin' wrote down there and you read it, so that couldn't have been any real complaint form. OK, so that was just to get us to shut up. They throw us in jail and we knew it was bogus, we just took it as it was, $110 apiece. Then our Nigger, he was about the last one to come in. We hollered across the monkeybars over to his cell and we say – "Hey, Win' how we gonna get out?" And he says: "You know, I don't know, my bail's $1100."

'That jail is like the inside of a toilet bowl in a place where everybody's got the backdoor trots, know what I mean? We had to take a shit, well, we had to get a Look Magazine and tear the pages and put it on the seat it was so grubby. The shitter didn't really have a seat on it. They had some drunks over in the bullpen but they didn't say nothin' to us, nobody said nothin'.

'There were cops crawlin' out of the ratholes, we must have scared the pricks off of 'em. Here's eight guys in jail, right? They had six Highway Patrolmen there, they had five guys from the city police department, they had five guys from the sheriff's department, about seven policemen from the surrounding towns in the county.'

The chief of the fire department, Harry Miller says, 'Yes siree, G. M. Allen comes in all aflutter. Had this little red firehat on, Number 4. He says, "Did you get 'em all? Anybody hurt?" G. M. walks up and down real slow, looking' at us, looking' us over, lookin' us in the hair, and then he says: "Where's The Nigger? I got somethin' to say to The Nigger." '

Win Allen says: 'Dig, here I am, under arrest, in the clink. And this dude comes up to me in his little cute firehat and I expect him to say somethin' to me about what happened. So he comes up to me, gets really friendly allasudden and whispers, "Win, I want you to come see me tomorrow about that bill you owe me." He has the fuckin' audacity to come to me in the clink and talk to me about a loan my family owes him.'

A 16-year-old dimple-cheeked high school dropout named Robin Armstrong, a strangely vague and muted farmgirl whose father blew his brains out two years ago – 'I'm fed up with everything; people are just so fuckin' ignorant anymore' – was standing in front of the firetruck. All of her friends were in jail and she was screaming, 'You fuckin' pigs!' and the firemen were clutching their gleaming hatchets.

Her mother drove up then and Robin Armstrong, trembling with fear and fury, started running like a panicked jackrabbit down an alley.

'I saw it from the window,' Harry Miller says. 'Robin starts boogeyin' in between the jail and the rest home, she's gonna run down this old road because she don't want her mother to capture her ass. So the firetruck has a tank with 200 pounds of pressure in

it and you know that big hose they have – well, they open that big
hose up and hit Robin in the back with it and knocked her on the
ground. They skidded her face across the gravel.'

Mrs. Armstrong, 40ish and sagging but dressed as if she still knew
how to please, went up to her sobbing daughter whose mouth was
bleeding, and slapped her hard. She called her daughter a 'little hoor'
and then she sashayed back to the fireman who was still holding the
hose. And then she thanked him.

The outlaws spent their night in the crabseat wiping their asses
with Look Magazine and organizing their Saturday parade, wondering all the time how they'd make bail. One of their bros was up all
night, making phone calls and asking the parents to bail their kids
out and getting nowhere. They didn't want to spend their money.

As the sun came up, red-eyed Ootney Simpson had figured out
only one way to get his friends out of jail. At 11 o'clock Friday
morning, Ootney Simpson, smiling like a dimwit fool, worn down
to the edge, showed up at the sheriff's office. The outlaw looked the
sheriff in the eye and put $1500 in cash on the counter. It was his
life's savings, the bankroll for the plot of land he dreamed about.
His dream was dead. A sweat of fatigue caked his face.

'Simpson's the name,' the dreamer said, 'revolution's my game.
Free The People!'

4 Ootney Simpson's dream

They called him 'Ootney' because of a shrivelled old geezer named
Jimbob Jones who runs a carry-out grocery on Number Seven
Highway about four miles from town. Jimbob Jones took a weird
shine to Charles Simpson and whenever he and his friends would
wander in for their quarts of strawberry wine and sixpacks of beer,
Jimbob Jones would cackle: 'Well, looky here, Rootin' Tootin' Mr.
Simpson.' So Rise and Win called him 'Rootin' Tootin' ' at first, and
then 'Tootney' and gradually bastardized it into Ootney.

When Ootney showed up at the jail that Friday morning with his
packet of liberating $100 bills, Rise and Win weren't surprised. It
was just like Ootney – whenever something had to be done, Ootney
was there to do it. As his father says, 'All his life he'd go out there
in the hayfield and keep up with the best of 'em.'

He was of the hayfield and the barn, grew to manhood there and loved it. He lived in Holden, a town smaller and even more backwoods than Harrisonville, a place where the cemetery is still called 'the boneyard', a police station is a 'booby hutch', and the mentally retarded are 'cabbageheads.'

Ootney's father, Charles B. Simpson, is 53 years old and looks 75. He looks like a man who is going to die and has looked that way for years. He stands 5'9", weighs 102 pounds, sports a Hitler moustache, a red baseball cap, and a cardigan sweater which the moths have savoured for years. He walks with face-twisted pain and a briar walking stick with a vulcanized rubber tip, his leg having been broken into pieces by shrapnel on the African front in WWII. He raised three kids and supported a wife, did as much work as he could, pinched pennies, lived on hot dogs and beans, and waited for the disability checks. Four years ago his wife left him, and, except for Charles, the kids got married and left him too.

The corpse-faced veteran and his boy were never too close and it was only in the past year or so that they did much talking. It was hard for the old man to move and he spent long hours sitting in his rocking chair in the room with the calico rug and the big calendar filled with bone-chilling winter scenes. He sat in the rocking chair with his baseball cap pulled over his grey eyes, the cane draped over a thigh, staring at the walls and the dates on the calendar. The boy would come into the room, his long hippie hair in his face, squat down on the rug, and they would talk. They talked about the land and the crops and the war, about policemen and guns and steer, about Henry David Thoreau and Abbie Hoffman and General of the Army Douglas MacArthur. 'The boy expressed his feelings too plain,' the old man says. 'You can't do that.'

He was always telling the old man about Thoreau and although the old man didn't know too much about him, he listened. Thoreau lived by a pond and his friends were plants and animals. He didn't pay his taxes because he wouldn't support a government which practised slavery.

The old man didn't have too much to say about Henry David Thoreau but a man talking to his son has to have something to say, so he told the boy stories about General Douglas MacArthur. The old man admired General Douglas MacArthur as much as the boy admired Henry David Thoreau. So he told his stories. How General MacArthur won the Philippines from the Japs. How he could have beat the Chinese across the Yalu River if Harry S. Truman hadn't stopped him. How Harry S. Truman once wanted to be a piano player in a whorehouse and that's where he belonged. How General Douglas MacArthur should have been President and the country wouldn't be in the fix that it's in.

The old man didn't know exactly what the boy did all the time in Harrisonville. One time Al Wakeman, the Holden police chief, came over and told the old man to keep his damn boy the hell out of trouble. Charles was always roaring up and down the streets on his motorcycle. 'Disturbing the peace,' the chief said.

Ever since he was a kid, Ootney had a bad case of asthma. He'd have an attack and his nose and throat would swell up, shutting most of his breathing off. That kept him out of the Army. 'One shot-to-hell veteran's enough in the family,' the old man says. 'He went to high school but he didn't graduate – he had mumps real bad his senior year.' Rise Risner adds: 'He just farted school off. He said, "Man, you fuckers are just teachin' me a bunch of lies, you're not teachin' me anything I wanna learn." He finally got into a big hassle with a teacher one day, just never did go back. He was real intelligent, he could see through shit. He'd always tell you the truth, even if it hurt. He'd say, "Look you motherfucker, you've been layin' down some phony shit." '

When he dropped out of high school, Ootney Simpson went to work at a foundry in Kingsville. He was bored with the job but worked at it for more than a year. He said he wanted to save enough money to build himself the world's most souped-up drag racer. 'He saved up a bunch of money,' Rise says, 'and he got fired 'cause he took off one weekend. He told his supervisor, "Well, I'm not gonna be at work a few days." So he came back and they said, "Well, you know, since you didn't notify anybody that you were gonna be haulin' ass for these few days, you're fired." So he started thinkin'. He went back raisin' hell. He went right into the personnel department and said, "Look you motherfuckers, I did notify you. I want this changed. I still wanna be fired but I want this to read that I notified you and you let me go," and so after that he started collectin' unemployment.'

Ootney was spending a lot of time in those days with his younger brother, Elwyn, 23. 'Bubber' looks like a chunkier Ootney – the same coal-black eyes, hair as long and parted the same way down the middle. Bubber also worked at the foundry and, together, they were building their dream drag racer, blowing most of their money on new manifolds and sparkling chrome treasures.

Win Allen says, 'Like the cat and Bubber, they used to race their drags in Kansas City, makin' cars and doin' some racin' and then one day Bubber says, "We're just gettin' screwed, people are just takin' our money," and so they stopped racin'.' Rise adds: 'They put $10,000 into their dream car, Ootney was just floatin' along, searchin', he broke his back on that car. And they put ten grand into it and that's when Bubber got married and Bubber's wife said, "All right, you gotta get rid of that race car." Well, Ootney and Bubber were in a partnership, you know, he says to his wife, "OK, honey, I'll get rid of that racin' machine for you." And they sold the major part of it for $1000. So they took a $9000 beatin' right there.

'Bubber and Ootney broke bad after that, like Bubber's wife was always hasslin' Charles even. Bubber picked up all this pseudo-shit – shit like trailers and pickup trucks. Like he was working 16 hours a day in two different foundries. He worked at one in Harrisonville and he got off work there at 3.30 and he had to haul ass to punch in on time to get to the other foundry by 4. Just to feed his wife. Well, that's about when Ootney's head started to spin. He didn't give a fuck about the money, but he just knew that whatever he was searchin' for he couldn't find at a drag strip. That's when he started showin' up around the square with us and gettin' into readin'.

'After a while he started talkin' to us about Thoreau,' Rise says, 'and he said the only thing he and Thoreau differed on was women. Like Ootney man, he dug on women. I mean he didn't fall in love with 'em or get stuck on 'em he just dug to fuck, just P-down, man. He just loved it. He could fuck all night and he still couldn't have enough. He was crazy about it. But he said he had to have women around him all the time and that's the only thing he and Thoreau differed on because Thoreau says in one of his books, he goes, "A Woman would be a foe to my career," and Ootney goes, "Old Henry David, he must not have liked to fuck."'

'If Ootney felt like takin' off his clothes, he didn't give a fuck who was there, no, he'd take his clothes off and jump in a river and take a bath or somethin'. Nothin' embarrassed him, nothin' natural. And he was crazy-good with women. Any woman you ever seen in your life, Ootney Simpson could scheme her into the fuckin' bedroom. It was like he was above women, they owed it to him to fuck him. He was a peach, true beautifulness. He had this long black hair and he had this big beard for a while that was like right under his eyes, hair all over him, skinny. His eyes had a sparkle, the whites were real big, this hooked nose, a real freak, a freak all the way. When he let his beard grow, the only thing you could see was his eyes – just the whites of 'em, 'cause the rest of him was dark. Sometimes he wore great big baggy Army pants. He was a real killer, man.

'He was real weird in a lot of healthy ways. Like he hated telephones. He'd fuckin' drive 40 miles to tell a dude some little-ass thing rather than call him on the phone. He hated phones. He said, "If you can't look a man in the eyes when you're talkin' to him to tell him somethin', it ain't worth nothin'." He said, "Anything that you lay on somebody that you feel is a part of you, you gotta look them in the eyes, feel their soul right there." '

Harry Miller says, 'He was full of feelings, just look at him and you could tell. Just look at his face and you'd say, "Man, that guy there, he'll give me a dollar to get somethin' to eat," It seems like anytime somebody was depressed, he was around to help them out. His feelings were so sensitive, like you couldn't gross him out, but he had such feeling for his friends. He could stand 50 feet away and somebody would jump up on you and the vibes from Ootney would knock him down. If we were havin' a hassle in town, fuckin' Ootney would pick up the vibes 30 miles away.

'Some of his fuckin' acts you could never forget,' says Harry. 'One time an ex-Marine from out of Vietnam, been home three months, comes up to Pat and Ernie's Bar and drinks 15 beers and an old guy that we used to know in high school brings him over to Rise's house, we called it the Hippie House, and Ootney is there. So they come in and the Marine starts throwin' down shit about – "Gawddamn, you don't faaght for your country, ya oughta be shawt." I was in bed but Ootney heard it. This guy was gonna fire on Rise's ass. Ootney gets up stark nekid, walks in there, and comes down into shit like Rubin jumpin' a Chicago pig's ass or somethin'. And jumps all over the Marine. He looks the dude back about three steps and he grabs his prick and shakes it at the Marine and turns around and just shoots him the moon and then he gives him the finger. Man, that Marine, he ran away.'

Rise says, 'But he was always gettin' into some shit. Like there was a cloud over him and it rained pigs everytime Ootney made a move. Like even when he wanted to do nothin' but listen to a rock and roll concert. He dug Black Sabbath. Black Sabbath cost him $150. He went up to Kansas City to see 'em and, first, he lost his ticket so he had to buy another ticket when he got up there and there was another dude there, a friend of ours who didn't have any money and didn't have a ticket either. So Ootney bought him a ticket. Plus all the other shit, miscellaneous money bullshit from that day. Then after the concert he was takin' a piss outside, you know, in the street, and he got busted for his piss and it cost him $100.

'Another time he was with a dude and the dude was drivin' through Kingsville, the town where the foundry is, and the pigs busted this guy for a faulty exhaust or somethin'. And so they were sittin' in the pig's cruiser and they had to wait for the county pigs to get there and give them the ticket because those pigs were just flunkies or somethin'. So Ootney says to the pig, "Am I under arrest?" And the pig goes, "No, you're not under arrest." So Ootney gets the keys from the dude who drove the car and he just jumps in and speeds away at like 100 mph, makin' a U-turn and givin' the pigs the finger and everythin'. He keeps racin' on at 100 mph and the pigs put out a roadblock for him 'cause he's tearin' up the countryside. He stops off at his place in Holden and puts his brother Bubber's motorcycle helmet on and some gloves and comes roarin' back to Kingsville 'cause he knows the pigs must be after him. Well, he roars right around that roadblock at 100 mph and drives right back up to where his friend is sittin' in the pig's car. One of the pigs pulls out his gun and he was pointin' the gun and shakin' and sayin', "Get your ass over here, Simpson." And Ootney has on his helmet and gloves and he just freaked them out. 'Course he spent that night in jail too.'

Win Allen says, 'Like the time we were over in Holden and I was found guilty of contempt of court, that was an outasight scene right there. Like Rise and Ootney and I and his brother Bubber were there and Bubber had a traffic violation that he was found guilty of and he didn't do nothin' wrong. So when the judge tells him that he's guilty, seeing that I dig on freedom of speech, I say, "Bullshit" and the judge fined me. After a while the judge calls me up there and he says, "Do you know the prior defendant?" And I say, "Yeah, I know him, he's a citizen of America." So after a while one of the pigs says, "Boy, come along with me." "Boy" dig? And I was gonna slide with him you know. So Ootney says, "Stop the music, I'll pay the nigger's fine." They freaked out. They didn't know how to react. They smiled. And Ootney says, "We'll teach the nigger a lesson once we got him into his cage." Sheeit, we laughed all the way out of town. The judge musta thought Ootney was gonna cut my dick off and put it down my throat or somethin'.'

Over and over again, in the past few months, Charles Simpson told his friends about the plot of land that he was going to buy. 'I'm gonna live just like Thoreau,' he told them, 'just like old Henry David.' He'd laugh. 'Fuck all you longhaired hippie dudes.'

'He was gonna buy these 12 acres,' Rise says, 'aww, fuck, that's all he did for a couple of months – just dream about and plan his land. That's all he wanted and the fuckin' red-neck farmer told him, "Yeah, I'll sell it to you." It is a shitty piece of land but Ootney liked it, just rocks and all barren, real freak's land. The redneck tells him, "All we gotta do now is send off to the capital and get a few papers, make out the forms and everything" and so Charles, he had the money, he made all the arrangements, all he had to do is give the redneck the money and take over. It would be his land. He used to take us out there and we'd sit around on the rocks and smoke a few joints and Ootney would say, "Welcome to my land, this is my land." Well, somethin' happens and the redneck goes, "Aw, hell, I don't wanna sell it, there's too much red tape and I don't wanna sell it to no hippie anyway." That broke Ootney's back.'

On Wednesday, April 19th, Charles Simpson found out he couldn't have his barren rock-filled dreamworld. On Friday, the 21st, he withdrew his dream money to bail out his outlaw friends.

He went home and told his father he'd gotten the money from the bank and the shot-apart, ashen-faced old man sitting in the rocking chair said:

'What about the land?'

'It don't matter now.'

He reached into a closet and took out the M-1 semi-automatic carbine he had bought from a friend and said he was leaving for Harrisonville to get his friends out of jail.

'What you takin' the gun for?' the old man asked.

'Gonna shoot me some targets,' his boy said.

5 *The shit comes down from the sky*

'Simpson's my name, revolution's my game' didn't go over very well with Sheriff Bill Gough, but he didn't say anything about it. Those longhairs were making noise all morning and driving him batty. It would be a real pleasure to get them out of his jail. He'd take those friendly old juiceheads any day. It looked like a long weekend was cropping, what with the fire-fighters coming in that night and those crazy longhairs still talking – right in jail – about holding their protest march tomorrow.

So he didn't give the Simpson boy any trouble when he said, 'Free The People!' in a shade louder voice than the sheriff liked to hear in his office. He counted the stacks of bills and looked up just how much the bond was and told his deputy to start getting the longhairs out of their cells. Simpson had a big grin on his face, but he looked like he hadn't slept for weeks. The whites of his eyes were more red than white and his hands were skittery. When the Anderson boy came in, Simpson looked at him as if he were going to kill him and before the sheriff could do anything, Simpson had the Anderson boy by the lapels. 'Now listen here,' the sheriff said, 'you fight in here, both of you are gonna go to jail. I don't care how much money you got.'

Rise Risner had just been brought out of his cell and was standing next to the counter when John Anderson walked through the door. 'Anderson works at TWA with some computers, but he always made out that he was a friend of ours, rappin' to us and stuff. Anderson was there the night before, Thursday, when we were being taken to jail. Well, he had enough money on him to get some of us out and he didn't do it. He didn't want to spend his damn money. Ootney found out about it and when he saw Anderson he said, "Look you fucker, you're supposed to be a friend of ours. I don't want you to ever fuck me over like that." '

Ootney looked strungout to everyone. 'He was tired, yeah,' Win Allen says, 'but it was more. He was pissed off bad. I think the money had a lot to do with it – like, this was the money he was gonna buy his land with, dig, and it had turned into jail money. And he was pissed off about me, too. Like Charles really dug me. So when he found out my bond was so high, a thousand dollars more than the others, that really pissed him off bad. He told me after he got us out, he said, "Nigger, if your face was as white as my ass, you wouldn't be havin' all this shit." He goes, "These fuckin' crackers, they gonna lynch you up against a tree one night." Then he laughed. Ootney was like that. He was jolly and jivin' but the vibes were like off center, it was like there was a bomb inside his head.'

Standing around the watertower outside the jail, they decided it was more important than ever to stage their anti-war march. They went to George Russell's house, where Ootney 'leaned up against a wall and looked like he was gonna fall asleep.'

'You fuckin' jailbirds kept me up all night,' he said.

'Ootney lost his beauty sleep,' they hooted.

Rise says, 'We were real determined we had to be in that square the next day marchin' with those signs and screamin'. The bust was the best example of the kind of shit we had all felt. Old Lloyd just had to point his finger and say "Him and Him" and it was enough to send us all to the crabseat.'

Win Allen decided they'd hand pamphlets out Saturday as they marched around the square 'so the Truth can be put up on the walls.' Hasty essays had to be written about war, repression, racism, and the new town ordinances.

'Come on, Ootney,' Win said. 'Help us write some of this shit.'

'OK,' Simpson said. 'I'll write how much I like fuckin'.'

They raspberried him and threw him lip-smacking mock farts, figuring, as Rise says, 'We better leave old Ootney alone 'cause he looked pretty tired.' But Simpson brightened after a while and, before the meeting ended, offered to help after all. A friend of his in Holden had a mimeo-machine and he would take the essays over there and have them run off.

'Ootney's the production manager,' Rise yelled, and, as the others laughed, Simpson came alive, dancing around, his fists flying, shadow-boxing Rise's belly.

'Come on, come on,' he yelled, 'Charles Simpson's gonna take on all you creepo fuckers.'

Rise says, 'After a while we split up and Ootney took the stuff we wrote up and he was gonna take it over to Holden to the friend of his that had the machine. He asked me if I wanted to go over there with him and I said sure. We piled on into his 1952 Chevy. That was Ootney's batmobile. It was an old, fallin' apart car that made a lot of noise. He loved the car, said it was a real Hippie car. So we drove on and out and we got outside a place called Strasburg and the goddamn car blows up. So we sat there not believin' it, you know, here we are and I just got out of jail and Ootney didn't get any sleep and now the goddamn car blows. Well, we couldn't believe it. We were so pissed off we couldn't do nothin' but stand there and mumble and say fuck it and laugh.

'So we decided we were gonna hitchhike into Holden and then hitchhike back to Harrisonville. Ootney had his sleeping bag in the back and the M-1 but I didn't think nothin' of it 'cause he and I were always goin' target shootin' with the thing. So he puts the rifle into his sleepin' bag and we're standin' there hitchhikin' and the car's still smokin'. Then this dude from Harrisonville that we know comes along and picks us up. He's goin' back to Harrisonville so he drives us back there and we get my car. We drive into Holden and drop the shit off with the mimeo guy and then we had nothin' to do. So Ootney says, "Let's just take the gun and shoot some target practice." We were gonna spend the night out in the woods.'

As Charles Simpson and Rise Risner drove from Holden to Harrisonville late Friday afternoon, they talked. The radio was thumping and Rise only half-listened. The conversation was like a hundred others they had had. 'Nothing much,' Rise says, 'Just a lot of shit, rap talk. Maybe he was trying to tell me somethin', but if he did, maybe I wasn't listenin' that close.'

They talked about astrology. Ootney was a Pisces and as they speeded past the wheatfields and around the greening countryside, he talked to Rise about being a Pisces, about how he'd read a book that said he'd be nothing but a dreamer all his life and he'd never make any money. He said that this book said a Pisces was 'self-destructive'.

'So what does this mean?' Rise asked.

'I don't know,' Ootney laughed. 'Maybe it means I'm fucked up.'

'Yeah, it means you'll fuck yourself to death,' Rise said.

They talked, too, about dope. Ootney said he hadn't done any dope for some time and didn't want to do any dope, 'because everytime I smoke a joint I think about how everybody's fuckin' us over and I get all depressed and down.'

As Rise drove into town, he heard Charles Simpson say a few quiet sentences that would forever stick in his mind.

'Everytime I turn around, I'm gettin' fucked up somehow. My old man's dyin' and my old lady leaves and the pigs are always hasslin' me. Shit, I can't buy a piece of land even when I got the money. I can't drive around without my car blowin' up on me. It's always the same shit. Ain't it ever gonna stop?'

'When we got into town,' Rise says, 'We were stopped at the red light and the radio was playin' the new Stones song. I was beatin' on the dash and sayin' "Tumblin'-tumblin'," and all of a sudden Charles jumps out of the car and runs up the street. He was out of the car and halfway up the street before I even knew what happened. And I freaked right there. What the fuck was he doin'? He had the fuckin' gun. What the fuck was he runnin' up the street for with that fuckin' gun in his jacket?'

Rise panicked. He made a U-turn, stepped on the gas, and 'started boogeyin' out of Harrisonville, goin' the other direction.'

When Simpson jumped out of the car, Charles Hale, Gary's younger brother, saw him and ran up to him. He asked Simpson if he had seen Gary.

'He just shook his head,' Charles Hale says. 'The only thing I noticed was, he had this great big beautiful smile on his face.'

Gary Hale was on the other side of the square with Win Allen and some of the others. 'So all of a sudden,' Win says, 'we heard this *rat-tat-tat-tat-tat* like. And I said, "Hey Gary, that sound like some caps, man, like somebody bustin' some caps," and he said, "That's what it sounds like to me." We looked at one another and we got vibes instantly, we said, "Wait a minute, man, who's all here?" So then we see people startin' to run and we started boogeyin' and we heard these two pigs were shot. And then we heard, "There's a dirty hippie down there, dead," and we all – like we saw Charles' body – and like we couldn't identify with that blood.'

Rise drove around for a while, scared, and then, finally, drove back to the square. 'By the time I got there the two dead pigs had been taken off the street but Charles was still layin' in the street where he had shot himself, all covered up. All I could see was his boots stickin' out from under the plastic bag. My knees just kind of buckled and I was leaned up against this building and I just kind of went down. I just passed out on the sidewalk and I lay there a few seconds. There's this woman who runs the cleaners and I've known her all my life and she goes:

' "Well, he tried to shoot me, Johnny" and I didn't say anything.

' "Why did he try to shoot me, Johnny? I didn't do anythin' to him," and I just screamed, "Shut up, goddamn you, just shut up." '

G. M. Allen was about to leave the bank for the day when he saw people running and heard the police sirens. He ran over to the other side of the square, saw the people in front of the Allen Bank and Trust Company, and heard about the two policemen killed and the Simpson boy in the alley with his head blown off. He wasn't surprised. He expected something like this all along. He felt it in his bones. He turned and headed back to his office as fast as he could. He had to activate the Civil Defense sirens and get on the CB band and tell his volunteers to get into town. Gary Hale saw him rushing across the square and went up to him.

'You satisfied now?' Gary Hale said, 'You see what you've done?'

'Get out of my way, you little bastard,' G. M. Allen said.

He got to his office and as he pushed the button and the sirens started screaming, G. M. Allen had a comforting thought.

It was 6 o'clock and the firefighters coming for their convention would be checking into their motels. They'd have more than enough manpower in Harrisonville that night to handle whatever would happen. 500 firefighters from all across the State of Missouri would be there.

And right then G. M. Allen said a prayer. He thanked the Lord for giving him the wisdom to plan the convention for the right time – 'when the hippies started doing their killing.'

6 Life among the razorbacks

Firefighters watchdogged the street corners that night with hatchets and shotguns in their hands. The square was barricaded and police cruisers shadowed all the streets leading into town. A rifleman armed with a carbine very much like Charles Simpson's perched in the courthouse belltower, which commands an overview and a clear shot to every cranny of the square. Around 11 o'clock a thunderstorm rolled in with its gnarled bolts of field-lightning and the rain sent the gunmen scurrying to their cars.

About an hour after the shooting, Win Allen was walking across the square and a policeman went up to him and said, 'You got two of ours, now it's time we get some of you.' When a curfew was announced that night, Win and Rise and the others got out of town fast and decided to stay out.

'There was blood in those people's eyes,' Rise says, 'It was like we'd all pulled that trigger, not just Ootney. They couldn't do anything to Ootney because he was smart and blew his brains out, but we were still there. I was really scared. Those people were crazy. The pigs were lookin' at us like they could hardly wait to tickle their triggers. We knew that if any of us like made the smallest wrong move, one of us would be dead and they'd just make up some bogosity and get away with callin' it justifiable murder.'

G. M. Allen says, 'I was just happy we had all those men in town. Besides that, we had policemen come from as far as 50 miles away. We didn't know what to expect, but we were ready. We thought some of the hippies might wanna shoot some more policemen or some innocent people. It didn't make sense, not any of it, unless you figure the whole thing was planned and Simpson was just talked into killin' those policemen for the sake of their revolution.'

On Saturday, the 22nd, the national day of protest to end the Vietnam War, the curfew was lifted – but only during the day, until six o'clock that night. Some of the firefighters and policemen got some rest, but gunmen still patrolled all sides of the square and a rifleman still stood guard in the belltower, using binoculars to scan the alleys and the rooftops. Harrisonville's first anti-war protest was, naturally, canceled, and after only brief debate, the firefighters decided to cancel their parade.

'You mean we drove those trucks all the way out here for nothin'?' a firefighter asked G. M. Allen.

'It ain't fair, sure,' G. M. Allen said, 'but I figure a lot of people are gonna be too scared to come into town.'

He was wrong. Except for the longhairs, everyone within a hundred miles seemed to drive to Harrisonville that day. Traffic was backed up for half a mile, all the way to the FINA gas station, and people stood in clusters around the spots which had been pools of blood the day before.

In the course of florid descriptions, rumor fed upon rumor. The Simpson boy had eaten LSD just before he did his killing. The gun was traced to the Black Panther Party in Chicago. Simpson had belonged to a Communist hippie group in Kansas City. FBI men were coming into town. The longhairs had decided to kill the whole town, just like Charlie Manson had killed those people in California. They found some dynamite hidden in the MFA silo. The courthouse would be burned that night. The hippies had a list with the names of townspeople who were going to be killed on it. The National Guard was coming in.

And the pickup trucks carrying whole families of people who hardly ever came to town kept coming in on this day. Excited little kids stood by the Retirement Home's grey walls and asked, 'Is this where he killed himself, mommy?'

Saturday night, the gunman in the belltower saw something move on the roof of the Harrisonville Hotel. He yelled to the firefighters across the street and, within minutes, the hotel was surrounded by dozens of men carrying all sorts of weapons – from Colt .45s to mail-order Lee Harvey Oswald specials.

'Give yourself up,' a deputy's bullhorn echoed. 'You're surrounded.'

There was a crash on the pavement and an old wino who'd found a comfortable place for the night yelled, 'Don't shoot, don't shoot, I'm comin',' and miraculously no shots were fired. The doddering old drunk had dropped his pint of whiskey from the rooftop in pants-pissed fear and a deputy was assigned to sweep the glass off the street.

The burials were held Monday. Patrolman Donald Lee Marler's was the first. More than 50 policemen came to the funeral, some of them from Kansas City. Marler's open casket was in the church foyer but was closed minutes before his wife and family got there. The minister said, 'The fact that everyone dies is proof that all have sinned. But God says it does not end there. Our friend took the short cut home.' The city council held a meeting before Marler's funeral and voted to pay for both Marler's and Wirt's funerals. A reporter asked if the curfew would be extended and Mayor M. O. Raine, the dentist who'd once pulled one of Charles Simpson's teeth, said, 'This is a black day and I don't like to have too many decisions made when people are so emotional, so I'm not gonna make that decision now.'

Charles Simpson was buried last – in Chilhowee, a tiny town not far from Holden, where his grandparents are buried. Rise Risner, who was one of the pallbearers, says, 'There was a whole lot of people there. I think about half of 'em were pigs because a lot of 'em had cameras. This dude, this minister, like you could tell he wasn't too happy about havin' to bury Ootney. He was just goin' through the motions, like he was the one who got stuck with buryin' a sack of shit. That's what the vibe was, that's what his face said. The minister was talkin' about how Jesus died and all this shit and he didn't say one fuckin' thing about Charles. They didn't have anything about him even, they didn't say one fuckin' thing about his life. Nothin'. He was rappin' shit about fuckin' buryin' Jesus and "He rose" and all this shit. I thought he was talkin' about Charles for a long time until I figured out what he was talkin' about. John Thompson was singin' "Blowin' in the Wind" and we all chimed in.'

After the ceremony, as they were bringing the casket out of the church, in the glare of television cameras and wire service photographers, the pallbearers clenched their fists and held them to the sky, their other hand on the wooden box that had Charles

Simpson's body in it. 'We gave the power fist 'cause we figured that
would be a way of showin' everyone that Ootney was a brother,' Rise
says. 'No matter what kind of shit they were sayin' about him. He
was one of us. We did it 'cause we loved him.'

Some of the townspeople saw and others heard about the pallbearers' clenched fists and, at first, no one knew what to make of it.
But then G. M. Allen told Mayor Raine he heard it meant someone
else was going to die and Mayor Raine told some of the councilmen
and by nightfall the word was out all over town: The hippies were
going to kill another policeman. So the curfew was extended still
another night and the rifleman still crouched in the bell-tower.

The curfew was lifted, finally, the next day, but Win Allen and
Rise Risner and Gary Hale and the others still didn't feel safe going
into town. They drove out to the City Park about a mile from town
and were surrounded by guns within minutes.

'You gonna get your asses outta here,' a policeman told Rise
Risner, 'or we gonna get even.'

Win and Rise collected all of their friends and left town, camping
out in an open and nearly inaccessible field about six miles away.
'I was afraid they'd come to one of our houses like one of those
lynching parties on TV and just take us,' Rise says, 'It was cold out
there and it rained and we were wet as hell, but we were alive.

By Friday, feelings ran so ugly that the Rev. W. T. Niermeier,
who had sermonized at Patrolman Marler's funeral, wrote a column
for the Democrat-Missourian that said:

'A word of God for our community at this time. Recompense to
no man evil for evil. Live peaceably with all men. Dearly beloved,
avenge not yourselves. Thou shalt not follow a multitude to do
evil.'

That day's Democrat-Missourian carried a news story about the
shooting but nothing about the circumstances. 'Well, I didn't want
to write too much about Simpson,' said J. W. Brown, the editor,
'not after all the trouble he caused us. I figured folks just wouldn't
want to read about him and if folks don't want to read about
somethin', I don't print it.' That same day, the newspaper was
awarded its 16th Blue Ribbon Weekly Newspaper citation by the
Missouri Press Association– for 'outstanding performance in the
field of journalism.'

The next issue of the paper carried a new two-column ad. The ad was the result of all the funerals J. W. Brown had to attend that week. He talked to some of the directors and they determined that the funeral homes didn't do much advertising in the Democrat-Missourian and the next week, the bold black-bordered ad, which in a perverse way Charles Simpson had solicited, said:

A HOUSE WITHOUT A WOMAN

is like a body without soul or spirit. Benjamin Franklin's words of wisdom recognize that a house becomes a home through the loving touch of a woman and the warm glow of a friendly hearth. Likewise, we believe, a funeral director becomes more than a business man since his prime object is to be of service to those in need. It is with humble pride that we serve the citizens of this community.

Friday afternoon, a week after the shooting, G. M. Allen was talking to one of his friends about the list the hippies were supposed to have with the names of the people they were going to kill on it. G. M. Allen said he heard that he was Number One on that list. 'I don't hold too much by it,' G. M. Allen said. 'Maybe there isn't even any list – but, by God, they try somethin' – well, I was in the Infantry during the War, they better think about that.'

A few days after that, Luke Scavuzzo, who runs Scavuzzo's Grocery and is an alderman, was doing a radio talk in Kansas City and he said: 'Maybe some people in town pushed those kids too much.' Now, Luke Scavuzzo said, 'Some people have learned they better *ease up*.' By nightfall, town scuttlebutt held that Luke Scavuzzo was saying they were going to '*give up*.' The next day about 20 people came in to tell Luke Savuzzo they weren't going to buy his groceries anymore becaue of what he said.

'Luke had to go around for a whole week tellin' everybody he never said that,' G. M. Allen says, 'He should have known better. Nobody's gonna give up or ease up. Are we supposed to wait around 'til someone else gets killed?'

A few weeks after Ootney Simpson fired his M-1 on the town square, the Civil Defense sirens screamed again and people ran to their citizens' band radios expecting to hear the worst of their fears confirmed. More trouble. Another killing. The voice of G. M. Allen was as breathless and garbled as the last time. But this time there was

little to worry about. It came out of the east and overturned a mobile
home and knocked down some outhouses and then it was gone.

Just another goddamn tornado.

I got into Harrisonville about two weeks after the shooting. The
first person I saw was Win Allen. He was lying on the courthouse
steps, pressed flat with his face to the cement. He didn't move and
he stayed that way, as still as the pennies on a dead man's eyes. Win
and Rise and the others had decided it was safe enough to go back
into town. The old mock-heroic game for the town square would go
on. Four dead men weren't going to get in the way.

I got out of the car and walked into the drug store for a pack
of Luckies and an old man behind the counter was staring out the
window at Win Allen. He watched me get out of the car and his
eyes must have picked out the Missouri plates on it because when I
walked in his tone was conspiratorial and trusting. 'See that nigger
boy up there,' Lloyd Foster said, 'he's been climbin' those steps
every day for four days now and just layin' down up there. He
goes up there and he looks around and he puts his fist up in the
air and then he lays down on top of his face. He pretends he's dead.
They say it's a way of rememberin' the crazy hippie that killed our
policemen.'

I was wearing a tie and a blue blazer and the next few days I
wore the same get-up, exaggerating the effect, walking around with
a fat Special Corona 77 cigar sticking out of my mouth. I sought out
townspeople in the most razor-backed bars in town, buying them
beer and malt liquor and getting them to talk. I slicked my hair
back above my ears and bought a bottle of gooey hair-oil and – with
cigar and coat and tie – I must have looked respectable enough to
them because pretty soon they were buying me beers. I told them
I was from a magazine in San Francisco and forgot to say which
one. I think the cigar and the slick hair got through. When I got
back to the motel at night and looked in the mirror I saw some guy
I remembered from somewhere but I couldn't place him.

When I was finished talking to the townspeople I drove back to
my motel and washed my hair and changed. I put my jeans on and
let my hair fall down over my ears and put on my leather jacket and
drove back into town. I was getting pretty tired of cigars anyway.

I found Win Allen and told him I was from ROLLING STONE and wanted to talk about Charles Simpson, and Win Allen almost cried he was so happy . 'Man,' Win said, 'we been watchin' you watchin' us and we figured you was FBI. With that cee-gar.' We laughed.

That night we gathered near the square – one of the cops I'd talked to spotted me and gave me a fixed hard glare – and drove about ten miles out of town into the middle of a wheatfield. We found a clearing that suited us and built a bonfire. It was a cloudy spring night, about 70 degrees, and the lightning was already playing patterns off to the east. There were about a dozen of us and we had eight or nine bottles of red wine and a dozen six-packs of beer. We also had a bagful of tongue-burning Missouri weed.

The fire was roaring and Rise Risner's red Volkswagen, which had been pulled as close as possible, played Dylan, Hendrix, and, what the hell, Jose Feliciano. The people here were Charles Simpson's best friends. We were talking about a man who had killed three innocent people in cold blood. They were calling him a brother and telling me how much he loved people and how he believed in The Cause.

'Sometimes Ootney said he thought violence was the only kind of revolution there was,' Rise said. 'But dig,' Win said, 'as far as violent revolution – anytime someone infringes on me and fucks me, it makes me mad, that's the way Charles was thinkin' too.'

'A lot of freaks you meet in places,' Rise said, 'somebody will rip them off or something and they'll haul ass. But we're not that way. We're country boys. We're willin' to fight the motherfuckers if they wanna fight us.'

'Ootney was smart,' Rise said. 'He killed himself to keep the pigs from havin' the satisfaction of killin' him or lockin' him up in some honky jail. He was into so much cosmic shit, man. He was so heavy with that, it was a religion to him. Like some religions say, self-destruction is the best thing you can do for your God, that's why they burn themselves. I know Ootney had to feel the same thing.'

'One time Ootney was in a black neighborhood,' Win said, 'and somebody said somethin' about Jesus to him and Ootney said, "The only way that Jesus and I differ is that he was willin' to die for the people around him and I'm not ready for that yet." '

'I think he was Jesus,' Rise said, 'as far as I'm concerned he was Jesus.'

'Because that cat just laid down truth, man,' Win said. 'Everything that came out of his mouth was truth and supposedly like Jesus laid down the same thing. And when he got up the stuff to die for The Cause, Charles became of the same instance. He was groovy, outtasight, he had so much compassion for people, sentimental about a lot of things, sensitive.'

It had been a long few days and I had scrutinized too many vivid details of four vicious killings and something in my mind flailed out now – Jesus Simpson, murderer, cold-blooded killer, compassionate, sensitive, sentimental. It could have been the fatigue or the Missouri weed or the beer mixed with wine, but I saw too many grotesqueries leaping about in that blazing bonfire.

'As far as I'm concerned,' Rise said, 'Charles isn't dead. It is just somethin' Charles wanted to do and if Charles wanted to do it, I can't say anything about it.'

'Yeah,' I said, 'but what about the people killed and their wives and kids? Don't you care about that?'

'Well, you know,' Rise said, 'how can I criticize it? It's Charles' thing. Like it was a far-out thing to do.'

We were gathered around this bonfire on a spring night in Missouri and the date was the fourth of May, 1972. I've never had much luck with the fourth of May. On this day in 1971, I was standing around a green field at Kent State University listening to requiems and eulogies. And on this day in 1970 I was running dazedly around those same lush fields looking at pools of blood and asking National Guardsmen why they had killed four innocent kids.

And now I was talking to some kids asking them why one of their best friends killed three innocent people with the same kind of gun the Guardsmen used and all they could say to me was:

'Like it was a far-out thing to do.'

I told them the story of my May fourths and Win Allen said:

'Well, dig, man, now it's four to three.'

'Right on,' Rise said.

'Old Ootney,' Win said, 'Old Ootney. That gun was outtasight, man. Like the first time I went to his crib I saw it and I said,

"Ootney, is that yours?" and he said, "Yeah, a friend of mine gave it to me," and I said: "Wow, man, sometimes when you and I go fishin' and out in the woods, maybe I can dig on it." Like Charles had this big Buck knife with a holster on it and this most beautiful fishin' pole and he said – he said whenever he went home, he just fondled the stuff all the time, felt it up and dug it.'

'Yeah,' Rise said, 'Ootney loved nature.'

Who Dunnit? – The Fascination of the Unsolved

AMANDA MITCHISON

In The Grip of Murder

It all began with the Boojum. He was the first one to make any
sense of the mysterious death of Hilda Murrell. The Boojum first
appeared in August 1984, five months after her death, and he started
coming down to Dorset to stay with Hilda's nephew Commander
Robert Green. The Boojum was a man possessed. A small, pallid,
podgy, owl-eyed, double-barrelled, disestablishmentarian depositer
of crumbs and leaver-behind of old, worn socks. Rob's wife Liz was
reminded of the shadowy monster in Lewis Carroll's *Hunting of the
Snark* and she called him the Boojum.

One day Rob gave the Boojum a lift in his car and the Boojum,
as was his wont, talked incessantly. A car coming in the other
direction scraped the side of Rob's brand new Peugeot. Rob
swerved, screeched to a halt and, rather shaken, got out to look
at the damage. The Boojum just continued talking. At 2 am in
the sitting-room of Joan Tate, a friend of Hilda's in Shrewsbury,
the Boojum was still talking as he gulped back wine and jumped
from chair to chair. He re-enacted Hilda Murrell's murder. It was
a breathtaking performance, for the Boojum did the murderers in
different voices.

These were the main facts known at the time of the Boojum: Hilda
Murrell, a 78-year old retired businesswoman and well-known rose
grower, disappeared from her home in Shrewsbury about midday
on Wednesday 21 March 1984. She was an intelligent, highly
educated woman who had just completed a paper on nuclear waste
management and was going to present the work at the Sizewell B
inquiry. Witnesses later told the police they saw her white Renault
being driven very erratically towards the centre of Shrewsbury at

lunchtime. A man was in the driving seat and someone wearing one of Hilda's large floppy hats was slumped in the passenger seat. Later that afternoon a local farmer reported twice to the police that the Renault had been abandoned in the ditch of a country road at Hunkington, five miles from Shrewsbury.

Three days later, Hilda's semi-naked body was discovered in a copse on the other side of an open field near where her car had been abandoned. She had a broken collar bone, severe bruising on one side of her face, several small stab wounds in the abdomen and one in the upper right arm. But, according to the pathologist's report, the stab wounds were not deep enough to have killed her and she probably died of hypothermia.

Traces of semen had been found on the corpse and on a hand-kerchief in the house, but Hilda Murrell had not been sexually assaulted. Her house, however, had been thoroughly searched – some pictures had been removed from the walls and left on the floor, her old handbags were found lying open in a row on the kitchen table, her papers had been gone through. Yet nothing of value had been removed, except a small amount of cash.

At the inquest in December 1984 the police said they had interviewed 2,000 witnesses, but many people in Shrewsbury felt the investigation was being carried out with remarkable ineptitude. Police statements were inconsistent or often at odds with what local witnesses knew to be true.

The police have given at least three different accounts of the follow-up to the farmer's report that the white Renault was in the ditch. It is also difficult to understand why a policeman visited Hilda Murrell's home at six o'clock on Saturday morning – before the body was found – and stayed for two hours. What he did during that period remains a mystery but he apparently did not go into Hilda Murrell's bedroom and left at nine, still not sure whether she was in the house or not.

The evidence itself seemed incomprehensible. Why did the mur-derer – or murderers – abduct Hilda Murrell and leave her to die, rather than simply kill her outright in her own house? Was driving her car – and driving it so conspicuously badly – towards the centre of town, and even past the police headquarters, not asking for attention? Who was the man seen running in a lane near the scene of the crime, and why was he wearing running shoes and a dark suit with trouser bottoms wet and stained with mud? Why, also, did the police issue two entirely different Identikit pictures of the man they wanted for questioning? Why, when there were plenty of wild areas nearer to the road, less exposed and closer to Shrewsbury, was that particular copse chosen?

What about the evidence of Ian Scott, husband of the owner of the copse, who the day after Hilda Murrell disappeared, walked through the copse examining and marking the trees which were due for felling. He saw nothing and claims that he would have noticed 'a dead rabbit, let alone a person'. And why was Scott not called as a witness at the inquest? Why was there a stabbed orange found in Hilda's car and what did the slash marks on the dashboard signify?

The Boojum's hypothesis was that Hilda came home unexpectedly and found someone rifling through her papers. Although very frail and frightened she confronted the intruder. The man, who was not a trained killer, panicked, beat her senseless and perhaps stabbed her and bundled her into her own car. Near the copse, Hilda finally came round, tried to take over the steering-wheel and the car drove into the ditch.

The Boojum believed that the murder was carried out by MI5, or by a private detective agency working on their behalf. According to Rob, 'He introduced us to the mentality of the private agent and gave us an idea about the sort of paranoid world they live in.' The Boojum's hypothesis took into account Hilda's bravery and the fact that she had once confided to a friend that, if she surprised a burglar, she would not fight over her possessions, but *would* battle for her papers.

The Boojum's scenarios were only one of a wide variety of hypotheses about who killed Hilda Murrell and why. According to the West Mercia police, the murder was a random burglary which just went horribly wrong. The Labour MP Tam Dalyell maintains Hilda was killed by British intelligence men who were searching for stolen documents about the sinking of the *Belgrano*. Some of Hilda Murrell's friends and her nephew Robert Green claim she was killed by private investigators working for the nuclear industry. Rob, a former naval intelligence officer who now works as a thatcher and has continued his aunt's campaigning work against nuclear power, and Don Arnott, a retired nuclear scientist whom Hilda had consulted on physics, are key figures in the story.

Rob left the navy because he could see no prospect of promotion and was offered early retirement. A neatly built, bearded man in his forties, he has eyes which pierce with the irrepressible intensity of someone who has been through a momentous experience which has given a new sense of purpose to their life.

Rob has scoured his aunt's diaries, consulted pathologists, tried to jog the memories of her friends, doorstepped many of the witnesses and knocked on every door within two miles of the copse at Hunkington where Hilda's body was found. He keeps assiduous diaries, and when he discovers new evidence he types it out in full and telephones journalists.

Don, a vigorous advocate of inductive methodology, probability theory and the like, suggested to Rob that they make a systematic study of Hunkington copse and other areas of woodland near Shrewsbury. They were looking for a 'safe house', anywhere Hilda could have been held before she was dumped in the copse. On 24 March 1986 – almost exactly two years after Hilda's murder – Don and Rob discovered a green, windowless, wooden stable virtually hidden by trees at the back of the copse. The stable was locked and, according to the owners, had not been used for several years. Inside was an earth floor covered in a thin layer of manure and rubbish.

Robert consulted a forensic specialist who said that so long after the murder it would be most unlikely the floor litter would contain any conclusive evidence that Hilda had been kept in the stable. But, just in case, Rob and Don scraped up the contents of the stable floor, piled them into boxes and took them to a secret place for safe-keeping.

Rob still travels up to Shrewsbury frequently and visits Don in his large, draughty, crumbling Victorian country house where three generations of Arnotts live in bucolic penury. Don is a clever, erudite, prickly sort of man with a shuffling gait and a back cruelly hooped as a result of polio. He used to be a consultant to the International Atomic Energy Agency, then in the late Seventies he changed his mind about nuclear power and joined the opposition. In late 1982 he was employed as a scientific adviser to a consortium of trade unions and pressure groups presenting evidence at the Sizewell inquiry.

At this point Don claims strange things began to happen – he says he was warned by the UK Atomic Energy Authority security agents that he was under surveillance by another organisation, a file of his documents was stolen, he was called to consortium meetings which didn't happen.

Four months after the inquiry opened Don went to a GLC anti-nuclear rally in London and was struck down by a heart attack. He withdrew from the inquiry.

During the year before his heart attack, Hilda visited Don several times to ask him questions about nuclear physics. Each session lasted three to four hours. After Hilda's death, Rob decided to present his aunt's paper at Sizewell and started consulting Don about nuclear physics. Rob went on to give evidence at the Hinkley C inquiry, which has completed its sessions and now awaits the inspector's report. At the inquiry Don concentrated on one small and hitherto neglected weaknesses in the reactor's design – the control rods.

The control rods are neutron absorbers which move in and out of the core to control the heat-generating fission reaction. In case of an accident or overheating, the control rods are designed to drop down into the core and shut down the chain reaction. Don, however, noticed that the control rods specified in the design for Hinkley C – and already cleared for use at Sizewell – are made of silver, indium and cadmium. This alloy has a melting-point of 800°C, lower than anything else in the core of the reactor. Also the stainless steel cladding around the rods is very thin – less than half a millimetre – and would be subject to enormous strain because of the pressure within the reactor and the movement of the rods.

Don claims that if an accident involving the overheating of the core occurred and the cladding of some of the control rods was worn or broken, the reaction from the melted alloy landing in the core would increase the nuclear reaction and 'might turn a damaging but remediable accident into one that was irremediable'.

Rob believes her awareness of this fault may be the key to his aunt's murder. There is also the *Belgrano* conspiracy theory. In December 1984 Tam Dalyell announced in the House of Commons that, according to 'a reliable source', Hilda Murrell's intruders were looking for sensitive naval intelligence documents which they thought Rob, who had worked in signals during the Falklands War, might have passed on to his aunt. Dalyell says that Rob had been known to be unhappy about certain aspects of the Falklands War and had left the navy shortly afterwards.

Rob denies that he was 'disaffected' and believes that Tam Dalyell, who has in the past called himself 'the most pronuclear man in the House', was the most obvious choice for anyone wishing to set up a false trail. Moreover, Dalyell was campaigning to prove that the Government knew the *Belgrano* was returning to port and sank it in order to pre-empt any peace negotiations.

The day after Dalyell made this allegation about the Murrell case, the flat of Lt. Cdr. Peter Hurst, the only other officer on the staff of the naval intelligence headquarters at Northwood to have left the navy since the Falklands War, was broken into, his papers were searched but nothing of value was stolen. The following month, Hilda's house on the Welsh border was the subject of an arson attack, but not of the type associated with Welsh nationalists.

Those who believe that Hilda's murder was connected with her anti-nuclear activities point to evidence that the Sizewell B objectors were a target of surveillance. In January 1985, the *Observer* reported that Peter Hamilton, a former military intelligence officer and managing director of the private detective agency, Zeus Security Consultants Ltd., said that his company had been commissioned to collect information on the objectors for 'a private client', who apparently believed information had been leaked to some of the pro-testers. Earlier this year, David Coghlan, a freelance security adviser and expert on bugging, claimed that Zeus Security Consultants had asked him to help with bugging the Sizewell objectors. He claims he was told the job was commissioned for MI5. The parent company of the Zeus group, Zeus Security Ltd, includes some influential figures on its board of directors, including Lord Chalfont, who has a military intelligence background and is now Deputy Chairman of the IBA.

Hamilton says he subcontracted the work to Barry Peachman of Sapphire Investigations Bureau, and Peachman in turn passed the job on to Contingency Services, a company in Colchester run by Victor Norris. Shortly after Hilda's murder, Peachman shot himself. The inquest recorded a verdict of suicide after hearing that he had been suffering from severe depression after the end of an affair. Victor Norris, who admits that he did some surveillance work on the Sizewell objectors, has a formidable past. In 1969 he was jailed for six years for a long list of sex offences against children, including his own daughter. At various times he has also run a satanist church, two extreme rightwing groups, and A H Services, a company named after Adolf Hitler which markets Nazi regalia.

Mr. Norris is now retired. In 1985 he professed to specialising in 'delicate work' and said, 'I do the work that the Home Office don't want their own people to do.' There is no suggestion that any of these companies were necessarily involved in the murder of Hilda Murrell. However, these admissions would tend to reinforce the indications that Hilda was under surveillance when she died.

Several witnesses have claimed that Hilda believed her telephone was tapped and seemed to be worried about her safety. Many of those who have followed up Hilda's case have been dogged by mysterious happenings: opened post, prowlers in the garden, break-ins where filing cabinets are opened but nothing valuable is stolen. Judith Cook, author of *Who Killed Hilda Murrell?*, claims that before her book was published, she received a series of anonymous telephone calls. 'At first they were joking in tone and said things like, "You don't want to make a fool of yourself." Then they got more serious, "Look what happened to Hilda Murrell." ' Chris Martin sent Rob a copy of his play – also entitled *Who Killed Hilda Murrell?* – and the script arrived torn and well-thumbed.

Portman Productions, a small independent company which is working on a film about Hilda Murrell by the playwright Christopher Haydon, also reports strange goings on. A production assistant who called the coroner's office in Shrewsbury for a transcript of Hilda Murrell's inquest was told by a man who answered the telephone to send in a written application. He added that she would probably not be given a copy. Later that day the assistant received an unexpected call from the same man, this time introducing himself as a police officer, who went on to say he was a bit of a botanist himself, and offered to do his best to get them a copy of the transcript. The company heard nothing more until a month later when West Mercia special branch visited Portman Productions and interviewed the assistant, claiming that she was under suspicion of trying to corrupt a police officer.

Rob is keenly aware of being under surveillance. His post is periodically opened and his telephone suffers from strange noises – single rings in the night, repeated faults and bizarre cross lines. Friends phoning his number have overheard conversations about times and dates of Rob's movements.

The local police are clearly exasperated with the case and in 1985 a spokesman told the Press, 'We've had every amateur detective in the country putting forward hair-brained schemes and theories about the killing.' But while West Mercia police has closed their incident room and to all appearances the case has been shelved, the police are still maintaining secrecy over the inquiries and have done little to allay fears about how the matter has been handled. An internal police inquiry into West Mercia's original investigation of the case was carried out by Peter Smith, then the Assistant Chief Constable of Northumbria. But the results have never been published.

Over this case there reigns an air of wakefulness and distrust in which even some of the investigators watch each other with suspicion and a flat tyre or a bump in the night can become capitalised, magnified, and interpreted as suspicious. Why was one of the firemen who attended Hilda's Welsh cottage after the arson attack told by the police not to talk to Rob? Why was he subsequently sacked? Was Central Television acting on orders from above when it decided recently to cancel a documentary film on Hilda Murrell?

The most hag-ridden person involved is Gary Murray, a disaffected private eye and now a part-time journalist, who claims to know what happened to Hilda and who was in her house. They were, he said, 'private people' not 'Government people'. Murray says that he has received death threats, had his car wired up with bombs, been dragged out of his car at dead of night and had a gun cocked at his head. But Murray also believes that he is being persecuted by the inland revenue and that his publishers, Bloomsbury Press, have suspicious links with the security services. He discounts the control rods theory and believes Hilda was killed for quite another reason 'very contentious and to do with top secret signals and intelligence information'. When I asked him to be more specific, he said, 'How do I know you are not working for Lord Chalfont?'

Rob says he has reliable information proving that his aunt was killed by private operators working under contract to part of the nuclear industry. Rob's hypothesis is that Hilda returned home on the Wednesday for an appointment with an 'Inspector Davis' from London, who wished to interview her, although she did not know why. She was overcome by two or more private security agents. Two of the agents, one of them wearing a wig and a big floppy hat of Hilda's, then got into the Renault and drove wildly towards Shrewsbury before turning off into the countryside, where they left the car in a ditch. Meanwhile one or more security agents drugged Hilda and bundled her into the back of another car, turned the other way out of her front gate and drove out of town. Rob believes Hilda was taken to a secluded, disused stable at the corner of a field near the copse. Here she was questioned, tortured, drugged and later carried out to the copse and left to die. The stab wounds may have been intended to disguise injection points. Her murder was also intended as an example to others.

According to this scenario, the abandoned Renault, the men running in the lane, the semen stains, the clothes strewn in her house in Shrewsbury were all intended to make the abduction look like a bungled burglary. Other disconcerting pieces of evidence – the knife stabbings on the dashboard of the Renault, the orange found in Hilda's car – can be interpreted as red herrings, warnings or as traps. According to this last theory, the evidence is a double bluff, a stratagem to lure the investigators into offbeat interpretations which would discredit them.

Rob's murder scenario all sounds improbably clever and some of his theories smack of wild speculation. There is, for example, no evidence that Hilda was drugged, but Rob has always been suspicious that the pathologist made no toxicology examination. The private detective dressed up as Hilda also seems overly elaborate. Yet Rob's hypothesis is more credible than may first appear and, at least, does square some of the more contradictory clues of the case. Even five years after the event, there is something about this unsettled murder which draws persistent attention. For Rob the case has provided a moral purpose in life and a means of self discovery.

Rob's mother committed suicide in 1964 when he was a 19-year-old navy midshipman posted abroad and afterwards Hilda seems to have acted as a substitute maternal figure. In some remote depth of Rob's mind, clearing up his aunt's murder is connected with coming to terms with unresolved feelings about his own mother's death.

But many artists and writers, with no strong personal ties to Hilda, have taken up the case or used loosely based Hilda prototypes in their work. The protagonist of Maggie Gee's novel *Grace* is an 85-year-old bohemian whose niece is campaigning against the transport of nuclear waste through London and trying to write a book about Hilda Murrell. In *The Lazarus File*, a thriller by the *World in Action* producer Stuart Prebble, a single-minded elderly spinster writing a paper protesting about the building of a new nuclear reactor is brutally murdered by private investigators in search of secret documents. Often these works are preoccupied with the personality of Hilda. In Chris Martin's play *Who Killed Hilda Murrell?* Hilda chairs the inquest into her own death and is the central dramatic character. Christopher Haydon has written and produced *Celestial Blue*, a play with only two actresses who act the young and the old Hilda.

The usual press image of Hilda as an eccentric, rose-growing spinster is inaccurate. She was reserved and outwardly very conventional – the type of woman obituaries like to describe as 'redoubtable'. As a commercial nursery gardener, growing roses was her business, and not a hobby. Extracts from her nature diaries, published posthumously by Collins, demonstrate a fine, poetic command of language and an observant eye. Hilda's lifestyle was typical of the respectable middle class in retirement. Her companions were just the sort of people who swell the ranks of local history extra-mural courses or collect for the local hospice. They are representatives of decent, democratic England – honest, caring, and somewhat staid. But Hilda held views well ahead of her times and refuted much of the what J D Galbraith has called 'institutional truth'. She joined the Soil Association in the Forties, long before organic farming was taken seriously by the public. In the Sixties Hilda was looking into acid rain and was predicting the oil market crisis. In the late Seventies she moved her attention to nuclear power.

No doubt she would even have appreciated the wider, long-term consequences of her own brutal end. According to Hilda's friend Joan Tate, 'I've always had this feeling she is sitting up there looking down with absolute astonishment at all these astounding stories and cover ups – all this stress now on the environment and the greening of Britain. And she'd find it funny to see herself as the inspiration for all these works of art. It would all have pleased her immensely.'

Hilda seems to have felt she was pitted against a positively evil force. She would refer to the 'nuclear *bruderbond*' and describe fission power as a 'devil's brew'. Similarly for Rob there are no shades of grey. His vocabulary is combative, redolent of the battlefield ('he was trying to make me break cover . . .') or of the court room ('I just put it to you that . . .'). As though in a modern fable, he plays the beamish nephew creeping with sword in hand through a dark wood and warding off hordes of freelance security agents in tight suits. Unfortunately, Rob is probably correct and someone, somewhere is out to get him or to keep him quiet.

But Rob also faces another more insidious, internal danger. For more than five years he has lived in an atmosphere of heightened fear and excitement. He is obsessed with Hilda's murder and the long, dark exploration will lead him either to oblivion or – worse still – to a culprit. If this happened, would he ever recover from the sense of anti-climax? What would he do next? Would his anti-nuclear campaigning lose some of its zeal? Victory can be the greatest danger for this type of quest. Like the snark hunter who finds his quarry, Rob's identity, his sense of purpose, everything he stands for, may just 'softly and suddenly vanish, and never be met with again'.

PATRICK MARNHAM

The Devils of Nancy

On 1 December a French examining magistrate, seven lawyers and assorted policemen, all dressed up in rubber boots and plastic aprons, spent five hours in a tiny kitchen in the city of Nancy cutting up lumps of raw meat on the bone with a chainsaw. They were trying to reconstruct a crime that may never have been committed – the murder of Bernard Hettier, a middle-aged factory foreman, by his former mistress, a widow called Simone Weber. It is a suspected crime which combines some of the classic attributes of French provincial life – anonymous telephone calls, inquisitive neighbours and a prim exterior concealing the passion and violence beneath. After the revelations of the last three years, the local papers have dubbed Madame Weber, 57, and her sister Madeleine, 54, who is accused of being her accomplice, 'the devils of Nancy'.

Bernard Hettier was a handyman and he loved the company of women. His life was an example of how someone of non-descript appearance, twice divorced, with no particular talent, no money, no family, no prospects and the misfortune to work in a factory in provincial France in the last quarter of the twentieth century could still have a very good time.

Unfortunately Mr. Hettier has stopped having a good time. Neither his three children nor his two sisters, nor any of his five other mistresses, have seen him since 22 June 1985. According to the police, he was drugged, shot in the back of the neck and dismembered with the aid of a chainsaw by Simone Weber. Madame Weber then packed the bits and pieces of her former lover into 17 black plastic dustbin bags and drove off from her sister's three-room apartment at 158 avenue de Strasbourg into the night. The head is still missing, as are the four limbs, but a torso has been recovered from the river Marne near Poincy; Judge Thiel, the examining magistrate, is confident that this will turn out to be the greater part of Mr. Hettier.

Bernard Hettier was known as someone who would always help you out. He was delighted to pop round, whether to mow the lawn, change a washer or mend the vacuum cleaner. He worked on the night shift in a chemical factory, which meant that he was available during the day, when the lady of the house was usually alone and in need of a hand. Bernard was very charming as well as being a skilful mechanic. He knew when life was about to become complicated and it was time to move on. He tried to remain on good terms with his old friends, and even went on mending their machinery. Then one day in October 1981 he met Simone Weber . . .

Any woman who has ever refused to change an electric plug or remove a spider from the bath can draw inspiration from Simone Weber. Here is someone who should have been a classic case of the helpless female. Middle-aged, widowed, unlucky in love, she also lost two of her five children. Her daughter Catherine, 16, drank two litres of Theralene (a soporific) and her death was recorded as a suspected suicide. Her son Philippe, one of twins, shot himself in unexplained circumstances while doing military service in Germany.

Simone might have been content to overfeed her dachshund and develop a dependency on Valium. She could have retrieved her self-respect by misdirecting strangers, or short-changing tourists, or even going in for a little mild shoplifting. To look at her today – short, stout, slightly lost among the tall policemen who accompany her on every outing she makes from the prison in Nancy where she has been living since October 1985 – she could be on the verge of a self-righteous old age, with button-up boots, a furry bowler hat and free bus pass. There is a large community of such old ladies in Nancy, but Simone Weber will never qualify for it.

For, instead of collapsing, Madame Weber went decorously berserk. First, refusing to accept the explanation of her daughter's death, she sued a nurse at the hospital in Nancy for manslaughter. Then she turned to revolutionary politics. This was during the late 1970s, the last kick of Euro-Maoism. Simone Weber attended the meetings of Truth And Justice, a group of Nancy militants, and told her new comrades that her daughter had been imprisoned and killed by a hospital nurse.

But she was not just a one-issue revolutionary. She was preparing for the big day. She obtained three containers of nitro-glycerine, a detonator, two rifles, ammunition and two silencers. She became a forger of identity documents. Had she lived 50 years earlier she might have been a formidable recruit for the French Resistance. She had a real talent for the life of deceit which was one of the resisters' most important survival techniques. She learnt to pick pockets and took to buying second-hand cars, camouflaging them as better models and reselling them for a profit.

She adopted several false identities. She claimed to be a philosophy teacher, a couturier, a nurse, a company director. She was known as 'Monique', 'Sophie' or 'Françoise'. In the hope of contacting her two dead children she went to 'black masses' held by spiritualists. She withdrew from straight society and became what is known in France as *une marginale*. Losing touch with her living children, she spent more time with her sister Madeleine, who was also rather strange.

Simone and Madeleine were brought up by their father in a suburb of Nancy after their mother abandoned them. They have led curiously similar lives. They married brothers, both were widowed, both had little dogs (Simone a dachshund, Madeleine a poodle). Both continued to live in Nancy and search for Mr. Right. Madeleine favoured Catholicism over Marx. Her apartment on the avenue de Strasbourg is still full of devotional objects. On the wall is a reproduction of the *Mona Lisa*. Madeleine's place was always very tidy. Simone's, in the rue de Cronstadt, was a pit, and the pictures on her walls were always of the dead – her mother, her two husbands, her children Catherine and Philippe. There was also a picture of Bernard Hettier.

The obvious place for a widow living in Nancy to look for Mr. Right is in *les petites annonces* of *L'Est Républicain*. They have a certain brutal charm. 'Company director, 33, earning £25,000 a year, ready to open up a world pillowed with tenderness to a woman of 48 with a good figure.' Simone had a good figure before she was exposed to three years of prison food. She herself might have placed this one: 'Former businesswoman, aged 45, sporting, great sense of humour, will enrapture a captivating gentleman willing to compromise.'

With similar promises Simone attracted the attention of a stubborn old soldier, Marcel Fixard, aged 79, living in Strasbourg, and discovered quite quickly that he had a little nest egg. She decided to marry him, but thought it better not to let him know. So in April 1980 she went to the town hall in Strasbourg with another old man, who was on day release from a nearby asylum and who stood in for Fixard. Fifteen minutes later, unknown to himself, Fixard had a new wife. Then Simone drew up a will in which her loving husband disinherited his family and left her all his money. Then she forged his signature with the help of tracing paper. Six weeks after his wedding, Mr Fixard, who had been in good health, suddenly died. And the widow, despite the protests of his two nephews in Bordeaux, became quite rich.

Just over a year later, in October 1981, Simone's lawn mower broke down. (The lawn came with the house in the village of Rosières which she had inherited from old Fixard, to the great scandal of the villagers.) She was selling Wanda beauty products when she bumped into Bernard Hettier in Nancy town centre. They had met once before. She was a friend of one of his former girlfriends. Once he had fixed her lawn mower, Bernard helped her to move house. As Madame Weber was to put it later, 'We lived the life of a couple for two years.'

At 55, Bernard Hettier considered himself a shrewd judge of character, and he was confident that he had met cuddly, rather solitary women like Madame Weber before. He didn't know about her hidden talents. He didn't know that the spare pressure cooker in the kitchen at the rue de Cronstadt was full of official stamps stolen from the town hall, or that the television remote control had been dismantled and reassembled around her false identity card. He never went through people's drawers, or he might have found the pad of prescription forms taken from a doctor's desk, blank air tickets, model wills, false car registration plates, bugging devices, a collection of men's watches and assorted jewellery. In all the time they spent together, Bernard apparently noticed only one odd thing about her: she slept with a pistol under her pillow. When, after 18 months, in June 1983, he found a new friend, he warned his family to keep away from Simone. By then she had taken a photostat of Bernard's identity card and his cheque book and popped them into a box of chocolates.

Louise, the new girlfriend, who lived in the northern part of Nancy, not far from Bernard's little-used flat, had just been treated for alcoholism. Simone found out and decided she was not going to be replaced by a 'sot'. For the first time, Bernard's legendary powers of disengagement proved inadequate. She telephoned him incessantly. He would come home and find Simone inside his flat, which was odd because he had never given her a key. So he changed the locks and went to bed. He woke in the night to see her face peering in through the first-floor bedroom window: she had installed herself on a ladder.

Driving around Nancy in his (blue) Renault 9, Bernard would glance in his rear-view mirror. All too often there was her (white) Renault 9, with her eager face behind the steering-wheel. At the traffic lights it was, '*Coucou* – Bernard! Could you drop by? I think the sink's blocked again.' Sometimes, when she got tired of following him round Nancy, she would pay a female neighbour to do it for her. If he managed to shake her off by fast driving, she would punish him later by disconnecting his car battery. Occasionally he found her peering through the window of his car, checking up on the mileage. His neighbours used to note the hours she sat in her car outside his flat, waiting for him to come home. This went on for two years. Bernard's family says that during this period she twice drugged his coffee.

The avenue de Strasbourg is not as grand as it sounds. It is a wide street, but most of the houses are broken up for multiple occupation. No 158 is an unusually narrow building. Madeleine's apartment occupies the first floor, two windows squashed together in a crumbling façade, the shutters now permanently closed. The shutters of the ground-floor apartment also seem to be closed until one notices as one gets closer that the right-hand one is raised about eight inches. Behind the shutter – dazzling white net curtains. One almost expects to see the snout of a telescope emerge. This is the home of an elderly couple, Marie and Nicolas Haag, who are the chief witnesses for the prosecution. In their old age, the Haags have become devotees of a national pastime, spying on one's neighbours.

They say that on the evening of 22 June they saw a middle-aged man climb the worn steps to the first-floor flat with Madame Weber but did not see him come out again. Two days later Madame Weber came to their door to ask if they knew how to fix the blades on to an electric carving-knife. And early the following morning they watched her carry the 17 black plastic dustbin bags down to her car.

Today the Haags are still on guard. One has the distinct feeling, as one walks down the wide parade of the avenue de Strasbourg towards No 158, that one is under observation. Before, there were just the neighbours to survey, the comings and gongs at No 158, Messrs. Gout, Bensacki and Meyer, to say nothing of Simone and Madeleine. But now the Haags also watch for journalists. At the front door, the name beside the bell for the first-floor flat has been chiselled out. The other bells do not produce a reply.

In the café bar a little further up the street, they are more interested in the football results and the darts board than in the interminable case of Simone Weber. A tramp comes in out of the rain and is given *un petit rouge* and a bag of food. He tries to take the food discreetly, but slips on his way to the door. 'You don't have the right to take the chair as well,' says the *patron*. Musing about the Weber case, Madame, behind the bar, said, 'How do you think she got her family to help her? She must have paid them a bit.' Madame is thinking of the telephone calls apparently from Bernard Hettier after his disappearance, actually made by Simone Weber's cousin. The café is a place for people who have nothing to do. They can pass the time and forget their problems. '*Sont contents, les garçons . . .*' says the fat lady who has spent all afternoon watching the darts players.

In here, among her neighbours, one is startled enough by the mere details of Simone Weber's love life: the possibility of a chainsaw massacre as well seems a bit far-fetched. But there is a shop opposite the café which hires out chainsaws. They are laid out in the window in neat rows. For £20 a week you can have the basic model. For £30 you can have a Stihl Rollomatic ('Not to be missed'). The display may have given Madame Weber an idea. She actually hired hers from a shop in the suburbs; she later reported it stolen and forfeited the deposit. The shopkeeper says it was the first time in 20 years that he had supplied a chainsaw to a woman.

The kitchen of No 158 is a narrow corridor with plastic tiles on the walls and a strip of lino on the floor. If you lean out of the front window of the flat you can just see the convent of the Poor Clares to the right and to the left the roofs of the hospital where Simone's daughter died. In the kitchen the fridge, gas heater and three-ring cooker are in impeccable condition. In fact the whole kitchen is in a suspiciously clean state. The fact that there are no stains of any kind is considered to be a major point against Madame Weber. Someone has been at work with the bleach.

The third major character in this story is also the new man in Simone's life. Tall, thoughtful, black-bearded, he has spent 180 hours talking to her and has made a 7,000-page record of their conversations. She has known him for three years. It is a steady relationship. He is called Gilbert Thiel and he is an examining magistrate. Before that he was a tax inspector. Judge Thiel checks everything. When he found a bloodstain on the sofa, Simone told him that Poupette, her sister's poodle, had probably been in season. The judge found the blood was human, not animal, group A or AB. Bernard was Group A.

Before he even met Simone, Gilbert Thiel tapped her telephone. She spent hours talking to Madeleine, who now has a flat in Cannes. They talked about 'a new school for Bernadette'. Judge Thiel realised they were talking in code. Madeleine was arrested and proved less stubborn than Simone. She said that 'Bernadette' was the name they had given to Bernard's car, which disappeared shortly after he did. The 'new school' was a new garage. Madeleine told the judge where he could find the car, in Cannes. The missing chainsaw was in the boot.

When a suitcase containing a male torso was found after a memorable '*déjeuner* on the banks of the Marne', Judge Thiel was encouraged. He is now waiting for a genetic test to establish whether the torso, with private parts still attached, is that of Mr. Hettier. The exhumation of Marcel Fixard revealed no suspicious circumstances. Judge Thiel has nevertheless charged Simone with two murders, as well as with theft, illegal possession of explosives and possession of false car registration plates. Madeleine has been charged as her accomplice and released on bail.

You can believe all this, or not. After 180 hours of questioning, Madame Weber denies everything. She says she is still very fond of Bernard and that he is probably in Majorca. She ridicules the theory of the chainsaw: far too noisy, she says, and it would have spattered blood everywhere . . .

According to her lawyers, the official reconstruction of the crime in the tiny kitchen on 1 December tended to support her objections. Other observers say that Madame Weber followed it with close attention and became very critical when Judge Thiel proposed using white veal meat. 'She wanted red meat, freshly killed and full of blood.' As for the chainsaw found in the car boot, she says she just wanted a chainsaw. Bernard might have found it useful.

There is at least one man who does believe her. Joseph Tournel, formerly leader of the Maoist group Truth And Justice, an ex-miner living in Béthune with a 75 per cent disability pension, is convinced of Madame Weber's innocence. He has come out of retirement to fight one last battle, and has formed a committee of support for his old comrade. 'I firmly believe that she did not commit the crime,' he says. 'And anyway it is inhuman to lock her up for so long without a trial. She has been in preventive detention for longer than anyone else in France. This is against the European Convention on Human Rights.'

But Monsieur Tournel has not been allowed to visit Simone, and in France an examining magistrate can keep a suspect in prison for as long as it takes him to gather his evidence. Meanwhile Simone Weber has hired and fired 20 lawyers in the last three years. She is capricious and, in a case as well-publicised as hers, the lawyers do not always expect a fee. So far, 16 demands for her release have been turned down. The fact that it is taking so long to prepare a case against her is, perhaps, the strongest argument in her favour. But if she did not do it, what has happened to Bernard?

There remains the possibility, until his body is found, that he is alive, not in Majorca, perhaps, but a little further away. Looked at from his point of view, his life had become impossible. Even if he had left Nancy and found a job elsewhere, Simone had enough money to follow him.

The solution lay in having that woman locked up while he got away. All he had to do was tell her to hire a chainsaw, leave a bloodstain on her sofa, enter the flat while the Haags were on the look-out and leave it without being seen. Then he disappeared. The suitcase fished out of the Marne was an unexpected bonus.

So let's imagine him sitting on a terrace overlooking the beach sipping a rum and Coke. He's grown a beard, he's probably running an electrical repair business and, ever since he learnt the Portuguese for 'dishwasher', 'lawn mower' and 'fuse box', he's had a little Brazilian friend. Perhaps he sometimes remembers driving round Nancy looking in his rear-view mirror, and reflects that the quickest way from the rue de Cronstadt to the avenue de Strasbourg is past the city prison.

BRIAN MASTERS

Fiona Jones

Fiona Jones just disappeared. Brian Masters, whose account of the Nilsen case, *Killing for Company*, broke new ground in the understanding of murder, went to France to join Fiona's husband, mother, father and brother in the search for clues. Here he carefully confronts each possibility: is she dead, is she hiding, did someone organise her disappearance or, worst of all, is she being held 'for loathsome purposes'?

Logic is not a cerebral, cold companion in life; on the contrary, it consoles and comforts, for it assures us that our routine expectations are indeed reasonable. It makes us feel safe, secure and optimistic to a degree we take far too much for granted. We depend upon logic to deliver life's normality in daily bundles and it is only when it fails us, when it falters and lets us down, that we recognise the stark bewilderment and despair of a world without rule or necessity.

It is the 'contingent' world which Sartre described with horrific vividness and it is in such a world, viscous and hostile, that the family of Fiona Jones has lived.

Fiona Jones went for a bicycle ride alone in France on 14 August and vanished into nothingness, removed from the face of the earth as surely as if she had been snatched up by some demonic jackdaw. Both she and her bicycle appear no longer to exist, because they are not there for anybody to observe. Since 15 August Fiona's mother, father, brother and husband have been trapped in this new world where logic refuses to behave, and they are visibly shaken by what they have been forced to contemplate. For what happened to Fiona is impossible.

The facts are straightforward. Mark Jones, 26, whose business is in sports equipment, had an appointment to discuss the design of a golf course at the Chateau de Bellinglise, a large rather posh hotel in its own grounds about seven miles from Compiegne in north-eastern France.

As he was about to celebrate the first anniversary of his marriage to Fiona Cottrill, also 26, the couple decided they would both go to France and stay on at the hotel after Mark's business was over. They travelled from their home, a pretty converted school house in the old village of Kingsbury, Warwickshire, on Sunday 13 August, arriving at Bellinglise late the same day.

Mark's appointment, which he would attend with his partner Colin Snape, was for the next morning, after which he and Fiona would have time to themselves.

On Monday morning Mark left Fiona in the hotel room, where she indulged herself with breakfast in bed. She said she would pass the time until he was free by hiring a bicycle and going for a ride along the country road perhaps as far as Compiegne. Bikes are readily available from the hotel. She was given a metallic turquoise model by the head receptionist and went happily up the drive towards Route D142 at 11.30 am. She was wearing bright pink shorts and a white top with short sleeves. It was a beautiful day, warm, clear and windless.

Fiona cycled through the villages of Elincourt Ste. Marguerite and Marest-sur-Matz as far as the tiny hamlet of Rimberlieu. We know this because she was seen by four motorists who either overtook her or passed in the opposite direction before 12.30.

Then there is a blank of two and a quarter hours when she was spotted by no one. The area is thickly wooded and below the woods there are fields high with corn. There are access roads to expensive private houses and paths into the woods, but no other road for traffic. Fiona may have taken a side turning to explore further.

I would have done the same, for the area is enchantingly pretty. There are no shops at Rimberlieu, just a few houses and a restaurant, La Bergerie, where the owner is cook, waiter and cleaner to the very occasional motorist who might stop. Apart from the passage of about four cars every minute, Rimberlieu is one of the most peaceful spots imaginable.

Fiona was seen again at 2.45 pm, also at Rimberlieu, but facing the opposite direction. She was on her way back to the Chateau de Bellinglise; Mark had said to be home by 3.30 and she was in good time. She was drinking from a half-bottle of mineral water she had taken with her. Apart from that, she had only a 200 franc note (about £20) and the key-card to her hotel bedroom.

Mark Jones and Colin Snape had spent the morning in discussions with two others, one of whom was an American golf architect. Their meeting at 8.30 am had finished by 10.30 whereupon they all proceeded to examine the grounds. Then they had lunch at the hotel. Colin said, 'Is Fiona joining us?' 'No,' said Mark, 'she's gone out on a bike.' Lunch was over by 2.30. One of the other businessmen was leaving for the airport and offered Colin a lift, but his flight was not until 7.30. 'There's no hurry,' said Mark. 'Fiona will be back soon and we'll both take you.' They lingered for the rest of the afternoon, had a cup of tea and waited.

When Fiona did not return by 5 pm, Mark left a note on her bed to say he had driven Colin to the airport and would be back after six, as indeed he was. The note had been moved to a sideboard which led Mark to believe his wife must be waiting for him somewhere in the hotel. She wasn't. The receptionist had not seen her since she left that morning. (Did a housekeeper move Mark's note? The bed had been made long before).

Mark then drove the length of the road to Compiegne and back but found no sign of Fiona. He was alarmed and informed the police, though he still suspected she had got hopelessly lost and would probably turn up the next morning, dishevelled and distraught, having spent the night in a barn somewhere.

He looked forward to having to apologise to the gendarmerie for causing unnecessary trouble. At least Fiona spoke good French so she would not need to feel isolated and abandoned. As it later turned out, the motorist who saw her at 2.45 pm did not say she looked isolated or abandoned, nor even lost.

By Tuesday morning, alarm had turned to fear. Mark called his father in North Wales, Tony Jones. 'Look, dad,' he said, 'I've got a problem. Fiona is missing. Should I tell Bruce and Pat (her parents) or wait until later? I don't want to upset them.'

Tony Jones thought it was better to tell them straight away; he would do it as he lived just down the road from them. The two families had known each other for years. Bruce Cottrill and his youngest son Simon went immediately to Manchester airport where they caught the first flight to Paris.

They were in Compiegne by Tuesday evening. They have been there ever since. Fiona's mother, Pat Cottrill, is there too, on her second visit. She once went home to Wales but could not bear the uncertainty at such a distance.

By this time Fiona Jones was a 'missing person'. It was the audacity and determination of her frantic husband which turned the beneficent glare of international publicity upon the case.

He urged a colleague to inform Central TV, who in turn got in touch with their counterparts on French TV, and within 24 hours the Chateau de Bellinglise was besieged by over 150 reporters. Bruce Cottrill prepared a 'Have you seen?' poster which he photocopied at the hotel and then distributed, with Simon, in every village on the route of Fiona's unfortunate journey and for 10 miles around.

This was done by Wednesday. Meanwhile 50 policemen were joined by 40 volunteer firemen, and later 200 soldiers, to search the forests. Frogmen scoured the stagnant ponds which abound in the area and the underground tunnels dating from the First World War (the Armistice of 1918 was signed in the famous railway carriage which is still at Compiegne). Dogs were brought in and a helicopter flew low for a radius of 15 miles.

There was no sign whatever of either Fiona or her bicycle. On Wednesday evening, 16 August, the first, last and only clue was discovered by police. Fiona's hotel key-card lay in a field on the way out of Rimberlieu in the direction of Bellinglise. It was about 12 yards from the road.

There was nothing with it, no thread from clothing, no hair, nor any indication of a struggle. The clue was almost as silent as the mystery it should have dispelled.

Since then only the persistence of Fiona's family has made her presence felt. Captain Ster, the police chief in charge of the case, was obliged after eight days to follow French procedure and hand the matter over to a *juge d'instruction*, Madame Pagenelle, who may speak or not as she sees fit and is likely only to offer information if it is concrete and factual. She will not speculate and must not reveal the line of her inquiry however sympathetic she may be (and is) towards Mark Jones and the Cottrills.

So far there is nothing to relate. The police are now under her command but they are by their own admission *tetus* (stubborn) and will not rest until Fiona is found. To an especially crass English journalist who asked if they were looking for a body, Captain Ster said, 'No, we are looking for Madame Jones.'

Was that journalist merely voicing the thought in everybody's mind? What are the alternatives, in fact, to a tragic outcome? And who is Fiona Jones?

Bruce and Pat Cottrill started their family in Liverpool where their eldest child, Fiona, and their first son, Jonathan, ('Jonty', now 25) were born. Just before the birth of the third child, Simon (now 22), they moved to Old Colwyn in north Wales. It is a small community, friendly and supportive. Fiona, Jonty and Simon all went to the local school where another boy, Mark Jones, became a family friend.

By the time Mark was in the upper sixth, Fiona came into the lower sixth, and they began going to dances together. It was the beginning of a nine-year courtship. Fiona was pretty, with an open character and a ready smile. She was also academically bright, reading from the age of four, and by now a devoted admirer of Thomas Hardy.

She studed Italian and French at Leicester University and graduated with upper second-class honours. Meanwhile Mark decided to read for a civil engineering degree. He and Jonty both went up to Liverpool University where they too graduated with honours.

Fiona's knack with languages enabled her to widen her reading still further. Dante became a great favourite, much to the amusement of Mark who found some of the stories 'cracking' and far more risky than those in the Sunday papers.

Mark and Fiona married at Llanelian church in 1988. For Bruce, by now safety officer for Hotpoint in Llandudno, it was quite simply 'the happiest day of our lives'.

They set up home in Warwickshire where Fiona took a job as a primary school teacher. After work, when Mark returned from the office, they liked nothing better than to go out for a meal, particularly an Indian curry. At weekends Simon might come and stay. He was studying at Sheffield Polytechnic.

All perfectly ordinary and unremarkable. Until one day the French countryside swallowed Fiona Jones whole and refused to surrender her. Could she have met with an accident? Hospitals in the area were contacted. There was no accident. Could she have decamped, run off with someone, a new lover perhaps? Hardly. It would have been far easier to let Mark go to France and make her escape during his absence. And why would the elopers encumber themselves with a bicycle?

Fiona's photograph has been published in all corners of France; it is doubtful if she could have passed unnoticed for so long a time. And she left everything at the hotel, her passport, even her private building society account. An absconder does not walk into a new future so unprepared.

Despite all this, the flight theory is still the one most favoured by local barmen and gossips; in France everything boils down to illicit love. Has Fiona been kidnapped? This is the hope her family and husband cling to. Mark thinks it possible that kidnappers assumed she was from a rich family because she was staying at the Chateau de Bellinglise, and realised their mistake later.

Again, why bother to kidnap the bicycle as well? Mark experimented to see how long it would take to dismantle a bike and shove it into a car. Four minutes, during which time 20 cars could pass. A van, of course, could accommodate the bike easily, but then there would need to be more than one man to cope with Fiona *and* the bike.

Perhaps Mark Jones has organised the disappearance himself? He admits surprise that he was not told to surrender his passport and report to the police station every day (he does, but of his own accord). Colin Snape, who was with him the entire day of 14 August, has still not been questioned by anyone. The idea is obviously too fanciful to merit investigation and has rightly been dismissed by the police.

Another possibility is that Fiona wandered back into the forest for an unknown reason and got into difficulties. In this case, the army, the police, the firemen, the dogs, the frogmen and the helicopter have all passed her by.

The harshest scenario holds that Fiona has been the victim of a crime, that she has been taken for loathsome purposes and that she will only be released, if at all, when the criminal or criminals have been satisfied.

Route D142 is not a road to travel if you are looking for a potential victim. Far better to try Paris or the Cote d'Azur. If Fiona fell into the clutches of ruthless men, then they were travelling on the least likely road and encountered their prey entirely by accident. The snatch would have been impulsive. Did they then throw the key-card into the field? No, it weighs little and would not travel 12 yards. Fiona dropped it in the field.

The question again arises, why bother to steal the bicycle as well? What else? Amnesia? She would have turned up by now. Imprisonment by an innocent madman who wants company, like Clegg in John Fowles's The Collector? This is an attractive idea, for at least Fiona would be unlikely to come to any harm. On the other hand the collector might keep her for months.

Meanwhile Fiona Jones's family stay on in Compiegne, assaulted by these corrosive thoughts, and more, every day. They have a flat which has been given to them indefinitely by a well-wisher.

They rarely eat out, but are seen walking in the town, where everyone recognises them and keeps a respectful distance. Pat Cottrill is the kind of naturally elegant woman one would want to meet and talk with, but circumstances forbid. Bruce Cottrill reveals the weight of worry in his face.

They are never apart. They would each cry, with Juliet,

Is there no pity sitting in the clouds
That sees into the bottom of my grief?

Mark is white-faced and weary. He goes to the gendarmerie every day simply to establish that he will not cease until something is discovered. 'I must do everything possible to help my wife,' he says. 'They know I am going to turn up every day. They can't forget about the case.'

Talking with this tall, good-looking, amiable man, one makes a conscious effort to speak of Fiona in the present tense, but in the end it is not entirely honest to smother thoughts in this way.

After a couple of hours, Mark grabs the thorn. 'We have thought about it in circles,' he says. 'You are an outsider. Tell me what you think. What are the chances that my wife is still alive?' I reply that I give her more than a 50 per cent chance, because I pin hopes on the harmless lonely madman who wants to look at her.

Simon Cottrill spends much of the day playing computer chess. He will soon have to make a hard decision. He is due to begin a course at Leeds University and will have to leave Compiegne.

Simon is scrupulously honest with his thoughts. I suggest we go for a drink and I am careful, for once, not to talk about Fiona but to be light and discursive. 'It is more false to talk about something else,' he says, 'and pretend Fiona is not on our minds. Even to think about something else is a kind of disloyalty, a failure of love.' So we talk about Fiona. When she turns up, I will want to wean her off Hardy and introduce her to Anthony Trollope. That, I hope, will be my small share of the celebration.

Rich, Famous –
and Dead

MARTIN AMIS

The Case of
Claus Von Bulow

There are two sides to every marriage, and two sides to every murder. Husband and wife can regale you with their rival versions of reality; we all know those long-running sanity contests that many marriages turn into. But murderer and victim seldom have equal access to the sympathetic ear.

Look at them now. On a typical summer evening Clause von Bulow might be hosting a dinner party in the fourteen-room Fifth Avenue apartment of scarcely describable opulence. The guests include people like Lady Annabel Goldsmith, Mercedes Kellog, Elizabeth of Yugoslavia. Behind every other chair stands a liveried footman . . . Meanwhile, across town on upper Broadway, among the flophouses and retirement hotels, Von Bulow's wife Martha is being well taken care of by money too, in a sense. She lives in a guarded room. She is visited every morning by the family doctor. Full-time nurses clean her tubes and catheters and adjust her body every two hours to prevent bedsores. Rumour – in the form of the *New York Post* – has it that a hairdresser and manicurist attend her daily. Her limbs twitch. She makes gurgling noises. Her eyes open and stare but she is probably blind.

'What do you give the girl who has everything?' runs the joke, often told – if not actually originated – by Von Bulow himself. The answer is 'Insulin'.

Martha von Bulow, known as Sunny to her friends, has been in a coma for two-and-a-half years. Claus has been found guilty of putting her there, at the second attempt, with an insulin injection. Sunny is worth $75 million. Both parties have their advocates. Family, friends, acquaintances – and the whole of tabloid and small-screen

America – are split down the middle. Hardly anything in either version is demonstrably false.

I Sunny's Story

'Claus Bulow – born Claus Borberg and yet to invent the "von" – was a middle-class Danish adventurer. His father was practically the *only* Dane to be prosecuted for collaboration with the Nazis. That'll give you some idea. As far back as his London days Claus was always shady. He stood bail for Stephen Ward during the Profumo scandal. He hung around with Lord Lucan – now there's another man who bungled the murder of his own wife.

'Claus never had any money of his own to speak of but he contrived to live on the edge of the high life. He was an art dealer and businessman, a courier, a fixer. He had languages, presence, a phoney aristocratic aura. In 1966 he met and carefully courted Princess Sunny von Auersperg.

'Sunny was a dream, the classic American heiress. She was the only child of George Crawford, the utilities magnate. She looked like Grace Kelly, a long-legged rose. Between them, she and her mother had about $150 million. At the time she met Claus, Sunny had just been amicably divorced from her first husband, an Austrian prince of great charm but no great wealth. She had two beautiful children, Alexander and Ala. She was a quiet, self-contained woman, perhaps even a little withdrawn. She regretted her lack of education and read widely. She liked to stay in. A private person, not a hostess.

'Claus seemed right for her, at first. They had one of the grandest apartments in New York – it makes the Astors' place look like a pigsty – and a dazzling mansion in Newport, Rhode Island. They poured a lot of time, energy and money into those places. They went on buying trips to Europe, and so on. But their style wasn't ostentatious. It was just family life at the highest pitch of polish. And they had a daughter of their own by now – Cosima. Cosima von Bulow! Named after the woman who started life as a Liszt and ended it as a Wagner. Poor old Hans von Bülow, the most famous cuckold of the nineteenth century.

'But Claus was bored. So was Sunny, in her way. Let's get one thing straight. It's garbage about Sunny being an alcoholic and a pill-popper. We have the testimony of the maid and the butler that she drank far less than the average American. She may have used aspirin, aperients, but not twenty a day of each. As the prosecution lawyer said, anyone who took that many laxatives for twenty-four years would have spent eighteen of them on the toilet. All the rumours about Sunny's addictions go straight back to Claus. She was stable. It was he who was changing.

'For one thing, he was in love – with Alexandra Isles, a socialite and minor TV actress. And he wanted to work again. He was tired of being a kept man, or so he claimed. So he started sounding out a divorce. Sunny was absolutely amenable and he knew her to be generous – the first husband had gotten well over a million. Claus dithers. Alexandra gives him a deadline: "Let's be together for Christmas."

'This was 1979. On the night of December 26, Sunny goes into a coma. Well, what do you know? All the next day Sunny lay unconscious on her bed. Maria, the maid who had been with Sunny for twenty-five years, was incensed, hysterical: "Call a doctor!" she told him. "No," he said, "she's just sleeping." It wasn't until late afternoon, when Sunny's breath started to rattle, that Claus finally gave in. All day he just lay by her side, fully clothed, waiting. He must have been tranquillised to the eyeballs himself. Why didn't he just tell Maria to get lost? It came out in court that Claus was heavily reliant on Valium.

'At the hospital Sunny's blood-sugar count was found to be abnormally low. After several glucose shots it was even lower! Something was eating her blood sugar. Insulin, for instance. But she recovered, and the doctors diagnosed reactive hypoglycemia . . . In February, while tidying a closet of Claus's, Maria found a little black bag. There were drugs in there. She showed it to Ala. From then on they monitored the bag's contents. One day they found a vial marked INSULIN. "Insulin?" said Maria. "What for, insulin?"

'And the following Christmas it all happens again. Another showdown with Alexandra Isles, another morning of stall and bluff at Clarendon Court, another coma. This time Claus had obviously given her the shot the night before, and seen to it that Maria stayed in New York. And this time Sunny did not recover . . . The family – Sunny's mother and stepfather, Alexander and Ala – initiated a private investigation. When they got hold of the black bag the vial was gone but there was a dirty needle, tipped with insulin. Richard Kuh, a lawyer, an ex-DA talked to Sunny's doctor, who said simply, "Either you go to the police or I will."

'At the trial everyone was amazed at the strength of the prosecution's case. Maria's testimony was devastating. So was Alexander's. (He and Ala had no financial motive, by the way – a few million here or there, in their forties.) Even Alexandra Isles, when asked if she still believed in Claus's innocence, said, "I don't know." All that can save the defence is a rescue-job from Claus himself. He refuses to take the stand. Why? Because the prosecution would have murdered him. It's open and shut. They mystery is *not* that such a clever man could commit such a dumb crime. The mystery is that he came so close to getting away with it.'

2 Claus's Side

'Let's be clear on one thing. Of *course* Claus is a bastard. Of *course* he's a snob and a money-worshipper. But he's not a murderer. And he isn't dumb. And this was such a dumb murder.

'Claus never made any secret of his origins. He always said, "My mother's Bulows are middle-class Danes. They have nothing to do with the German family." His father was no Lord Haw-Haw, just a fuddled playwright who neglected to resign from the Danish-German Literary Society. The "von" was Sunny's idea. Claus was legitimate. He wasn't the kind of bogus Eurocrat who gets a dukedom on the transatlantic Jumbo.

'In London Claus lived well. He worked for Getty, who doted on him. "What would I do without Claus?" he used to say. Claus would regularly have 200 people to dinner in his vast flat in Belgravia. He would take sixty people out to lunch at Wiltons. He was in the dead centre of the money world. He could have had any number of rich women.

'Claus always wanted the best. He waited – and he got Sunny. Incredibly beautiful, incredibly rich and, it seemed, incredibly easy to dominate. But Sunny proved to be surprisingly stubborn. Claus wanted to entertain, to splash money around. Sunny was reclusive. She never wanted to go anywhere or do anything – and she wanted

Claus with her at all times. The marriage soon developed into a kind of Faustian contract for Claus. He could do what he liked all day, while she was flower-arranging or at her exercise class. But at six o'clock he went home, had a TV dinner and watched *Bonanza* with his wife.

'Now Sunny. She might not have been a chronic drinker but she was always high on something. Often it was just nerves. She was the most discombobulated woman you ever met. At parties she would be dead silent, then catastrophically indiscreet. Someone might say, "There's nothing more boring than married sex." And Sunny would say, "Yes, but you're queer." Half the time you couldn't tell whether she knew you were in the room. The first husband, that titled ski-instructor or tennis-pro – he couldn't take it. She winked at his infidelities. But *he* left *her*.

'You probably don't understand about these rich American ladies. They have nothing else to worry about except their looks and figure. When money lets you live at such a pitch of perfection, ageing is intolerably ugly. A hint of flab is an abomination. These women are arrested anorexics. They doctor themselves with diet pills, laxatives, emetics. They eat a sundae and stick a finger down their throats . . . Sunny had a face-lift long before she needed one. Maria, the maid, she wouldn't discuss that at the trial, on principle. Her oath to Sunny superseded her oath to the court. Who knows what else she wouldn't discuss, on principle?

'Clearly Sunny and Claus used to mess around with drugs. Syringes were so much a part of the furniture that the kids used to use them as water-pistols. And here we have Truman Capote piping up, saying that now he comes to think of it Sunny von Bulow once told him that insulin jabs were a great way to lose weight! Truman's affidavit is included in the submission for a retrial. It'll all come out then.

'As for the two comas, I agree it looks pretty bad for Claus, particularly the first one. It's certainly possible that he was guilty of a degree of negligence here. Maybe he thought, "She's bombed herself out again. If that's what she wants, let her get on with it." Maybe he was bombed himself. No one said Claus was Captain Nice. But he isn't stupid. If he was going to kill his wife – there are dozens of more effective poisons.

'From then on you just have to look at the family set-up. With Sunny still technically alive, Claus controls her fortune. In league with the kids, Sunny's mother, who loathed Claus, hires this whole army of private dicks. They had the black bag in their possession for weeks. The insulin-tipped needle could easily have been a plant. Anyway, why didn't Claus destroy the evidence? As he says, he had the Atlantic Ocean at the back of his garden.

'Two more points. It's been said that Claus murdered for love. Claus wouldn't cross the street for love, let alone kill his wife for it. She had already settled an allowance on him: the income from a million-dollar investment. Now, if Claus were the sort of man who wanted really spectacular wealth, why didn't he wait a couple of years? Sunny's mother was past eighty and in poor health. With her gone, he'd have come into some serious money – $150 million.'

3 The Life of Pure Money

What's the difference between $75 million and $150 million? Hardly any difference, surely, in our terms. But in the life of pure money, $75 million and $150 million are chalk and cheese. What's the difference? The difference is $75 million.

Look around at your life. Look at your flat, house, your car, the sort of holidays you take, restaurants you eat at, clothes you wear. Not bad, eh? All right for now, at any rate. But in the world of pure money, your life is no kind of life, a nothing life. Your life is too poor to be lived.

'That house is owned by the top Mafia man in Providence,' said my contact, as our tour of Newport began. 'He burnt the place down for the insurance. His wife was in it at the time . . . That's the drive where the heiress ran over her Italian lover. He kept her locked in the attic . . . Alcoholic . . . Get rid of the mother . . . Suicide attempt . . . Disinherited . . . He controls all the money.'

We were driving down Bellevue Avenue. Huddled together on either side of the road are Gothic and Palladian mansions – laughingly known as 'summer cottages'. As Von Bulow once said, houses of this size in Europe would be surrounded by 30,000 acres. Here, they are practically terraced. Clarendon Court had comparatively extensive grounds: eleven acres. Clarendon Court had eleven gardeners. You cannot see the house from the road. The tall gate wears a buttoned bib; it looks as anomalous as the vest of a Scottie dog. A few mansions away stands Sunny's mother's place, also screened from the street.

Many of these grand follies are now wholly or partly deserted. Some eccentrics live on in the wings of mansions which are either abandoned or open to the public. The evening Atlantic mist enfolds the ocean lawns (the scenes of legendary parties), watched by the spectres of lost Bouviers, aged Oelrichs and vanished Vanderbilts.

You cannot get into Clarendon Court – few people ever did during Sunny's custodianship. Under an earlier reign, *High Society* was filmed there. I settled for Rosecliff, where they made *The Great Gatsby* and Harold Robbins's *The Betsy*. The blazered young guide led us up the heart-shaped marble staircase, through the silk and brocade of the bedroom, under the coffered ceilings of the salon, into the great ballroom ('the scene of many brilliant entertainments'), and into the baronial dining-room, where the table was set for thirty guests. 'Excuse me, sir,' a tourist asked the guide, 'but would they like eat *lunch* here?'

I slipped past the imported tapestries and pre-faded panelling – out into the Court of Love, designed by Augustus Saint-Gaudens on the model of Marie Antoinette's sanctuary at Versailles. Gum-chewing, super-coiffed young housewives pointed out features to their sleepy, plump-bellied men. Children in *ET* T-shirts skidded in the gravel. Plastic urns, filled with sand, now silted up with bubblegum and triple-band, extra-low-tar filters. Von Bulow gossip suffused the Court of Love. These people like to see how the other half lives. These people want to know how the other half dies.

4 The Clausettes

During the Von Bulow trial, the longest in Newport's history, Claus dwelt at the Sheraton Islander Hotel, hard by the innocuous court-house. The hotel staff loved him. 'So gracious. And every morning, always $10 for the maid.' Every morning, too, The Clausettes – informal cheerleaders in Von Bulow T-shirts – would jolly him along to his daily ordeal. Each night, as Von Bulow sorted wearily through his fan mail, there would be incessant long-distance calls from

assorted vampish lonelyhearts. 'It was extraordinary,' said a friend
who did a lot of hand-holding during the trial. 'You know: "It's
Suki from Hong Kong" . . . "It's Merouka from Tangiers . . . "'

Claus von Bulow is, to put it mildly, an unlikely folk-hero, yet
he has a great deal of solid public support, particularly among the
ladies. This can partly be attributed to the uncontrollable nature
of fame in America – where, for instance, multiple rapists and
winners of ugly-contests are promptly bombarded with love-tokens,
marriage-offers, and so on. Von Bulow, the stylish Eurocrat, the
man of façades, is particularly strong on such appeal. But it goes
a little deeper than that.

William Wright, in his solid, thorough, very pro-Sunny *The Von
Bulow Affair,* has an excellent point to make on the subject of
Bulowmania. It transpired that the jurors, in their six-day media-
tions, had one crucial difficulty in reaching a guilty verdict. It had
nothing to do with the medical evidence, the permissibility of the
black bag, the family 'vendetta'. The jurors were unable to accept
that *anyone* could commit such a crime.

Now there is a subtext here. By 'anyone' the jurors meant anyone
human, anyone familiar, anyone they knew. They had seen Von
Bulow every day for several months; however cold and remote,
Claus was palpably human. The Von Bulow trial was televised in
its entirety. The whole of America 'knew' Von Bulow. And nobody
one knows injects his wife with insulin for money, and then reclines
at her side watching her begin to die.

5 The Art of Manipulation

'Martin!' said *my* New York hostess in a hoarse whisper, on the
day of my return from Newport: 'It's *Claus von Bulow* on the
telephone!' Murders don't travel well, so it is necessary to account
for my friend's scandalised awe. The British equivalent of such an
exchange would have gone as follows: 'Who shall I say is calling?'
'Oh, it's the Yorkshire Ripper here.'

'Mr. Von Bulow,' I said. 'How do you do. How kind of you to
call.'

'Well, I heard you were in town', he said in his Wildean drawl,
'and that you were interested in my case. I don't think we'd better

meet, but I thought it only right to respond to that interest. I admire your writing. It seems a little obvious to say that I admire your father's writing too.'

Well, well. I asked my new friend Claus if I could prepare some questions and call him back. He nonchalantly agreed. We then talked for fifteen or twenty minutes. In terms of content, Von Bulow said very little that he hadn't already said in published interviews. But the style was markedly different – more droll, more florid, more literary. Here are some gobbets.

'I am innocent of this cowardly and despicable act. After all, it's hardly a *crime passionnel*. It would have required a great deal of premeditation, a great deal of malice.' When asked if his demeanour at the trial had told against him: 'Unquestionably. I am very tall, I look extremely arrogant. A Kraut general who happens to talk like Professor Higgins.' When asked why he didn't use some of his more eloquent sympathisers (Alan Pryce-Jones, for instance) as character witnesses: 'Well of course I absolutely adore Alan, but in Newport they'd need a *translator*.'

Expatiating on his love for Cosima, Von Bulow offered an ambitious quotation from Chesterton. When he ruled out the possibility that he might jump bail and flee to his native land, I bounced back with 'Denmark's a prison.' He guffawed obligingly. It is a pleasant laugh; the laugh takes off, takes over . . . 'Why didn't you take the stand?' I asked. 'I can't answer that,' said Von Bulow.

I confess that, as we talked, I hoped for Von Bulow's innocence. I also confess that I failed to ask the overwhelming question, the question to which there is no answer unless there was indeed a vendetta, an elaborate conspiracy. Experts agree that the coma was caused by an injection of insulin. Either Sunny did it, or Claus did. When Von Bulow was first questioned by the investigators – the first suspicion of suspicion – he was asked: 'Would your wife have any reason to inject herself with insulin?' Von Bulow didn't say, 'Why should she?' or 'Yes, she took it to lose weight' or 'You mean it was the *insulin*.' He said, 'My God. That's the last thing she should have!'

Everything about Von Bulow points to an obvious character type: the Manipulator. In my experience, Manipulators are always incompetent or transparent manipulators: the true manipulator never has a reputation for manipulating. Everyone harbours their theory about the night of December 19, 1980. Here, for what it's worth, is mine.

The theory rests on the inscrutability of marriage. I don't think Von Bulow covertly administered a fatal injection. He must have prepared some mitigation for his conscience; there must have been collusion, however innocent, on Sunny's part. In the ritual, the intimate theatre of the marriage bed, Sunny might have injected herself, sleepily half-deceived about the contents of the syringe. Or perhaps it was an offer of painless death to the tranquillised woman. 'Here, you do it. You press.' Then, the next day, the stalling, the play-acting, the vigil.

Von Bulow's appeal is imminent. A squad of lawyers is beavering away at the Harvard Law School, orchestrated by the famous loophole-specialist Alan Dershowitz. The crux of the defence's submission has to do with the large-scale use of private investigators: a private army of gumshoes (answerable not to the public, not to justice, but to the client) which then empties its confiscation cupboard into the lap of the police. As revealed in court, the cost of the operation was $100,000.

Dershowitz is on record with the boast that few of his clients are innocent. His services will take Von Bulow's legal expenses far beyond the million-dollar mark. But then this has always been a story about the very rich. At a cost of $1,500 a day, Sunny lives on, incapable of thought, helplessly reliant on the vigorous organism and its separate will to live.

Observer 1983

*   *   *

Postscript Von Bulow and Professor Dershowitz won their appeal. But in 1985 the new attorney-general of Rhode Island, an ex-nun called Arlene Violet, ordered a retrial. Again the prosecution's case was dismissed on technical grounds: the inadmissability of the black bag; the use of private investigators.

An intriguing, and representative, character in this drama is a 'flamboyant' young man called David Marriott. During preparations for the appeal he worked closely with the Claus camp; he was to testify that he had often supplied drugs and needles to Sunny and her son Alexander (Sunny's interest in dope of all kinds is no longer seriously denied). Later, Marriott said that the drugs 'didn't go to Sunny or Alex, they went to Claus'. While working with Claus and Dershowitz, Marriott was paid between $10,000 and $100,000 (claims vary) for expenses and 'lost wages'. Marriott has also signed up with a New York literary agent.

Climbing from his limousine, Marriott answered questions put to him by the *New York Times*. How did he support himself? 'It's nobody's business,' he said. 'Since 1976, I've had the use of a limousine. I've never really worked. And I don't work now.'

So much for 'lost wages'. So much for the strange life of pure money. Von Bulow has challenged – so far unsuccessfully – the estate's control of Sunny's fortune. He lunches most days at Mortimer's, on the Upper East Side. He has not spent a day in jail (indeed, there isn't an embarrassment of millionaires in what America likes to call its 'correctional facilities'). At the time of writing, Sunny is still alive – or, more accurately, not yet dead.

CLANCY SIGAL

Brando: A Family Affair

'The shooting was not an accident' – Cheyenne Brando, to the LA police.

Too symbolically, morning glories and barbed wire adorn the 10-foot high black steel gates of Marlon Brando's secluded estate high above Beverly Hills. All around the tightly guarded compound Brando shares with Jack Nicholson – the world's other most bankable movie star – the landscape is crumbling literally as well as psychologically. In one of the great acts of ecological violence, the Santa Monica Mountains are lopped off and bulldozed to make way for the mock-Victorian, two-million-dollar-per-house strip developments that threaten to strangle Mulholland Drive, the Hockney-ish, twisting road that separates Hollywood from San Fernando Valley. Visibly, dramatically, people are killing this once wild, gracious area.

We are used to lurid murders in Hollywood: William Desmond Taylor; the Fatty Arbuckle case; Thelma Todd; the knifing of hoodlum Johnny Stompanato by Lana Turner's daughter; Sal Mineo slain in his own garage (while I slept through his screams across the street). And most recently, Erik and Lyle Menendez, two sleek Princeton products, accused of using a 12-bore shotgun to blow out the brains of their wealthy showbiz parents in the smart family residence just off Rodeo Drive. Death in Hollywood is not democratic. You rate a screaming headline and massed TV cameras only if you're either famous or have a good address.

Marlon Brando qualifies on both counts.

On the night of 16 May, LA paramedics, summoned by the frantic 66-year-old actor, found his daughter Cheyenne's lover sprawled on a couch in the den of Brando's 12-room mountaintop home at 12900 Mulholland Drive. According to police, the lover, Dag Drollet, the 25-year-old son of a prominent Tahitian civil servant, was lying, almost tranquilly, holding a cigarette lighter in one hand and a TV remote control in the other. Drollet looked like any other couch potato in front of the continuously flickering television set. Except that a bullet from a .45 handgun had shattered his face and exited through his neck, and he was quite dead.

The gun belonged, it is said, to Marlon Brando's 32-year-old son, Christian, who immediately confessed to killing Drollet. Police also confiscated a Beretta shotgun, a carbine, an M-14 assault rifle, a MAC-10 machine pistol and a silencer.

It looks open and shut. Christian couldn't wait to spill his guts even if, as detectives commented drily, 'The suspect's account of what transpired changed with each telling.' The common thread of Christian's rambling admissions was that Drollet, the assumed father of Christian's 20-year-old half-sister Cheyenne's unborn child, had been slapping her around. Christian told Drollet to stop hitting her. There was an argument, a struggle, a shot. 'He fought for the gun,' the police report quotes Christian. 'I told him to let go. He had my hands, then boom! Jesus, man, it wasn't murder . . . Please believe me. I wouldn't do it in my father's house.'

Where might he do it? 'If I was going to kill that guy,' Christian burbled to furiously scribbling cops, 'I would have taken him to [nearby] Franklin Canyon and hit him in the head with a baseball bat and pulverised the guy.'

Clearly, Christian Brando, despite his father's leaning to Eastern mysticism and Zen doctrine, is no pacifist. Nor is Marlon Brando. For all its private luxury, Mulholland Drive – a favourite venue of teenage drag-racers who kill themselves fairly regularly by crashing over its steep cliffs – is full of crazy people. 'We have nuts coming up and down all the time,' Marlon has complained. One of the Hillside Strangler victims was found in the back of his own LA house, and his next-door neighbour was strangled in his bathroom. Roman Polanski's former wife, Sharon Tate, was murdered in Benedict Canyon, a minute away. Charles Manson terrorised rich hill-dwellers, like Brando, who has admitted to pulling a gun on intruders 'three or four times'.

Money is the honey, violence is the bee. Or, as one ex-MGM star told me, 'Fame plus available guns is lethal.' Even without guns, fame is a killer. If it misses the rich and famous, it gets their children.

'It helps to have something – it helps not to have everything,' the daughter of an Academy Award-winning screenwriter told me about the Brandos. She should know, because she grew up in Malibu's gilded colony where her best friends and surfing companions were movie stars' brats. She had gone to the same Montessori school as Christian, an overcrowded classroom packed with Hollywood's big-name children. Typically, it was run by Tom Laughlin, an aspiring screenwriter who was later reincarnated as 'Billy Jack'. The kids do not remember him fondly. 'I was a horrible child,' my friend says, 'but I wasn't so bad that I deserved that nasty mixture of contempt and adoration from the teachers who wanted the Hollywood connection but needed to show their independence of it.'

Her mother, who cut short her acting career to raise a family, adds, 'Something about our image on the screen makes people doubly toadying – and hating. This falls on children in a bad way. For stars' kids the middle option simply doesn't exist. They have to be as successful as their parents – or fail catastrophically. Either way it's an attention-getter.' And a Beverly Hills psychoanalyst, who was herself an actress married to a hunky star, mused, 'It's all this nutty pretence: on the one hand, lavishing money and cars on them, on the other, "I don't want our kids to know they're rich" nonsense. It's crazy – and makes for crazy youngsters.'

Hollywood is not unique in spoiling its children. (Though I must say I gasped slightly the other day when the 13-year-old son of a producer-director drove past in his own limousine.) Literary London, for example, can be fiercely self-involved too. But LA's cultural narcissism, coupled with the movie industry's almost Japanese caste system, can feel like hammer blows to the unwary or thin-skinned. The 'creative community', as it likes to call itself, is so transcendentally egomaniacal, so innocent of curiosity about the outside world, so breathtakingly in love with itself, that it's wonderful to behold – at a distance, if you have strong defences. Weaker egos like Christian Brando's – he's a self-described 'welder' or 'tree surgeon' who rarely worked and was utterly dependent on his father for money (including a $100,000 annuity) – wilted. Or waited for revenge.

But on whom, and why?

Christian hardly knew his victim. Dag Drollet's father had been the principal of Cheyenne's school in Tahiti and the families knew each other socially. Tarita, Cheyenne's mother and Marlon's wife, was in the house at the time of the murder but claims to have seen and heard nothing. She and Marlon have been together since he romanced her while filming the 1962 remake of *Mutiny on the Bounty* in French Polynesia. (Who can forget his amazing 'English' accent as the Bounty's mutinous leader, Fletcher Christian?) For what it's worth, Marlon's previous wife, by whom he had a child, was Movita Castenada, who played exactly the same 'native woman' role opposite Clark Gable in the original 1935 production. Christian's mother, Anna Kashfi, was Brando's first wife.

Tahiti, where his father owns a 12-island atoll, was Christian's personal decompresion chamber. He had good times on its lovely beaches, and even status of a sort as the son of a major landowner. The pressure was off, temporarily. But Hollywood is an overpowering magnet. Magnet may be the wrong image, more like oxygen tank for those craving the high, thin air of places like Mulholland Drive, insulated from, but part of, the only scene that matters, monies. Christian had lousy luck and even worse friends in Hollywood, but kept coming back.

He was dying to be what his father scorned, an actor. (Marlon: 'Acting has absolutely nothing to do with anything important.') But the only people who'd hire him – he once played a Mafia hitman in a cheap Italian film – wanted him solely as an entrée to his father. Without talent, deliberately sabotaging his auditions, strung out on God knows what, Christian gravitated toward the lower circles of the Hollywood inferno, the ex-cops and would-be starlets who would have refused him the time of day if he hadn't been his father's son. Take a look at TV news coverage next time he comes up for a court appearance and, among Christian's visitors and supporters, you will see a fair sample of the human locusts who feed upon famous names. Unless you have a taste for *Hollywood Babylon* or John Waters films, they aren't a pretty sight.

But Marlon Brando has been our public property for so long, why deny legitimacy to the more obvious gate-crashers?

No sane detective goes looking for clues to a murder in the film career of the killer's father. But the melodrama at 12900 Mulholland Drive – where, 13 years ago, Roman Polanski was accused of having sex with an underage girl in Jack Nicholson's house – may indeed owe something to the influence of Brando's screen personality on the actions of his son.

In jail photographs Christian, handcuffed and unshaven, looks suspiciously like 'Stanley Kowalski', the Tennessee Williams slob-with-dignity his father played so devastatingly in both the stage and film versions of *A Streetcar Named Desire*. What man has not been influenced by Marlon Brando's searing portraits (in *The Men, Viva Zapata, The Wild One and On the Waterfront*) of the male animal in pain? Then, in 1973, in *Last Tango in Paris*, Brando took the biggest risk of all by showing us an American man in the final agonies of an utterly vulnerable love. (While Brando was in Europe filming *Last Tango*, Christian's mother, Anna Kashfi, kidnapped the lad and took him to a Mexican hippie commune, in the umpteenth chapter of their ugly, 16-year custody battle.)

Probably not since Byron or Shelley, including Valentino, has a man made such an impact on our sexual imaginations as Brando. To make it worse, he is blusteringly modest. 'I'm just another s.o.b. sitting in a motor-home on a film set,' he once said, 'and they come looking for Zeus.'

How maddening to be the son of a genius who makes us feel like fools for admiring him.

Zeus indeed. In LA our gods are within reach: Marlon regularly broke from his well-publicised seclusion to dash out to K-Marts – tacky low-cost high-volume stores – to stock up on (for example) discount towels by the dozen. He was our very own Garbo, reminding us constantly, almost as an anti-presence, that he was somebody – a contender, perhaps? – outside his screen image. Father, like son, also had to fight for his identity against nebulous forces that he was constantly trying to pin down.

Together with lengthy psychoanalysis, politics helped Marlon to know who he was. He was dedicated and he took risks. Of course he always retired from the battlefield to the high ground of comparative luxury. But he gave freely to those in need, especially if they had coloured skin. A terrible guilt, possible personal in nature, drove him to feel he had to make up for the white man's crimes, whether in South Dakota or South Africa. He made enemies, but also comrades and friends.

That night, after vainly trying to revive Dag Drollet with mouth-to-mouth resuscitation, Brando instinctively reached for the phone to ring his old political ally, the great radical lawyer William Kunstler. ('Get me Bill Kunstler NOW. Not five minutes from now. Not 10 minutes from now. NOW!'.) Together they'd fought many battles, especially for Native American-Indian rights. Kunstler flew in from New York and, in demanding bail, leaned on the black woman magistrate by harping on his long record in the civil rights movement. When refused, he fizzed and fumed like a Yankee Rumpole ('an outrage'), then turned the case over to a young associate. Kunstler's next case is – what else? – the role of a lawyer in Oliver Stone's new film about Jim Morrison and The Doors.

Ah, Hollywood.

The Brando affair has become, like our other big social/legal event – Zsa Zsa slapping the Beverly Hills cop – an A-budget Technicolor production. Marlon is ready for the role. 'The messenger of misery has come to my house,' he intones to the world's press, their cameras whirring like deadly hummingbird wings. We gloat dutifully, feeding off the frenzied details because everybody is talking: cops, chums, secretaries, ex-wives, future mistresses (they hope), Brando's brother, old schoolteachers. There's an awful lot of 'payback' involved. So many people seem to have grudges, envy, long-simmering resentments. An agreed-upon fiction emerges of Marlon as a bad father, a paunchy old pasha who can't say hello to an exotic-looking woman without making her pregnant. (Among his nine or 10 children, four of them 'official', is the infant of his current live-in housekeeper.)

In this obviously overheated version, Marlon's ménage is a wild collection of avant-garde Beverly Hillbillies who, anywhere but the Hollywood Hills, would send property values plummeting. Unfathomable evils of the flesh and spirit are hinted at. Yet our response is sad and subdued. We can't fail to be impressed by the indestructible stoicism of Brando and his brown-skinned, superbly beautiful family in the face of the gawping courtroom mob.

In all senses, this family affair, between the Drollets and Brandos, and between us and the images we still carry in our psyches of a fiery young rebel, incarnating our secret pride and injury, who became just another ageing father with an out-of-control kid.

Only one person has a legitimate claim on Brando – Dag's father, Jacques. Dignified and truly patriarchal, M. Drollet – part-Norwegian, part-French, part-Tahitian – is also Nemesis. While Brando's $500-an-hour lawyers and the DA's office throw their legal bones to see in them Christian's fate (anywhere from murder one to involuntary manslaughter), Jacques Drollet keeps demanding a trial so that the 'whole story' can be told. Perhaps mistrustful of LA home town justice, he has started a civil-criminal action in Tahiti against Cheyenne, now charged with murder complicity.

And it's true that a lot of unanswered questions hang in the hot, dry air. Who did all those guns belong to? Was Christian really drunk when he stood so closely over Dag Drollet that the victim's face had a star-shaped powder burn? What did Cheyenne say over dinner with Christian just before the murder, that may have jacked him up enough to kill that night? How many people actually witnessed the shooting? (Cheyenne herself says she walked into the TV room, saw Christian with a gun, but left because she thought they were 'just playing'. She has since fled to Tahiti and given birth to a boy, presumably Dag's.) Why did she burn her lover's personal effects immediately after the shooting? Why was she so eager to insist to police that, contrary to Christian's story, it was no accident? And why was Marlon Brando, normally so reticent, equally quick to deny Dag had stuck Cheyenne – a key part of Christian's defence – and to point out that his son always had a violent temper when angry? (He also told police that ever since a recently disfiguring car accident

Cheyenne had begun telling falsehoods about several members of the family.)

In this cacophony of half-guesses and (so far) unasked questions, only Jacques Drollet's demand for justice sounds unambiguously clear. For Christian he feels only mild contempt. ('A coward, a coyote.') His animus is reserved for Marlon. 'He knows our Tahitian customs. He should have protected my son. In Tahiti the host is under an obligation to protect the guest, morally and physically.' This profound breach of Tahitian etiquette, and the fact that neither Marlon nor Cheyenne went to Dag's funeral, fuels an impressive rage that may help to send Christian to prison.

Or not. Even mass rapist-murderers and serial killers plea-bargain down. But Christian's bad luck is that the name that made, and crucified, him may force the authorities to play it straight for once – no leniency, no under-the-table deals to sell a screenplay to the defendant's father – rather than risk charges of favouritism. The rules of justice, which Marlon Brando has always tried to shape to the benefit of the underdog, he must now attempt to exploit for his spoiled, violent son.

What would Fletcher Christian, or Gauguin do? Trouble has come to Marlon's Paradise despite his best efforts. Brando had fought hard for a family life. He did not neglect Christian; perhaps better that he had. He went to school plays and constantly bailed his son out of scrapes. He tried 'tough love', too. He isn't the only parent in Hollywood, or anywhere else, who was alternately too soft and too hard in the face of the unparalleled craziness that American teenagers must cope with, a social madness of drugs and random killing a billion years beyond what Marlon 'Bud' Brando, son of a rambunctiously bohemian mother, experienced growing up in the Thirties in Libertyville, Illinois.

'Man's breath is fatal to his fellow man,' Marlon is fond of quoting Rousseau. Yet in his long search for a simple place that does not disgust him – on a Pacific island, in Eastern philosophy or Western activism, in his own soul whose tarnish he may have come to know too well – Marlon Brando finally came to rest in a house that, with its surveillance cameras, barbed wire and armed guards, looks remarkably like a miniature version of Langley, headquarters of the CIA, which he has so often cited as the root of many of our political evils. 'All the rich people do,' he has said, 'is move farther and farther away from the areas of trouble.'

But, as in a Raymond Chandler thriller, trouble turned out to be his business. Marlon Brando pursued Utopian dreams and found Hollywood nightmares.

ROBERT RAND

Nightmare on Elm Drive

The typical tourist wouldn't think of coming to Hollywood without taking a ride on Space Mountain at Disneyland or meeting Bruce, the man-eating shark from the movie Jaws along the Universal Studio Tour. For those with a sense of the macabre who want to go beyond the glitz and glamour, there is Graveline Tours, which for $30 will expose you to '100 years of death, sin, and scandals'. For three hours, camera-toting tourists ride in a long, black hearse for a visit to the dark side. The tour includes the home where Marilyn Monroe committed suicide and the hotel where John Belushi overdosed on cocaine and heroin.

Since last year, there has been a new stop on the Graveline Tour outside the gates of a $5 million Mediterranean-style mansion on Elm Drive in Beverly Hills. It is the home where Jose and Kitty Menendez were brutally murdered with 12-gauge shotguns on August 20, 1989. Twice daily, the hearse stops and people hear what sounds like the classic American immigrant's dream story including financial success, a beauty queen wife, and two loving children.

Everyone knew the Menendezes were a close-knit family – handsome, strong and successful. So it came as a great shock when, seven months after the murders, Beverly Hills Police announced that the couple's own sons, Erik, 19, and Lyle, 22, had not only masterminded the killings, but pulled the trigger on their parents. The motive: simple greed. Detectives believe the Menendez brothers couldn't wait to inherit their parents' $14 million estate. Relatives and friends refuse to accept the official theory of the crime, saying these two loved and often-hugged young men are innocent. Beverly

Hills officials will privately tell you they are 100 per cent certain the brothers committed the murders.

Jose Enrique Menendez fled Cuba at 16 – the son of a privileged class whose privileges had suddenly been revoked – to live in the attic of strangers near Philadelphia, Pennsylvania. In less than three decades, he transformed that inauspicious beginning into an entertainment conglomerate, a vision into a huge money-making reality. His friends and business associates were international celebrities – Sly Stallone, Kenny Rogers, Barry Manilow, The Eurythmics.

August 1989 had been a typical non-stop, hard-working whirlwind for Jose Menendez. During the first week, he had renewed his three-year contract as chairman of the board and president of Live Entertainment, a video and music distribution company. His base salary of $500,000 was bolstered by bonuses of nearly a million a year. The annual Video Software Dealers Association convention in Las Vegas had been a great success, as had several forays to New York to romance analysts and new investors on Wall Street. Live company officials announced several major videocassette releases and unveiled an impressive upcoming list: new movies on the way from Jessica Lange, Arnold Schwarzenegger, and the company's biggest and most reliable star, Stallone.

Sunday, August 20, late summer in Southern California, was warm and hazy with the usual orange cloud that seemed to be hanging off in the distance even though you knew the smog was all around you. Jose was home spending the day with his wife, Kitty, and their two sons. Family had always been very important to Menendez.

His weekly schedule might include stops in London, Berlin, and Tokyo, but on the weekend he would always try to be home with the boys, even if he had to be in Europe again the following week. Erik and Lyle had serious ambitions of joining the pro-tennis circuit. That Sunday, after playing on the court behind the eight-bedroom house, everyone relaxed in front of a big screen TV to watch Brad Gilbert compete in a tournament. Erik and Lyle's tennis trophies sat proudly on a narrow shelf lining the wood-panelled, high-ceilinged family room. The brothers were invited to a food tasting festival that night. Jose didn't want them to go, but later relented. Before going to the party, they stopped near the UCLA campus to catch the new James Bond thriller, *Licence to Kill*. The queues were too long, so they ended up seeing Batman.

Around 11 pm, Erik and Lyle called a friend and made plans to met at the Cheesecake Factory, a Beverly Hills restaurant. The brothers say they drove home to pick up identification cards so they would be able to drink beer. The friend waited at the restaurant for 45 minutes. Erik and Lyle never showed.

Just after ten, Jose and Kitty Menendez were settled in the family room watching a movie. It was the maid's night off and they were spending a rare evening alone together. Half-eaten bowls of fresh berries and cream sat on a wooden coffee table in front of the beige, L-shaped sectional sofa. Jose was dressed casually in shorts and a sweatshirt. Kitty was wearing a jogging suit.

Jose started to doze off. He was in a resting position with his arms folded across his stomach, his feet up on the coffee table. Kitty was sitting next to him. The house was equipped with an alarm system, but Jose rarely turned it on. The boys were always setting it off by accident. Besides, he felt safe in Beverly Hills.

A neighbour heard some 'popping sounds' a short time later but didn't think anything of it. The idea of gun shots just didn't fit in the neighbourhood. But it wasn't fire-crackers. The French doors behind the couch were open on this warm summer night. Two men with 12-gauge shotguns had quietly walked in and put the barrel of a gun to the back of Jose Menendez's head before pulling the trigger. Kitty turned to see a gun only inches from her mouth. Instinctively, she raised a hand to protect her face as the gun was fired. The blast threw her from the couch to the floor.

In all, five shots were fired at Jose. Kitty was hit ten times. The killers seemed to particularly dislike Kitty, disfiguring her with four shots to the head and one that nearly severed her wrist. After patiently picking up all the shell casings from the pools of blood on the Oriental rug and parquet floor, the killers vanished.

Veteran homicide investigator Dan Stewart says Jose was almost unrecognisable because of his wounds. 'The wounds were devastating, like a small fist going through you. I've seen a lot of homicides, but nothing quite that brutal.'

When Erik and Lyle pulled up to 722 Elm Drive just before midnight, the electric driveway gate was open and the front door unlocked. The first thing they saw inside was grey clouds of smoke still hanging lazily in the air. Beverly Hills police recorded a hysterical emergency 911 call at 11.47 pm. 'Somebody shot and killed my parents,' sobbed Lyle Menendez. As the dispatcher repeatedly asks, 'They were shot?' Lyle screams, 'Erik, shut up!' and later 'Erik! get away from them!' When the police arrived minutes later, a horrible, pathetic scream pierced the night. It was Erik Menendez rolled up in a ball, crying hysterically on the front lawn.

"I've never seen anything like it and never will see anything like it," Erik Menendez told me two months after the murders. Quietly, in a calm, low voice he said: 'It's probably the hardest thing I'll ever have to do. They weren't real . . . wax . . . it looked like wax. I've never seen my dad helpless. I hope it was sudden. Possibly, if Lyle and I had been here, we could have done something. Maybe my dad would be alive, maybe I'd be dead. I'd definitely give my life for my dad's. He was always there when I needed him.'

As the ambulances loaded with the bodies flashed down the street, neighbours stood helplessly on their magnificent lawns. 'Please, tell me he's a drug lord,' pleaded a woman who lived nearby. Another neighbour kept repeating: 'Things like this just don't happen here.'

But it had happened here; beautiful elegant Beverly Hills, home of the Polo Lounge, Giorgio, Zsa Zsa, and Rodeo Drive. The town averages two murders a year. In a few brief moments, 1989's quota had been filled.

One afternoon in 1954, 10-year-old Jose Menendez went to Havana Airport to meet his father, a successful accountant and former soccer star. Security was tight around the international arrivals area, but the young boy strode regally up to the Customs officer and declared, 'My name is Jose Enrique!' It was what Jose's mother called 'his king complex'. He never said his full name, Jose Enrique Menendez, because kings did not use their last name. She says, 'He was very proud of himself: he was He.' His imperious manner must have either charmed or flabbergasted. The officer stepped aside and let the boy pass.

He was bright, terrifically energetic, precociously self-possessed, disarmingly arrogant, born into wealth and position. But the traits that got him through airport security in 1954, and made him a sure bet for success in Batista's Cuba, just might have landed him in prison six years later. After Fidel Castro came out of the Sierra Maestra mountains, Jose's parents sent him off with his sister's fiance to the fiance's distant relatives in the United States. The two youths simply showed up with nothing and hoped they would be taken in. They shared an attic room, and Jose entered high school, his bright hopes up against long odds.

He married at 19, an American girl – Mary Louise Andersen. They called her Kitty. His father wrote saying he was too young to get married. Jose replied: 'If I'm old enough to live on my own at 16, I'm old enough to get married at 19.' He washed dishes and sold encyclopaedias to work his way through Queen's College. He had to wait for pay day to scrape up a $3 class fee. They ate a lot of salty ham and peanut butter.

In spite of the financial pressure, Erik Menendez says his mother remembered the struggling fondly. 'My mom says that's the closest they've ever been. The happiest days they ever had were during that time because it brought them so close together. Money kind of brings you apart. It loosens the ties because you no longer need to be as close.'

Jose Menendez made it through and put three letters after his name, CPA. An accountant trainee is not quite king, but Menendez didn't hang around at the bottom. By the time he was 25, he was a company comptroller making $75,000 a year. He moved on to Hertz, the car rental giant, where Bob Stone, former chairman of the board and CEO, said of him: 'I never knew anyone who worked harder, worked more toward goals. If he had stayed at Hertz, he would've become president of the company.'

Jose became known for solving problems inside troubled divisions. When he moved in, people were fired or reassigned and budgets were streamlined. Stone says Menendez was not a hatchet man but 'a demanding executive who made changes that were necessary.' When things got tough, Jose would compare problems to his own life and tell fellow workers: 'That's a problem, but it's certainly not as big a problem as losing your country.'

After being promoted to executive vice-president in charge of US operations, the long days and gruelling trips took their physical toll. Jose's hair started falling out and the skin on his hands began to peel from nerves.

Jose Menendez always wanted his sons to be the best at whatever they did. When they were nine and 12, he told them to choose between tennis and soccer because they couldn't excel at both. His preference was for tennis. You didn't have to depend on anyone else. The boys found themselves in tennis clinics three times a week with private coaches.

On weekends, Jose would hit balls back and forth for hours, drilling his sons on the techniques of the game. Erik Menendez says Jose insisted that everything he and Lyle did should be perfect or not be done. 'We are prototypes of my father. He wanted us to be exactly like him.'

Menendez rarely socialised outside work, preferring to stay at home at the end of his daily commute from Princeton, New Jersey to New York City. On the weekends, Jose's parents, sisters, and their children would gather together for at least one day of visiting, cooking a big meal, and watching sports on TV. Family members say they never saw major problems in the Menendez household. Jose ran things in a traditional Latin style with himself in the dominant role. Kitty fulfilled an important supporting role, making sure the boys were at school or lessons on time. Jose himself would often take time out of his busy day to check up and see if everything was going smoothly with his sons. He expected the best from his sons and rewarded them for it although he refused to settle for anything less.

One relative says Jose could get angry with his boys and often lectured them, but the discipline was never physical. People who knew the family in New Jersey remember the boys playing competitive sports when they were growing up, but never seeming to have much fun at it. Lyle and Erik were noted for spending a great deal of time with each other, being a bit isolated from other young people.

People around Jose thought he eased up a bit when he switched from Hertz to the less buttoned-down crowd at RCA Records in 1980. A job change from car rentals to pop music might seem odd, but Bob Stone says Menendez was 'a superb executive and could've put in any business'. The former dish-washer was making $500,000 a year and signing rock groups such as Duran Duran and the Eurythmics. He pushed for the signing of Latin music acts and RCA signed them: Emmanuel, Menudo, Jose Feliciano.

Menendez established a reputation as an inflexible straight arrow at a time when casual drug use was widespread and accepted in the music business. Erik Menendez says his father was threatened after warning some acts they would be dropped from RCA Records because they were users. He says his father never took the threats seriously.

In 1986, General Electric bought RCA, and when Menendez wasn't made president, he left. His settlement with RCA was almost a million dollars. He used to joke that Kitty needed three of him to support the family's free-spending habits, but he told his mother it was her money because she had supported him in school. The family had just moved into a beautiful stone mansion at the end of a half-mile long driveway. The 13-acre estate, known as Mountain Lakes, was once owned by Andrew Carnegie.

Jose had many job offers to work for somebody else, but his most intriguing option was a position in California with Carolco Pictures which planned to start a video division. The most attractive part of the offer was partial ownership of the company. For Jose, picking up and moving thousands of miles away was not difficult. His entire life was family and work, so there were few close friends to leave behind.

For years, Jose had been taking Kitty for granted. To her, the idea of moving to California from New Jersey was devastating. She had built her own world of friends, lunches and charity work. The thought of moving to a strange city after 16 years in Princeton upset her. One evening, Jose suggested that Kitty stay in New Jersey with Lyle who was planning to attend Princeton University. He would move to California with Erik who still had two years of high school left and commute on weekends. Kitty quickly said no to the proposal.

Jose went back to Carolco and asked for what he considered a ridiculous amount of money. When his offer was accepted, he took the job, regretting that he hadn't asked for even more

money. Kitty and the boys dutifully moved with him to Los
Angeles.

When they arrived in California first Jose rented a beach house
near Malibu to make Kitty feel better. She started a two year project
to extensively remodel the structure. The family bought the Beverly
Hills house while the work (including moving a swimming pool)
dragged on. Kitty's project was taking so long, Jose joked that they
would never get to live in it. He was, of course, proved right.

A police investigator told a reporter a few weeks after the killings
that 'the murders stink of organised crime. They went there to take
care of business and to make a message clear.' But as the late summer
turned into fall, no suspects were forthcoming.

The entertainment community in Los Angeles is like a small
town when it comes to gossip and the sudden killing of a leading
video executive kept phone lines buzzing for weeks. People who
knew Jose Menendez talked about a gang fight involving his son
and subsequent threats to the family. Some believed it must be
drug related simply because of his Spanish surname. But it was
just talk.

Officials from Menendez's parent company, Carolco Pictures
(which hit the jackpot after financing Rambo: First Blood, Part
2, which grossed over $250 million worldwide) released a statement
saying 'all who worked with Jose find it inconceivable that he was
involved in any unsavoury dealings that might have led to this tragic
event'. They considered the idea of the killings being a mob hit
'bizarre and offensive'.

That statement is at least naive. The home video business began
in the mid-seventies because people wanted to watch porno videos at
home. Long before corner video emporiums popped up everywhere,
there were little store-fronts selling grainy films of couples rolling
around under bright lights. The men never took their socks off. That
original distribution network was dominated by organised crime.

When adult films evolved into videos and mainstream movie
studios saw a potential gold mine, they moved into the business
and absorbed a number of people who had adult film experience
on their resumes. Today, porno films, once relegated to bachelor
parties and dingy back rooms, are now a $700 million a year business.
Home video is a $7 billion a year industry. Menendez was part of

the legitimisation of home video. Some people think he inevitably stepped on a few dangerous toes.

In the past three years, Live Entertainment has purchased interests in two companies from people identified by law enforcement authorities as having ties to organised crime. One of those men was the former owner of Caballero Home Video, the largest adult film company in the business. Live officials say they did exhaustive research into both companies and found them to be clean.

Menendez told his mother, four days before he died, about the pressures of the world he lived in. But he reassured her that he believed he had nothing to fear as long as he held his course. 'There's always somebody that will be a problem to you,' she says he told her. 'He wouldn't stop for money or fear. Only by removing him could they make him change his opinion.'

Despite all the talk of possible mob connections in the media, the Beverly Hills police investigation was quietly focusing in on Erik and Lyle Menendez. The behaviour of the boys had become a most intriguing lead. Detectives felt the brothers simply hadn't done a very good job playing the role of grief-stricken orphans. Usually, family members of murder victims take an active, aggressive role in the police investigation. Lyle and Erik didn't seem to care about the search for the killers.

Detectives asked the brothers to produce the ticket stubs of the movie they say they saw (they didn't have them), and subpoenaed phone records from a pay phone the boys said they used the night of the murders: there was no record of a call they said they made. They also tried unsuccessfully to recover a file deleted from Menendez's personal computer a month after the shootings that allegedly contained a reference to Jose and Kitty's will.

Marta Cano, Menendez's sister, says the family is upset that anyone would question the boys' love for their parents. Lyle deleted the file by mistake, she said. Besides, they would have no reason to tinker with the will. Jose had always been generous in providing for their future. A computer expert hired by Lyle says he erased family files that could have contained a reference to a new will, possibly one that would have left less to the sons (who inherited everything) and something to other family members. Beverly Hills detectives seized the computer last January after executing a search warrant on the Elm Drive mansion.

In the months just after the murders, Lyle Menendez spent over $500,000. The spending spree included a new Porsche, a gold Rolex watch, and $40,000 of new clothes. He also put down $300,000 to purchase a chicken wing restaurant near the Princeton University campus. Family members say this was Lyle's way of dealing with his grief, describing him as 'never having been very emotional'. They tell the story of Jose reacting to his own father's death, going into the bathroom so no one could see him cry.

As investigators dug deeper into the Menendez brothers background, they discovered that Erik Menendez had written a screenplay with a friend. Entitled *Friends*, it was amateurish and banal, unlikely to have ever been made into a movie. The script, which Kitty Menendez helped type, opens with the protagonist, Hamilton Cromwell, finding the family will and discovering he stood to inherit $157 million. He murders his parents, inherits the money, but in the end is killed and dies smiling.

On Friday, August 18, two days before the murders, someone used the driving licence of Donovan Goodreau, a former room mate of Lyle Menendez, to buy two 12-gauge shotguns in a sporting goods store in San Diego. Police believe that the shotguns, which have never been recovered, were the murder weapons. Information on a government form, filled out during the sale, had Goodreau's licence number but phoney San Diego address. Goodreau says he lost the licence when he moved out of Lyle's dorm room at Princeton University. Police also have information that Lyle showed the licence to a friend several days after Goodreau's departure.

Much of the case against the Menendez brothers seems to rest on circumstantial evidence. A friend of Lyle's allegedly found a shotgun shell casing in his jacket pocket but the credibility of that information is questionable since it was revealed that the pair had a falling out after the collapse of a potential business deal. The gun purchase records, located a few weeks after the arrest of Lyle and voluntary surrender of Erik (who was playing in a tennis tournament in Israel), could be more damning but not conclusive.

The prosecutor's key evidence is audiotape recordings of a psychologist's notes and at least one actual therapy session, involving both brothers, made several months after the murders. Police arrested Lyle a few hours after seizing the tapes, during a raid on the home of Dr. Jerome Oziel, a Beverly Hills psychologist, who was treating both Erik and Lyle. Normally, conversations between a patient and therapist are confidential but under California law, the privilege can be broken if the patient threatens violence or if the doctor reveals information to a third party.

Judalon Smyth, a former patient and friend of Dr. Oziel, reportedly contacted police after learning of allegedly incriminating statements made by Erik and Lyle Menendez. Oziel, 43, is the target of a lawsuit, filed by Smyth, 37, in which she alleges sexual assault and fraud. In the suit, Smyth claims that the psychologist developed an intimate relationship with her while she was his patient, threatened, choked and struck her on several occasions, raped her, gave her drugs and coerced her into signing a $5,000 promissory note she believed was a gift. Oziel denies the charges. His attorney calls the situation 'a real life enactment of the movie Fatal Attraction'.

In a major victory for the prosecution, a judge ruled on August 6 that the tapes on which the brothers allegedly confessed to the murders may be used as evidence against them. Judge James Albracht found that Dr Oziel had 'reasonable cause to believe' that Lyle and Erik Menendez 'constituted a threat and it was necessary to disclose those communications to prevent danger'. Defence attornies have called Oziel 'less than credible', saying they will appeal the ruling all the way to the California Supreme Court. The Menendez brothers showed no reaction to the ruling although relatives and friends in the court room gasped.

Erik and Lyle Menendez have pleaded innocent. They could receive the death penalty under California law if convicted. A trial is at least several months away until the issue of the psychologist's tapes is litigated and the appeals process exhausted. Meanwhile, the two brothers continue to sit in the tomb-like Los Angeles County Jail where they are being held without bail. At the continuing court hearings, they appear at ease, smiling at relatives and their attractive blonde girlfriends who visit them daily at the jail. Family members insist the brothers may have been set up by a third party to take responsibility for the murders. There is even speculation the boys may know who killed their parents but are keeping quiet out of fear.

At a news conference announcing Lyle's arrest, Beverly Hills Police Chief Marvin Iannone told reporters greed was the motive behind the murders. Pressed for a further explanation, he offered a non-answer saying: 'Who knows what goes on within a family?' The people who know the answer to that question believe the police have made a horrible mistake. Terry Baralt, the aunt of Erik and Lyle Menendez quietly says: 'We thought the murder was bad enough, but you grieve and life goes on. We felt 1990 had to be a better year. Now this is even worse than the murders.'

JAY ROBERT NASH

A 'Wronged'
Woman's Fury

Juanita Edwards, a woman in her sixties, sat in the examining room while Dr. Herman Tarnower took her pulse. At the time, Tarnower was not only a leading cardiologist but one of the most celebrated authors in America, his book *The Complete Scarsdale Medical Diet*, written with Samm Sinclair Baker, having sold more than three million copies and grossed more than $11 million since its publication in January 1979. Before Tarnower completed his examination of Mrs. Edwards, the doctor was called to the phone by his assistant, Mrs. Lynne Tryforos, a slim, attractive thirty-eight-year-old blonde.

Tarnower picked up the phone in the examining room, then told his assistant: 'I'll take this call in my office.' He excused himself, leaving the phone off the hook so that Mrs. Edwards accidentally heard part of his conversation whenever he raised his voice. 'Goddamnit, Jean,' Mrs. Edwards heard Tarnower yell over the phone, 'I want you to stop bothering me!' There was some muffled conversation, then the doctor again yelled: 'You've lied and you've cheated!' Later he was heard to say: 'Well, you're going to inherit $240,000.' The sixty-nine-year-old doctor hung up and returned, visibly agitated, to finish his examination of Juanita Edwards.

The 'Jean' he had just brushed off was his fifty-six-year-old mistress, Jean Struven Harris, whom he had been seeing for fourteen years. Dr. Tarnower would see her once again on this last day of his life.

Actually, there had been many mistresses in the long and lucra-tive life of Herman Tarnower, dozens of them whose names and addresses he kept in a little black book. Jean Harris had lasted the longest, but only because she had willingly become his slavish pawn, a role that she came to loathe, one that caused a self-hatred and a seething passion for either vindication or vengeance. On March 10, 1980, Mrs. Harris chose the latter course.

That Monday afternoon Jean Harris left her duties at the Madeira School and slipped behind the wheel of her blue 1973 Chrysler. She drove through a rainstorm for five hours from McLean, Virginia, an exclusive Washington, D.C., suburb, to the $500,000 six-and-a-half acre estate of Herman Tarnower outside of Purchase, New York, near Scarsdale in Westchester County and nineteen miles out of New York City. She had swallowed several amphetamines, and inside her purse rested a .32-caliber revolver with extra cartridges.

While Jean Harris was still on the road battling rain-coated roads, Dr. Tarnower was dining with intimate friends, including his attractive blond assistant, Mrs. Lynne Tryforos. His guests left the sprawling Tarnower home – with its Japanese motifs, its huge swimming pool, tennis courts, and private duck pond – by 9 P.M. A little less than two hours later Jean Harris arrived at the estate and made her way through the darkened mansion to a second-floor bedroom to face a pajama-clad Herman Tarnower.

Some minutes later shots rang out that awakened Suzanne van der Vreken and her husband, Henri. The housekeeper-cook told her husband, who was the grounds keeper for the estate, to go upstairs and check on the noise. He cautiously entered the doctor's room, to find his employer lying between twin beds and dying of four bullet wounds in the hand, chest, shoulder, and arm. His wife, meanwhile, had called police in nearby Harrison, New York. Putting down the phone, the housekeeper went to the window to see a blue Chrysler sedan parked in the circular driveway. Someone was sitting behind the wheel.

As she stared straight ahead into the dark drizzle that awful night, Mrs. Jean Struven Harris, a worldly, educated, and highly refined woman, must have thought deeply and desperately back to the time when fate had brought her into contact with Herman Tarnower. It was a time when she had been made to feel like Cinderella by a charming, urbane, but domineering man who had over the years utterly captivated her heart and mind (or so she later insisted) and, through his betrayals and her insane jealousy, brought about her ruination as well as his own violent death.

Jean Harris's background was one that would brighten the hustling heart of any personnel agent inspecting her resumé. Born in Cleveland, Ohio, to a career military officer, she lived as a child in the exclusive suburb of Shaker Heights and attended the Laurel School, a private academy for girls from upper-class families. She graduated with honors and then during the war years moved on to Smith College, where she graduated magna cum laude and Phi Beta Kappa in 1945.

Marrying James Harris, the son of a Detroit industrialist, who worked as an executive for the Holly Carburetor Company, Jean settled down in exclusive Grosse Pointe, where she taught history at the Country Day School. From 1950 to 1954 she stayed at home to raise her two sons, David and James. They were to grow up calling her 'Big Woman' in reference to her proper manner and insistence on etiquette; she was a gentle but persistent disciplinarian.

Mrs. Harris returned to teaching at the University Liggett School in Grosse Pointe. In 1964, Jean made two major decisions. She divorced her husband on grounds of cruelty and, after she was passed over as assistant to the president of her school, moved on to become the director of an exclusive Philadelphia girls' school, Springside, living with her two sons in the well-to-do suburb of Chestnut Hill. In 1972 she became the director of the now defunct Thomas School in Rowayton, Connecticut, another exclusive girls' school. It was here that Mrs. Harris first began to show signs of instability; she was subject to 'unexplainable emotional outbursts,' according to one faculty member. Her unruly temper may have caused her to look elsewhere for employment in 1977 after board members criticized her behavior.

It was in that year that Jean Harris became the headmistress for the Madeira School for girls in McLean, Virginia, which had graduated the likes of Katharine Graham, chairman of *The Washington Post*. Mrs. Harris had arrived at the top of her profession when she assumed the position at one of the most exclusive schools in America. It was here that Mrs. Harris earned the sobriquet of 'Integrity Jean' for her obsession with honesty and her near-rabid emphasis on discipline. Two weeks before driving to the Tarnower estate with a gun in her purse, Jean Harris had arbitrarily expelled four girls -- from some of the wealthiest families supporting Madeira -- for drinking and smoking marijuana.

Mrs Harris's attitude during this period was undoubtedly influenced by the vexing thought that her lover of fourteen years, the indefatigable Dr. Tarnower, was about to throw her over for another woman, a younger woman, a sleek, calculating blonde who, in Mrs. Harris's troubled mind, was out to destroy her. Her constant obsession with honesty, was, no doubt, a reaction to the incessant betrayals she experienced with Tarnower. In her public life as the prim and proper headmistress of Madeira, Mrs. Harris exhorted her female charges to concentrate on emotional integrity, not outward gloss and polish.

In one address to seniors at Madeira she stated:

> I have often talked with you about those useful study skills and good manners that we hope you have woven into the fabric of your lives during your years at Madeira. But it occurs to me I have seldom mentioned that most important ingredient of all, a stout and loving heart. It is not easily won and yet is one of those things we each assume we have and so neglect to give it the attention it deserves. Hard work, good intentions, politeness, even genius are not substitutes for it.

Mrs. Harris's own heart was lost long before to Dr. Herman Tarnower, to her beloved 'Hi,' as intimates called him. The two first met on December 9, 1966, at a Manhattan dinner party given in the home of Leslie and Marjorie Jacobson. 'It was an instant take,' Marjorie Jacobson later testified when referring to that first meeting between Tarnower, whom she had known for twenty-five years, and Mrs. Harris, who had been a childhood friend.

Herman Tarnower must have seemed to Jean Harris an exceptional man, if not a trifle odd in that he was eminently successful and had been for most of his life, yet he had never married. Tarnower was born into wealth; his father was a prosperous hat manufacturer in New York City. He had been expected to go into the family business but ignored that idea and entered Syracuse University, studying medicine and graduating in 1933. He served his residency at Bellevue. He traveled extensively through Europe on a 1936–37 postgraduate fellowship, specializing in the study of cardiology in London and Amsterdam.

He returned to White Plains Hospital in 1939 as an attending cardiologist. During World War II, Tarnower served as a medical officer in the U.S. Army Air Corps. After Japan surrendered, the doctor was a lieutenant colonel and a member of the Casualty Survey Commission, examining Japanese civilians injured in the A-bomb blasts of Hiroshima and Nagasaki, an unforgettable if not traumatic experience for Tarnower that he spoke of frequently during the remainder of his long and lucrative life.

After being mustered out of the Army, Tarnower moved to Scarsdale to open a medical practice. As his practice expanded he grew rich, establishing his own Scarsdale Medical Center in 1959. The doctor spent his leisure time traveling about the world and shooting big game, delighting in annual African safaris where he shot kudu, lion, rhino. The heads of these beasts Tarnower mounted on the walls of his new $500,000 house in Purchase, New York. The mansion itself, sitting on more than six acres, with its Japanese-style brick-and-glass architecture, was another trophy. Into it he brought art treasures and antiques and, at night, women of all kinds. Some were his patients, others were members of New York society. All of them were, like Jean Harris, sophisticated and intelligent. By the time Herman Tarnower met Mrs. Harris, he had the reputation of a ladies' man if not an out-and-out playboy. Yet she didn't seem to mind. His wealth and social position made him a prize catch for any woman, yet in affairs of the heart the doctor was like a wily trout, experienced at nibbling the worm away without ensnaring himself on the hook.

Three weeks after her first meeting with Tarnower, Jean received a 'nice note' from the cardiologist, who later told her over the phone that he was leaving on an African safari but would like to see her in New York upon his return. The couple did meet, dining in New York; and then, related Jean, 'we went to the bar at the Pierre [Hotel] which I have loved ever since. We danced. Hi was a wonderful dancer and I got better.'

Within a month Mrs. Harris was celebrating Tarnower's fifty-eighth birthday with him at his estate, with her two sons in attendance. Then Tarnower, after a few visits to see Jean in Philadelphia, began sending her roses regularly and calling her every night at 6:30 P.M. The doctor gave Mrs. Harris an enormous emerald-cut diamond in May 1967 and at that time asked her to marry him. Mrs. Harris accepted, and Tarnower made hasty plans to add a wing to his house to accommodate Jean's two growing boys.

The wedding plans never went beyond the talking stage, however. In August, Tarnower informed Mrs. Harris, according to her own later statements, that the wedding was off. Jean returned the ring, which she said was worth approximately $50,000, telling the doctor: 'You really ought to give it to Suzanne. She's the only woman you'll ever need in your life.' This remark, of course, was a reference to Tarnower's devoted housekeeper of sixteen years who not only maintained the doctor's palatial home but dutifully picked up after the many women who made regular nocturnal visits to see Tarnower. (The housekeeper had strict instructions to make sure that no female undergarments were ever left in his bathroom, an apparently overlooked chore on the night of Tarnower's murder.)

Tarnower's exceptionally active sex life, which appeared to be extraordinary for a man in his late sixties, might have been in keeping with his philosophy of good health and an energetic body and heart; his bedroom prowess certainly provided ample exercise. He also made light of his sexual dexterity. Above one of the twin beds in which Jean Harris slept on weekends at the Tarnower estate was a picture of the lizard-like-looking doctor with a caption beneath it reading: 'No strings on me.'

Another woman, one of many who also reportedly slept in that bed, was the tall and aesthetic-looking Lynne Tryforos, the doctor's assistant. According to Mrs. Harris the assistant slept with Tarnower whenever she was not present; before Mrs. Harris arrived on a weekend in Scarsdale, Mrs. Tryforos would sleep with the doctor, departing just before Jean arrived and returning just after she left for Virginia.

The nurse had dropped out of Endicott Junior College to marry Nicholas Tryforos, part owner of a florist shop. They divorced in 1976, and Mrs. Tryforos and her daughters, age ten and fourteen, moved to a small house in Scarsdale. Lynne was hired as Tarnower's assistant after the doctor took one look at her. From 1977 on she was the doctor's constant social companion whenever Jean Harris was not present, attending parties and dances with Tarnower. The doctor subtly acknowledged her presence in his diet book by wedging into the many recipes therein something called 'Spinach Delight à la Lynne' (creamed spinach made with yogurt).

Mrs. Harris discovered the presence of Lynne in Tarnower's personal life as early as 1977, when she found Mrs. Tryforos's coat in a hall closet at the doctor's estate. Jean confronted Tarnower, but he ignored her mild accusations. Over the next three years, Mrs. Harris insisted, Lynne tried to unnerve and agitate her by making anonymous phone calls to her, calling her when she was alone in Virginia or even phoning her when she was on trips to Paris or Miami with Dr. Tarnower. On New Year's Day, 1980, while Jean was vacationing with Tarnower in Palm Beach, she said she picked up a copy of *The New York Times* to find the following ad: 'Happy New Year, Hi. Love always. Lynne.' She showed this to the doctor and said: 'Herman, why don't you use the Goodyear blimp next year. I think it's available.'

'I hope none of my friends see it,' Jean quoted Tarnower as responding. She was later to quip: 'I was one of his friends, and I saw it.'

Lynne Tryforos's presence at the doctor's estate was another matter. The nurse first appeared in front of Jean with her two daughters, carrying buckets of paint. Mrs. Harris ordered her from the premises, but the nurse proceeded to paint the lawn furniture with her daughters, saying 'I'm allowed.'

The women, according to housekeeper van der Vreken, then took to open warfare, each cutting up the other's clothes whenever they found them on Tarnower's premises, and, when this tactic proved ineffective, spreading human feces upon designer gowns belonging to each other. According to Mrs. Harris, she persistently complained to Tarnower that Lynne was making obscene anonymous phone calls to her. The doctor, with the assistant 'simpering' next to him, banished Jean for a month from his Xanadu for making such wild accusations.

It was about this time, in November 1978, that Mrs. Harris visited Irving's Sports Shop in Tyson's Corner, Virginia, a few miles from the Madeira School, and purchased a .32 Harrington and Richardson revolver from clerk James Forst. It was for her own protection, Jean had told the clerk, since she lived 'back in the woods in a secluded area.' This was the very weapon that Mrs. Harris carried in her handbag on the night of March 10, 1980, a gun she intended to use on herself, she later told police.

Though Tarnower appeared to need Jean Harris less and less as a sexual prop, he did use her extensively in the preparation of his book. One report stated that Suzanne van der Vreken provided the recipes and Jean polished the manuscript, although she disliked the idea of the book and, like Lynne Tryforos, felt that it 'denigrated him' to where he was known as the 'Diet Doc.' The book, which became a stupendous success, promised readers that they could lose a pound a day if they followed the high-protein, low-carbohydrate regime dictated by Tarnower.

In the acknowledgements Tarnower thanked Jean Harris 'for her splendid assistance in the research and writing of this book,' but co-author Samm Baker later thought this nod of gratitude specious, stating: 'Whatever she did for him, I don't know.' Baker later stated that Tarnower was a dedicated physician: 'Medicine is his life.' Another friend labeled Tarnower at the time of his book's great success as unconcerned about his sudden fame. He was already wealthy and did not really need the fortune the diet book brought him. One person thought the doctor 'austere, humorless and egotistical.' Another, Sidney Salwen, said that the book's success never changed Tarnower, that 'the last thing he would have wanted was to be known as the diet man. The diet was incidental. He was first and foremost a cardiologist.'

In the eyes of Jean Struven Harris, however, Herman Tarnower had become, in March 1980, a man who was destroying her confidence, self-esteem, and sanity piece by piece through his mistreatment of her and his flagrant affair with Lynne Tryforos. She began to lose control at the Madeira School, with peers and board members criticizing her severe policies. She felt 'traumatized. I functioned until I couldn't function anymore.' She was, she claimed further, in a drugged state half the time, swallowing by the handfuls such addictive drugs as Desoxyn, which the doctor had prescribed for her ten years before when she began to complain of exhaustion. Other drugs urged upon her by the doctor included Valium, Nembutal, Percodan, Plexonal. She took painkillers, sedatives, stimulants, uppers and downers; Dr. Tarnower had Jean Harris popping pills almost on an around-the-clock basis.

As a final gesture toward reconciliation with her wayward lover, Jean wrote Tarnower a voluminous letter in which she poured out her heart, her insecurity, her bottomless sense of self-degradation, and her venomous hatred for Lynne Tryforos and for the way he had treated her. It was this letter that Mrs. Harris later fought desperately to suppress during her murder trial. That she had shot and killed Dr. Tarnower on the night of March 10, 1980, Mrs. Harris never denied; that it was murder, she would never admit.

When police cars arrived that night with sirens screaming and deck lights flashing in the Tarnower driveway, they passed Mrs. Harris, who was about to drive away. Patrolman Brian McKenna approached her.

'There's been a shooting in the house,' she told the officer.

He rushed inside, going upstairs to find the doctor on the floor of his master bedroom, mortally wounded. By then Mrs. Harris had reentered the house and was standing in the foyer. Patrolman Daniel O'Sullivan came near to her, and she looked at him squarely, saying: 'I shot him. I did it.'

O'Sullivan and Detective Arthur Siciliano took Mrs. Harris into the dining room. She quickly explained that she had just driven up from Virginia, where she was the headmistress of the Madeira School, 'with the hope of being killed by Dr. Tarnower.'

The policemen squinted at her in wonder. 'He wanted to live, I wanted to die,' she went on. 'I'd been through so much hell. I loved him very much. He slept with every woman he could. I had no intention of going back to Virginia alive.' She described how she had gone to the doctor's room and begged Tarnower to kill her, and how he had shouted at her: 'You're crazy! Get out of here.' She had produced her revolver and they struggled with it. Then the gun went off several times.

Siciliano asked her: 'Who had control of the gun?'

'I don't know,' Mrs. Harris responded.

'Who owns it?'

'It's mine.'

'Who did the shooting?'

'I remember holding the gun and shooting him in the hand.'

Mrs. Harris led police to her car and opened her purse, retrieving the revolver and turning it over to the officers. They walked back into the house, where Jean began to recite a litany of complaints against Tarnower, indicting him again and again for sleeping with numberless women. 'I had it!' she shouted, and made a wild gesture with her hands.

An officer came downstairs to report that there were fresh knicks on the bathroom tile, and Jean stated that there was where she had thrown the gun several times during her struggle with Tarnower.

She handed Detective Siciliano a list of names, telling him that they were the names of friends and relatives who were to be contacted after she had taken her own life or if Tarnower had been good enough to kill her. She mumbled something about shooting herself at the edge of the estate's duck pond 'where the daffodils bloom in the spring.' Mrs. Harris remembered staring down at the wounded Tarnower after the struggle for the gun, asking him: 'Why didn't you kill me, Hi?' She jerked her head from one officer to another. 'Why should he die? Can I see him? Who did he have over for dinner?'

The place was soon filling up with police. Ambulance attendants rushed upstairs with a stretcher to pick up the fatally wounded Tarnower. Police Lieutenant Brian Flick stood staring down at Mrs. Harris, who was seated in a chair. She looked up at him, saying: 'Isn't it ironic? He's dying and I'm alive. I wanted to die and he wanted to live.'

She began to get out of the chair but appeared faint and sank back, breathing heavily. She said she wanted to make a phone call, and Patrolman Robert Tamilio accompanied her to a phone in an adjoining room. Mrs. Harris called a friend who was a lawyer, blurting: 'Oh, my God, I think I've killed Hi!'

As she was led back into the living room, Jean Harris passed a mirror, stopped, and stood close looking at herself, noticing bruises on her face and arms. She touched a bruised lip and said in a soft voice: 'He hit me, he hit me a lot.'

Once more seated in the dining room, Mrs. Harris heard the hospital attendants upstairs. Tears welled up in her large eyes and she stood up, walking to Detective Siciliano. 'Can I see Hi?' she asked him.

'I don't think it's a good idea at this time,' he told her.

Just then the ambulance attendants appeared on the stairs,

carrying the stricken Tarnower. They passed Mrs. Harris, whose eyes were riveted to the doctor's exposed face. Jean suddenly grabbed Detective Siciliano, as if to steady herself, seeming to slip downward in a dead faint.

'Get a doctor!' shouted Siciliano as he lowered her to the floor.

'The police doctor just got here!' a voice shouted back from the open front door. 'He'll be right in!'

Siciliano was shocked to see Mrs. Harris make an immediate recovery, almost jumping up from the floor, brushing herself off, and saying in a calm voice: 'I don't need a doctor.' This abrupt turnabout in posture – from a fainting, confused person to a self-reliant and purposeful woman in a matter of seconds – had been repeated several times by Mrs. Harris in recent weeks. Only days before, Jean had written in the Madeira alumnae magazine: 'If my educational philosophy has a schizophrenic ring to it, perhaps the same could be said of myself as a woman.'

An hour after he was removed from his elegant estate, Dr. Herman Tarnower was dead of four gunshot wounds. A fifth shot had been fired, police learned a short time later, but had failed to strike the 'Diet Doc.'

Police booked Mrs. Harris on charges of second-degree murder. Two days later she was released on a $40,000 bond and immediately checked into a Westchester hospital for treatment. Her lawyer, Joel Aurnou, first stated that he would plead his client not guilty by virtue of self-defense. He described Mrs. Harris's many bruises, one on the lip, one near an eye, and a seven-inch bruise from her left elbow to her armpit. 'She is a poor, sick woman,' Aurnou told reporters.

Newspaper and TV reporters went wild with the case, gathering every morsel of gossip and rumor available, and there was much of that before Jean's trial commenced. It was high-society murder and millions were at stake, Tarnower's millions. His will was quickly unearthed. In it he had left Mrs. Harris $220,000 (not the $240,000 he was overheard to tell Jean by Mrs. Edwards) which would be forfeited if she was convicted of murdering him. He also bequeathed $200,000 to nurse Lynne Tryforos. Another $20,000 each was willed to Lynne's two daughters, along with a large sum for their college educations. The rest was divided among a phalanx of relatives, with

Pearl Schwartz of Larchmont, New York, Tarnower's sister, to receive his fabulous estate.

In Virginia shocked board members of the Madeira School quickly drafted a letter informing alarmed parents that the school would survive in spite of 'the tragic events involving Mrs. Harris.' Students came forward with reports of how Mrs. Harris had driven off on the day of the murder, leaving the front door to her home wide open. Some of them looked inside to see the place 'a perfect mess.' She was strict, some students carped to reporters, too strict. She had recently found orange peels littering the grounds of the school and had banned oranges on campus. 'Outlawing oranges,' sneered one girl. 'Can you *imagine?*' Another girl said: 'She was very intense. Even the littlest things seemed to get her off.'

'Mrs. Harris is most genteel,' *New York* magazine quoted one Madeira alumna. 'She's so very proper. The whole thing sounds so *incongruous.*'

Mrs. Harris's soap opera trial commenced the following November in a White Plains courtroom where she was tried before Judge Russell R. Leggett and a jury of eight women and four men. The public clamored for every word of testimony from the ninety-seven witnesses oozing scandal and sin in wealthy Scarsdale society. Hundreds, mostly women, packed the courtroom during the trial, spilling out into a hallway, fighting each day for a place in the visitors' gallery.

Jean Harris appeared composed throughout the many weeks of her trial. She busied herself with studying photographs and making notes, which she passed to her three lawyers – Joel Aurnou, Bonnie Steingart, and Victor Grossman. She reacted to witnesses in an animated fashion, frowning at those who made derogatory remarks about her, laughing – perhaps a bit too long and loud – with the court when any tidbit of humor presented itself.

The policemen who arrived at the scene of the killing gave their testimony, describing Mrs. Harris's actions and quoting her strange and damning words verbatim. Suzanne van der Vreken also testified. (She and her husband, Henri, received $32,000 each in Tarnower's will, $2,000 each for every year of loyal service to him.) Mrs. van der Vreken was neither sympathetic nor antagonistic to Mrs. Harris's cause, but she did say that Jean in one conversation 'used some words not very nice about' Lynne Tryforos. She quoted Mrs. Harris at the time as saying: 'I will make their life miserable.'

Jean herself took the witness stand in her own defense, and for six days she fenced with a determined prosecutor, Assistant District Attorney George Bolen. She displayed at first a cautious, even shrewd, demeanor, answering questions directly but always adding a bit more with each response as she became indignant and often angry at Bolen's queries. She was a lady of quality, her refinement and upbringing were apparently paramount to her as she sat stiffly in the witness chair, dressed all in black.

Jean told Bolen that three weeks before the doctor's death she and Tarnower had made love and that she had given him a gold tie clasp. She added that she was not seeking 'The Good Housekeeping Seal of Approval,' and that she understood from the start that Tarnower was 'not the marrying kind.' She smiled broadly, almost triumphantly, at prosecutor Bolen when she said: 'He made love to me that morning. We had a lovely conversation and that's when I gave him the gold caduceus.' (A tie clip with the medical symbol on it.)

When Lynne Tryforos's name was mentioned, Jean bristled, then blurted how her hated rival had slashed her thousand-dollar wardrobe and had even attempted to seduce the caretaker, Henri van der Vreken. 'This gets dirtier and dirtier,' moaned Mrs. Harris, but she plunged on, at Bolen's instigation, to say that 'I dried Suzanne's eyes when she came to me saying Lynne was trying to seduce Henri.' Then she added: 'I thought of possibly suing Tryforos when $1,000 of my clothes were destroyed.'

Bolen asked if Jean's salary in 1966, the year in which she met the doctor, had been relatively low.

'Yes,' she replied.

'And Doctor Tarnower took you on trips around the world?' inquired Bolen.

'I don't really like your saying he "took me." I sound like a piece of baggage! We went together.'

Always Bolen returned to Lynne Tryforos, attempting to show that out of hatred for this woman and her affair with Tarnower, Mrs. Harris had ruthlessly planned premeditated murder.

In an adroit move the defense produced a huge Christmas card
that Jean had once sent to Tarnower, one in which she poked what
lawyer Aurnou hoped the court would think good-natured fun at the
doctor's many female lovers and which would prove that Jean Harris
was never jealous of Tarnower's female companions, certainly never
to the point of killing him in a jealous rage. Jean's parody of 'A Visit
from St. Nicholas' was read aloud by her attorney to the delight of a
courtroom packed with sensation-seeking reporters and spectators:

'Twas the night before Christmas, . . . In the guest room lay
Herman, who, trying to sleep, was counting the broads in his life –
'stead of sheep! On Hilda, on Sigrid, on Jinx and Raquel, Brunhilda,
Veronica, Gretel, Michelle. Now Tania, Rapunzel, Electra, Adele;
Now Susie, Anita – keep trucking Giselle . . . ingenues, Dashers
and Dancers and Vixens. I believe there was even one Cupid – one
Blitzen! He lay there remembering with a smile broad and deep, till
he ran out of names, and he fell asleep.

(Let me mention, my darling, if this muse were inclined toward
unseemly thoughts or an off-color mind, it wouldn't be easy to keep
this thing refined!) But 'tis the time to be jolly – and very upbeat –
and for now that's not hard because Herman's asleep! Beside him
lay Jeannie, headmistress by jiminy – who was waiting for Santa to
come down the chimney. . . . Then all of a sudden there arose such
a clatter, Herm awoke from his sleep to see what was the matter.

And with Jeannie obediently three paces back, they tiptoed to
the living room to watch [St.] Nick unpack. . . . Now let's see –
there's Herman – with Tarnower for a monicka [*sic*]. It seems to
me he got his best stuff for Chanukah. . . . But here's one little
thing that I *know* he will use, if his evenings are lonely he'll have
no excuse. . .

Here's some brand new phone numbers in a brand new black book
(I'm not quite the innocent gent that I look!). This book holds the
key, and the hope, and the promise, of a whole bunch of fun with
some new red-hot mamas.

The result of exposing Mrs. Harris's kitsch to the world only
emphasized her knowledge of Tarnower's prolific lovemaking while
betraying the real thoughts that lay just below the surface of her

nail-scratching lines. The revelation of the poem also held her up to ridicule, and there was plenty of that the following day. One newspaper ran the headline: SLAIN 'DIET' DOCTOR WENT FROM BED TO VERSE.

On the following day prosecutor Bolen returned to the subject of Lynne Tryforos, asking Jean what she thought about her.

'I think she denigrated Hi and gave me a great deal of trouble with my own identity,' replied Mrs. Harris in a calm voice.

'Was it a question of her education?' probed Bolen.

'She lacked common sense and taste.'

'No taste?'

'You have to judge taste by the things people do,' replied Jean, as if instructing the prosecutor. 'Writing to a man for eight years while he was traveling with another woman is tasteless.'

'How many times did you tell the doctor that you were upset about Lynne Tryforos?'

'Not all the time I felt it. I didn't count.'

Bolen had repeatedly attempted to introduce into evidence the much-debated letter Jean Harris had sent to Tarnower on March 10, 1980, the day of his murder, but Judge Leggett stated that he would read the letter and decide later on its possible admission to the trial. Still Bolen persisted, trying to slip points made by Jean in the letter into her testimony. In one reference to the letter he asked: 'Did he accuse you of stealing two books and some money?'

'We read each other's books all the time,' replied Jean coolly.

'Why did you use the word "steal" in the letter?'

'Hi couldn't find them and I didn't have them.' She added, as she was doing increasingly in her long testimony: 'By Saturday and Sunday I was very deeply depressed, and I covered it up. Anything unkind from Hi was disturbing.'

'How did you refer to Lynne in that letter?'

'In many unattractive ways, as I had experienced her – dishonest, adulterous, a whore – that pretty well does it.'

Bolen raised his voice when he then asked: 'Did you say, "your whore"?'

'The letter was to Hi,' replied Jean stonily.

'And did you refer to "your psychotic whore?"'

'That's what Suzanne [van der Vreken] called her. Suzanne thought she was crazy.'

'What did Suzanne think of you?'

'I hate to think,' retorted Jean Harris wryly as the court let loose a ripple of laughter.

Bolen doggedly continued quoting Jean's letter, asking her if she used the word 'slut' in referring to Lynne Tryforos.

Jean turned in the witness chair, annoyed, her face flushed, asking Judge Leggett: 'At what point – ?'

'Mr. Aurnou is your attorney,' Judge Leggett pointed out. 'He can object.'

After a while Bolen went back to the same subject, asking Mrs. Harris to explain the word 'whore.'

Jean's face tightened and she replied: 'A whore is a whore is a whore.'

'Is that your usual language?'

'Those are not words I customarily use. I was in a struggle with my own integrity. I couldn't walk away, and I couldn't come to terms with it.'

Later, Bolen asked Jean if she had realized how relaxed Dr. Tarnower had become with Mrs Tryforos, that he actually found himself 'going out to get a pizza' with her. (Such posthumous heresy about Tarnower's eating habits raised many eyebrows; the doctor had once been quoted as saying: 'My cravings are not for Big Macs, but for low-calorie Italian white truffles.')

Munching on pizza, Jean responded, did not sound like Dr. Herman Tarnower. 'He was the only man I know who didn't know who Charlie Brown was, the kind of person who read Herodotus for fun.'

How did she feel about finding things of Lynne Tryforos's at the Tarnower estate, Jean was asked. She shrugged indifferently, then admitted that she 'threw some "Super Doctor" buttons' left by Lynne 'into the pond,' along with 'Valentines left on the front seat of his car,' items she said had been left on purpose by Mrs. Tryforos before Jean's regular arrival at the doctor's home. All of it was 'inappropriate' in Jean's estimation. She was cool at this point but then appeared to become upset and related how 'frustrated and hurt' she had been at finding Lynne's 'negligee' in 'her' bathroom.

This item, a green negligee, the prosecution would later contend, which was spotted by Jean Harris on her last visit to Herman Tarnower, found in 'her' bathroom, tacit proof that she was being two-timed by a 'tasteless' nurse, was a negligee that caused her to go for her gun and send four bullets into a cringing, begging Dr. Herman Tarnower.

The full image of the 'wronged woman,' or the 'scorned woman' releasing fury hotter than hell was not formed for the jury until the following day. The admission of Jean's March 10 letter was a bombshell that exploded the myth of Mrs. Harris as a woman who had jokingly accepted Tarnower's peccadillos and had remained aloof and unperturbed by his philandering. She was, as most concluded after hearing the letter, one certainly filled with pain and agony and lovesick hopelessness, capable of hating as deeply as any mass murderer in the history of crime.

February 4, 1981, was a high-water mark for the prosecution, George Bolen read Mrs. Harris's inflammatory letter to Herman Tarnower, which had been mailed by Jean at 8.30 am from Virginia on the day of the doctor's murder and had arrived a day later. The lengthy missive had been in the hands of the defense team, but Bolen had managed to pry it loose so that Judge Leggett could pass on it. The judge, in a surprise move, allowed Bolen to introduce the letter as evidence. Bolen stood before the court and slowly read Mrs. Harris's self-damning words. The infamous 'Scarsdale letter' read:

> I will send this by registered mail only because so many of my letters seem not to reach you – or at least they are never acknowledged so I presume they didn't arrive.
>
> I am distraught as I write this – your phone call to tell me you preferred the company of a vicious, adulterous psychotic was topped by a call from the dean of students 10 minutes later and has kept me awake for almost 36 hours. I had to expel four seniors just two months from graduation and suspend others. What I say will ramble but it will be the truth – and I have to do something besides shriek with pain.
>
> Let me say first that I will be with you on the 19th of April because it is right that I should be. [This is a reference to an upcoming dinner sponsored by the Westchester Heart Association at which Dr. Tarnower was to be honored for his contributions to cardiology; Tarnower had apparently told Mrs. Harris on the day of his death that he would not only be taking Lynne Tryforos to this dinner but had proposed marriage

to the nurse and she had accepted, the action that sparked Mrs. Harris's vitriolic missive.] To accuse me of calling Dan [a Tarnower friend who was making preparations for the dinner] to beg for an invitation is all the more invidious since it is indeed what Lynne does all the time – I am told this repeatedly, 'She keeps calling and fawning over us. It drives us crazy.' [An oblique quote attributed to housekeeper Suzanne van der Vreken.] I have and never would do this – you seem to be able to expiate Lynne's sins by dumping them on me. I knew of the honor being bestowed on you before I was [ever] asked to speak at Columbia on the 18th.

Frankly I thought you were waiting for Dan's invitation to surprise me – false modesty or something. I called Dan to tell him I wanted to send a contribution to be part of those honoring you and I assured him I would be there.

He said, 'Lee and I want you at our table.' I thanked him and assured him I would be there 'even if the slut comes – indeed, I don't care if she pops naked out of a cake with her tits frosted with chocolate!'

Dan laughed and said, 'And you *should* be there and we want you with us.'

I haven't played slave for you. I would never have committed adultery for you – but I have added a dimension to your life and given you pleasure and dignity, as you have me.

As Jackie [a mutual friend] says, 'Hi was always a marvelous snob. What happened?'

I suppose my check to Dan falls into the 'signs of masochistic love' department, having just, not four weeks before, received a copy of your will, with my name vigorously scratched out, and Lynne's name in *your* handwriting written in three places, leaving her a quarter of a million dollars and her children $25,000 apiece – and the boys and me nothing.

It is the sort of thing I have grown almost accustomed to from Lynne – that you didn't respond to my note when I returned it leaves me wondering if you send [*sic*] it together. It isn't your style – but then Lynne has changed your style. Is it the admiration of 14 years of broken promises, Hi – I hope not – 'I want to buy you a whole new wardrobe, darling,' 'I want to get your teeth fixed at my expense, darling.' 'My home is your home, darling.' 'Welcome home, darling.' 'The ring is yours forever, darling.' '[If you leave it] with me now I will leave it to you in my will.' 'You have, of course, been well taken care of it in my will, darling.' 'Let me buy an apartment with you in New York, darling.'

It didn't matter all that much, really – all I ever asked for was to be with you – and when I left you to know when we would see each other again so there was something in life to look forward to. Now you are taking that away from me too and I am unable to cope – I can hear you saying, 'Look, Jean, it's your problem. I don't want to hear about it.'

I have watched you grow rich in the years we have been together, and I have watched me go through moments when I was almost destitute. . . .

. . . I don't have the money to afford a sick playmate – you do. She took a brand new nightgown that I paid $40 for and covered it with bright orange stains. You paid to replace it – and since you had already made it clear you simply didn't care about the obscene phone calls she made, it was obviously pointless to tell you about the nightgown.

The second thing you paid for (I never replaced it) was a yellow silk dress. I bought it to wear at Lyford Cay [an exclusive club in Nassau in the Bahamas] several years ago.

Unfortunately I forgot to pack it because it was new and still in the box, rolled up, not folded now, and smeared and vile with feces.

I told you once it was something 'brown and sticky.' It was, quite simply, Herman Tarnower, human shit. [Mrs. Harris had accused Mrs. Tryforos of smearing this on her finest gown.]

I decided, and rightly so, that this was your expense, not mine. As for stealing from you, the day I put my ring on your dresser my income *before taxes* was $12,000 per year.

I had two children in private school. They had been on a fairly sizable scholarship until I told the school I wouldn't need it because we were moving to Scarsdale. It was two years before we got it back.

That more than anything else is the reason David [her son] went to Penn State instead of the Univ. of Pennsylvania. He loathed every minute of it – and there is no question that it changed his life.

That you should feel justified and comfortable suggesting that I steal from you is something I have no adjective to describe.

I *desperately* needed money all those years. I *couldn't* have sold that ring. It was tangible proof of your love and it meant more to me than life itself.

That you sold it the summer your adulterous slut finally got her divorce and needed money is a kind of sick, cynical act that left me old and bitter and sick. . . .

You have never once suggested that you would meet me in Virginia at *your* expense, so seeing you has been at my expense – and if you lived in California I would borrow money to come there, too, if you would let me.

All my conversations are my nickels, not yours – and obviously rightly so because it is I, not you, who needs to hear your voice.

I have indeed grown poor loving you, while a self-serving, ignorant slut has grown very rich – and yet you accuse me of stealing from you. How in the name of Christ does that make sense?

I have, and most proudly so – and with an occasional 'right on' from Lee [a mutual friend] and others – ripped up or destroyed anything I saw that your slut had touched and written her cutesie name on – including several books that *I* gave you and she had the tasteless, unmitigated gall to write in.

I have refrained from throwing away the cheap little book of epigrams lying on your bed one day so I would be *absolutely sure* to see it, with a paper clip on the page about how an old man should have a young wife.

It made me feel like a piece of old discarded garbage – but at least it solved for me what had been a mystery – what had suddenly possessed you to start your tasteless diatribe at dinner parties about how everyman [*sic*] should have a wife half his age and seven years.

Since you never mentioned it to anyone under 65, it made the wives at the table feel about as attractive and wanted as I did.

Tasteless behavior is the only kind that Lynne knows – though to her credit she is clever and devious enough to hide it at times. Unfortunately, it seems to be catching.

The things I know or profess to know about Lynne – except for what I have experienced first hand – have been told by your friends and your servants, mostly the latter – I was interested to hear from Vivian and Arthur's [mutual friends] next door neighbor in Florida – I don't remember her name though I'm sure Lynne does:

'I took her to lunch, she seemed so pathetic' – that you sat at the table while I was there and discussed Lynne and her 'wonderful family – brother a Ph.D.'

I can't imagine going out to dinner with you and telling my dinner partner how grand another lover is. . . .

My phone tells me this – that 'mysterious' caller – I hope to God you don't know who it is! Who pays him? [Apparently an oblique reference to the obscene calls Mrs. Harris said she had recently been receiving before Tarnower's death.]

When my clothes were ripped to shreds Suzanne said, 'Madam, there is *only* one person who *could* have done it. You must tell him.'

In my masochistic way I tried to downplay it in my notes to you, although in all honesty I thought it was so obvious you would know who did it. Instead you ignored it and went happily off to Florida with the perpetrator. Suzanne told me – and I would think would say so in court.

1. The clothes were not torn when she went into the closet to find something of Henri's on 'Wednesday or Thursday' while we were away.

2. On the Sunday morning before we came home Henri and Suzanne both saw Lynne drive hurriedly up to your house. They were outside and she did not see them. They saw her go in but not out.

3. Lynne knew you were coming home that evening and that she would see you by 8.00 the next morning. What business did she have at your home that morning?

4. When I discovered the clothes destroyed Suzanne was sitting in the dining room at the wooden table right next to the door. I said, 'My God – Suzanne, come look!' and she was right there.

When I called your slut to talk to her about it and see what she was going to do about it, she said, 'You cut them up yourself and blamed it on me.'

That was the first time it occurred to me they had been 'cut,' not ripped. Only someone with a thoroughly warped mind would decide that a woman with no money would ruin about one-third of her wardrobe for kicks. Suzanne still believes Lynne did it and I most certainly do, too. I think this is enough evidence to prove it in court!

The stealing of my jewelry I can't prove at all – I just know that I left some things in the white ash tray on your dresser as I have for many years. When I thought of it later and called, Lynne answered the phone.

When I called again and asked Suzanne to take them and put them away, they were gone. I only hope if she hocked them you got something nice as a 'gift.' Maybe I gave you some gold cuff links after all and didn't know it. I [don't for one instant] think Henri or Suzanne took them. . . .

Going through the hell of the past few years has been bearable only because you were still there and I could be with you whenever I could get away from work, which seemed to be less and less.

To be jeered at, and called 'old and pathetic' made me seriously consider borrowing $5,000 just before I left New York and telling a doctor to make me young again – to do anything but make me not feel like discarded trash – I lost my nerve because there was always the chance I'd end up uglier than before.

You have been what you very carefully set out to be, Hi – the most important thing in my life, the most important human being in my life, and that will never change.

You keep me in control by threatening me with banishment – an easy threat which you know I couldn't live with – and so I stay home alone while you make love to someone who has almost totally destroyed me. . . .

I always thought that taking me out of your will would be the final threat. On that I believed you would be completely honest. I have every intention of dying before you do, but sweet Jesus, darling, I didn't think you would ever be dishonest about that. . . .

I wish 14 years of making love to one another and sharing so much happiness had left enough of a [mark] that you couldn't have casually scratched my name out of a will and written in Lynne's instead. . . .

Give her all the money she wants, Hi – but give me time with you and the privilege of sharing with you April 19th. There were a lot of ways to have money – I very consciously picked working hard, supporting myself, and being with you.

Please, darling, don't tell me now it was all for nothing.

She has you every single moment in March – for Christ's sake give me April. T. S. Eliot said it's the cruelest month – don't let it be, Hi.

I want to spend every minute of it with you on weekends. In all these years you never spent my birthday with me. There aren't a lot left – it goes so quickly.

I give you my word if you just aren't cruel I won't make you wretched. I never did until you were cruel – and then I just wasn't ready for it.

Jean Harris had sat like a stone Buddha through the reading of the much-heralded Scarsdale letter, and when Bolen finished reading it, she continued to show a blank expression to the court. There was, however, a sigh en masse from those packing the courtroom, as if in relief that the truth was finally known: Mrs. Jean Harris had been jilted, thrown over completely by Tarnower for his nurse, the younger, attractive woman whom he vowed to marry and make his considerable heir. It took little imagination to envision Mrs. Harris's terrible thoughts after mailing the letter and how she must have exploded in rage to where she grabbed her revolver, hopped in her car, and set out for Scarsdale, a teeth-clenching, hand-clutching drive spurred on by jealous anger and having only one intent – murder.

Prosecutor Bolen hammered home the point again and again after having read the letter, asking if Tarnower had told her just that morning that he was through with her and would wed Mrs. Lynne Tryforos.

'No,' replied Jean. 'Did he tell *you*, Mr. Bolen?' she added bitterly.

'Isn't it a fact that the doctor told you he preferred Lynne Tryforos over you?'

'No.'

'And in that March 10 morning telephone call did he tell you that you had lied to him and that you had cheated?'

'No, indeed. That would have been a strange word from him.'

'And did he tell you that you were going to inherit $220,000?'

Defense lawyer Joel Aurnou stood up and shouted: 'I move for a mistrial!'

Judge Leggett denied his motion.

'No, he didn't,' Mrs. Harris finally responded.

'Didn't he say, "Goddamnit, Jean, I want you to stop bothering me"?'

Jean's face reddened and she shouted back at Bolen: 'No!' Then she turned to Judge Leggett. 'Is this going to go on forever?'

At this point the prosecution and defense lawyers exchanged challenges with Judge Leggett, asking if there was a witness to Tarnower's remarks. Bolen replied there was, meaning Juanita Edwards, and that he would later produce her as a witness for the prosecution.

Bolen finally turned dramatically once more to Jean, asking her his final question. 'And isn't it true, Mrs. Harris, that you intended to kill Dr. Tarnower and then kill yourself because if you couldn't have him nobody else would?'

Her response was soft and determined: 'No, Mr. Bolen.'

The prosecution has made telling and damning points during the six-day interrogation of Jean Harris. She had admitted killing Tarnower but insisted that it was accidental, that she had wanted him to kill her. She had tried to place the blame for her unhinged state on her troubles at Madeira, not Lynne Tryforos, saying that the hassles from the school board in recent months had destroyed her life. 'I couldn't function from then on,' she had testified. 'I wasn't sure who I was. I was a person sitting in an empty chair.'

She had decided to die, period. 'My only worry was what I would do if Hi said something that spoiled my resolve to die.' She admitted finding Mrs. Tryforos's green negligee in Tarnower's bathroom and then claimed that Tarnower had hit her repeatedly when she made a scene about Lynne's undergarments. 'The script was not working as I intended,' she had told the jury, and she remembered begging Tarnower at that moment to 'hit me again, and make it hard enough to kill me!'

It was then, she admitted, that she reached into her purse and pulled out the revolver, reportedly saying, 'never mind, I'll do it myself.' She struggled with Tarnower over the weapon. She remembered 'an instant where I thought I felt the muzzle of the gun in my stomach. I pulled the trigger. I thought: "My God, that didn't hurt at all. I should have died a long time ago." '

But, of course, it was Herman Tarnower who had been shot and it was Herman Tarnower, celebrity cardiologist and aging ladies' man who crashed to the bedroom floor, gushing blood from four bullet wounds.

In the final arguments Aurnou and Bolen put on a battle royal. The defense attorney brought to bear every plea for Jean Harris's sorry plight and how she had been driven half mad at the thought of losing every worthwhile thing in life. To Aurnou the entire affair was a tragic accident that took place when Mrs. Harris, 'masochist' to the end, tried to kill herself.

'She was obsessed with dying,' pleaded Aurnou. 'Everything that happened in that room that night had meaning to her only in terms of stopping the pain of dying.' He portrayed Tarnower as an ungrateful lover who was 'incapable of accepting the greatest gift a woman has to give,' but the doctor did try to save the woman's life and in the attempt was accidentally shot to death. 'There is no evidence that Jean Harris ever intended to kill Tarnower,' Aurnou pointed out to the jury. 'This suicidal, sick woman . . . was obsessed with dying. That's why she's not guilty of murder.'

Bolen addressed the jury to make only one thunderous point: Jean Harris murdered Herman Tarnower after finding Lynne Tryforos's negligee in the doctor's bathroom. 'She goes into the bathroom and sees the belongings of Lynne Tryforos for the first time. All the inward hostility to Lynne Tryforos – and how, in her mind, Lynne Tryforos had usurped her role as far as the doctor is concerned – emerges.

'She's enraged. She gets the gun. She's in control. She has the power now. If Herman Tarnower won't deny himself of Lynne Tryforos, she'll do it for him: "If I [Mrs. Harris] can't have him no one can."

'She intended to kill him, take him from Lynne Tryforos, then take her own life. The defendant confronts Herman Tarnower with the gun, points it, shoots it and the bullet breaks through Dr. Tarnower's outstretched hand and into his chest.' Bolen described how more bullets were sent into the errant lover, while 'the defendant retreats,' going into the bathroom where 'she's enraged, she's throwing, she's tossing' Mrs. Tryforos's belongings. Bolen then reminded the jury in mocking terms how Mrs. Harris had earlier insisted that at that point she went to get help.

'She's so concerned about the doctor,' Bolen sneers, 'she remembers to take her fur coat and gun.' The prosecutor paused, then added sarcastically: 'Yeah, she went to get help.'

He went on to demand that Jean Struven Harris be convicted of murder in the second degree, the highest form that she could be convicted of in New York State, first-degree murder applying only to the killing of law enforcement officers and prison guards, the maximum penalty for both being the same, twenty-five years to life.

On Tuesday, February 24, 1981, after eight days of deliberation, the jury of eight women and four men returned a verdict of guilty of second-degree murder. Foreman Russell Von Glahn pronounced the word 'guilty' three times for the murder charge and two weapon counts. Defense lawyers burst into tears when hearing the verdict, but Jean Harris gave the court and newsmen her 'stiff-upper-lip' expression, even leaning over sympathetically to console lawyer Bonnie Steingart by patting her knee.

On March 20, 1981, Mrs. Harris was sentenced to the minimum term for her crime, fifteen years to life. She had earlier told her lawyers: 'I can't sit in jail.' After being sent to prison, the one-time arbiter of social taste went on a brief hunger strike, saying that she 'only wanted to die.' She did not die, but gave up the strike and slowly adjusted to prison life.

Her ordeal was finally over; she no longer had to worry about sharing Herman Tarnower's affections with other women, or about the manners and morals of spoiled children from upper-class families, or count the sharp rungs on the social ladder she had tried to scale. She had time to reflect upon the social strata and life-style she valued beyond measure, one that undoubtedly gave her the notion, as it has many before her, that she could murder with alacrity and escape back into an insulated world that protects its own. She has plenty of time to think about it, at least a decade behind bars.

*Farewell to the
American Dream*

JOAN DIDION

Some Dreamers
of the Golden Dream

This is a story about love and death in the golden land, and begins
with the country. The San Bernardino Valley lies only an hour east of
Los Angeles by the San Bernardino Freeway but is in certain ways an
alien place: not the coastal California of the subtropical twilights and
the soft westerlies off the Pacific but a harsher California, haunted
by the Mojave just beyond the mountains, devastated by the hot dry
Santa Ana wind that comes down through the passes at 100 miles an
hour and whines through the eucalyptus windbreaks and works on
the nerves. October is the bad month for the wind, the month when
breathing is difficult and the hills blaze up spontaneously. There
has been no rain since April. Every voice seems a scream. It is
the reason of suicide and divorce and prickly dread, wherever the
wind blows.

The Mormons settled this ominous country, and then they abandoned it, but by the time they left the first orange tree had been
planted and for the next hundred years the San Bernardino Valley
would draw a kind of people who imagined they might live among
the talismanic fruit and prosper in the dry air, people who brought
with them Midwestern ways of building and cooking and praying
and who tried to graft those ways upon the land. The graft took in
curious ways. This is the California where it is possible to live and
die without ever eating an artichoke, without ever meeting a Catholic
or a Jew. This is the California where it is easy to Dial-A-Devotion,
but hard to buy a book. This is the country in which a belief in
the literal interpretation of Genesis has slipped imperceptibly into
a belief in the literal interpretation of *Double Indemnity*, the country
of the teased hair and the Capris and the girls for whom all life's

promise comes down to a waltz-length white wedding dress and the birth of a Kimberly or a Sherry or a Debbi and a Tijuana divorce and a return to hairdressers' school. 'We were just crazy kids,' they say without regret, and look to the future. The future always looks good in the golden land, because no one remembers the past. Here is where the hot wind blows and the old ways do not seem relevant, where the divorce rate is double the national average and where one person in every thirty-eight lives in a trailer. Here is the last stop for all those who come from somewhere else, for all those who drifted away from the cold and the past and the old ways. Here is where they are trying to find a new life style, trying to find it in the only places they know to look: the movies and the newspapers. The case of Lucille Marie Maxwell Miller is a tabloid monument to that new life style.

Imagine Banyan Street first, because Banyan is where it happened. The way to Banyan is to drive west from San Bernardino out Foothill Boulevard, Route 66: past the Santa Fe switching yards, the Forty Winks Motel. Past the motel that is nineteen stucco tepees: 'SLEEP IN A WIGWAM – GET MORE FOR YOUR WAMPUM.' Past Fontana Drag City and the Fontana Church of the Nazarene and the Pit Stop A Go-Go; past Kaiser Steel, through Cucamonga, out to the Kapu Kai Restaurant-Bar and Coffee Shop, at the corner of Route 66 and Carnelian Avenue. Up Carnelian Avenue from the Kapu Kai, which means 'Forbidden Seas', the subdivision flags whip in the harsh wind. 'HALF-ACRE RANCHES! SNACK BARS! TRAVERTINE ENTRIES! $95 DOWN.' It is the trail of an intention gone haywire, the flotsam of the New California. But after a while the signs thin out on Carnelian Avenue, and the houses are no longer the bright pastels of the Springtime Home owners but the faded bungalows of the people who grow a few grapes and keep a few chickens out here, and then the hill gets steeper and the road climbs and even the bungalows are few, and here – desolate, roughly surfaced, lined with eucalyptus and lemon groves – is Banyan Street.

Like so much of this country, Banyan suggests something curious and unnatural. The lemon groves are sunken, down a three- or four-foot retaining wall, so that one looks directly into their dense foliage, too lush, unsettlingly glossy, the greenery of nightmare; the fallen eucalyptus bark is too dusty, a place for snakes to breed.

The stones look not like natural stones but like the rubble of some unmentioned upheaval. There are smudge pots, and a closed cistern. To one side of Banyan there is the flat valley, and to the other the San Bernardino Mountains, a dark mass looming too high, too fast, nine, ten, eleven thousand feet, right there above the lemon groves. At midnight on Banyan Street there is no light at all, and no sound except the wind in the eucalyptus and a muffled barking of dogs. There may be a kennel somewhere, or the dogs may be coyotes.

Banyan Street was the route Lucille Miller took home from the twenty-four-hour Mayfair Market on the night of 7 October 1964, a night when the moon was dark and the wind was blowing and she was out of milk, and Banyan Street was where, at about 12.30 a.m., her 1964 Volkswagen came to a sudden stop, caught fire, and began to burn. For an hour and fifteen minutes Lucille Miller ran up and down Banyan calling for help, but no cars passed and no help came. At three o'clock that morning, when the fire had been put out and the California Highway Patrol officers were completing their report, Lucille Miller was still sobbing and incoherent, for her husband had been asleep in the Volkswagen. 'What will I tell the children, when there's nothing left, nothing left in the casket?' she cried to the friend called to comfort her. 'How can I tell them there's nothing left?'

In fact there was something left, and a week later it lay in the Draper Mortuary Chapel in a closed bronze coffin blanketed with pink carnations. Some 200 mourners heard Elder Robert E. Denton of the Seventh-Day Adventist Church of Ontario speak of 'the temper of fury that has broken out among us'. For Gordon Miller, he said, there would be 'no more death, no more heartaches, no more misunderstandings'. Elder Ansel Bristol mentioned the 'peculiar' grief of the hour. Elder Fred Jensen asked 'what shall it profit a man, if he shall gain the whole world, and lose his own soul?' A light rain fell, a blessing in a dry season, and a female vocalist sang 'Safe in the Arms of Jesus'. A tape recording of the service was made for the widow, who was being held without bail in the San Bernardino County Jail on a charge of first-degree murder.

Of course she came from somewhere else, came off the prairie in search of something she had seen in a movie or heard on the radio, for this is a Southern California story. She was born

on 17 January 1930, in Winnipeg, Manitoba, the only child of
Gordon and Lily Maxwell, both schoolteachers and both dedicated
to the Seventh-Day Adventist Church, whose members observe the
Sabbath on Saturday, believe in an apocalyptic Second Coming,
have a strong missionary tendency, and, if they are strict, do not
smoke, drink, eat meat, use makeup, or wear jewellery, including
wedding rings. By the time Lucille Maxwell enrolled at Walla Walla
College in College Place, Washington, the Adventist school where
her parents then taught, she was an eighteen-year-old possessed
of unremarkable good looks and remarkable high spirits. 'Lucille
wanted to see the world,' her father would say in retrospect, 'and
I guess she found out.'

The high spirits did not seem to lend themselves to an extended
course of study at Walla Walla College, and in the spring of
1949 Lucille Maxwell met and married Gordon ('Cork') Miller, a
twenty-four-year-old graduate of Walla Walla and of the University
of Oregon dental school, then stationed at Fort Lewis as a medical
officer. 'Maybe you could say it was love at first sight,' Mr. Maxwell
recalls. 'Before they were ever formally introduced, he sent Lucille
a dozen and a half roses with a card that said even if she didn't come
out on a date with him, he hoped she'd find the roses pretty anyway.'
The Maxwells remember their daughter as a 'radiant' bride.

Unhappy marriages so resemble one another that we do not need
to know too much about the course of this one. There may or may
not have been trouble on Guam, where Cork and Lucille Miller lived
while he finished his Army duty. There may or may not have been
problems in the small Oregon town where he first set up private
practice. There appears to have been some disappointment about
their move to California: Cork Miller had told friends that he wanted
to become a doctor, that he was unhappy as a dentist and planned to
enter the Seventh-Day Adventist College of Medical Evangelists at
Loma Linda, a few miles south of San Bernardino. Instead he bought
a dental practice in the west end of San Bernardino County, and the
family settled there, in a modest house on the kind of street where
there are always tricycles and revolving credit and dreams about
bigger houses, better streets. That was 1957. By the summer of
1964 they had achieved the bigger house on the better street and the
familiar accoutrements of a family on its way up: the $30,000 a year,

the three children for the Christmas card, the picture window, the family room, the newspaper photographs that showed 'Mrs Gordon Miller, Ontario Heart Fund Chairman . . . ' They were paying the familiar price for it. And they had reached the familiar season of divorce.

It might have been anyone's bad summer, anyone's siege of heat and nerves and migraine and money worries, but this one began particularly early and particularly badly. On 24 April an old friend, Elaine Hayton, died suddenly; Lucille Miller had seen her only the night before. During the month of May, Cork Miller was hospitalized briefly with a bleeding ulcer, and his usual reserve deepened into depression. He told his accountant that he was 'sick of looking at open mouths', and threatened suicide. By 8 July, the conventional tensions of love and money had reached the conventional impasse in the new house on the acre lot at 8488 Bella Vista, and Lucille Miller filed for divorce. Within a month, however, the Millers seemed reconciled. They saw a marriage counsellor. They talked about a fourth child. It seemed that the marriage had reached the traditional truce, the point at which so many resign themselves to cutting both their losses and their hopes.

But the Millers' season of trouble was not to end that easily. 7 October began as a commonplace enough day, one of those days that sets the teeth on edge with its tedium, its small frustrations. The temperature reached 102° in San Bernardino that afternoon, and the Miller children were home from school because of Teachers' Institute. There was ironing to be dropped off. There was a trip to pick up a prescription for Nembutal, a trip to a self-service dry cleaner. In the early evening, an unpleasant accident with the Volkswagen: Cork Miller hit and killed a German shepherd, and afterwards said that his head felt 'like it had a Mack truck on it'. It was something he often said. As of that evening Cork Miller was $63,479 in debt, including the $29,637 mortgage on the new house, a debt load which seemed oppressive to him. He was a man who wore his responsibilities uneasily, and complained of migraine headaches almost constantly.

He ate alone that night, from a TV tray in the living room. Later the Millers watched John Forsythe and Senta Berger in *See How They Run*, and when the movie ended, about eleven, Cork Miller suggested that they go out for milk. He wanted some hot chocolate. He took a blanket and pillow from the couch and climbed into the passenger seat of the Volkswagen. Lucille Miller remembers reaching over to lock his door as she backed down the driveway. By the time she left the Mayfair Market, and long before they reached Banyan Street, Cork Miller appeared to be asleep.

There is some confusion in Lucille Miller's mind about what happened between 12.30 a.m., when the fire broke out, and 1.50 a.m., when it was reported. She says that she was driving east on Banyan Street at about 35 m.p.h. when she felt the Volkswagen pull sharply to the right. The next thing she knew the car was on the embankment, quite near the edge of the retaining wall, and flames were shooting up behind her. She does not remember jumping out. She does remember prying up a stone with which she broke the window next to her husband, and then scrambling down the retaining wall to try to find a stick. 'I don't know how I was going to push him out,' she says. 'I just thought if I had a stick, I'd push him out.' She could not, and after a while she ran to the intersection of Banyan and Carnelian Avenue. There are no houses at that corner, and almost no traffic. After one car had passed without stopping, Lucille Miler ran back down Banyan towards the burning Volkswagen. She did not stop, but she slowed down, and in the flames she could see her husband. He was, she said, 'just black'.

At the first house up Sapphire Avenue, half a mile from the Volkswagen, Lucille Miller finally found help. There Mrs Robert Swenson called the sheriff, and then, at Lucille Miller's request, she called Harold Lance, the Miller's lawyer and their close friend. When Harold Lance arrived he took Lucille Miller home to his wife, Joan. Twice Harold Lance and Lucille Miller returned to Banyan Street and talked to the Highway Patrol officers. A third time Harold Lance returned alone, and when he came back he said to Lucille Miller, 'O.K. . . . you don't talk any more.'

When Lucille Miller was arrested the next afternoon, Sandy Slagle was with her. Sandy Slagle was the intense, relentlessly loyal medical student who used to baby-sit for the Millers, and had been living as a member of the family since she graduated from high school in 1959. The Millers took her away from a difficult home situation, and she thinks of Lucille Miller not only as 'more or less a mother or a sister' but as 'the most wonderful character' she has ever known. On the night of the accident, Sandy Slagle was in her dormitory at Loma Linda University, but Lucille Miller called her early in the morning and asked her to come home. The doctor was there when Sandy Slagle arrived, giving Lucille Miller an injection of Nembutal. 'She was crying as she was going under,' Sandy Slagle recalls. 'Over and over she'd say, "Sandy, all the hours I spent trying to save him and now what are they trying to *do* to me?"'

At 1.30 that afternoon, Sergeant William Paterson and Detectives Charles Callahan and Joseph Karr of the Central Homicide Division arrived at 8488 Bella Vista. 'One of them appeared at the bedroom door,' Sandy Slagle remembers, 'and said to Lucille, "You've got ten minutes to get dressed or we'll take you as you are." She was in her nightgown, you know, so I tried to get her dressed.'

Sandy Slagle tells the story now as if by rote, and her eyes do not waver. 'So I had her panties and bra on her and they opened the door again, so I got some Capris on her, you know, and a scarf.' Her voice drops. 'And then they just took her.'

The arrest took place just twelve hours after the first report that there had been an accident on Banyan Street, a rapidity which would later prompt Lucille Miller's attorney to say that the entire case was an instance of trying to justify a reckless arrest. Actually what first caused the detectives who arrived on Banyan Street towards dawn that morning to give the accident more than routine attention were certain apparent physical inconsistencies. While Lucille Miller had said that she was driving about 35 m.p.h. when the car swerved to a stop, an examination of the cooling Volkswagen showed that it was in low gear, and that the parking rather than the driving lights were on. The front wheels, moreover, did not seem to be in exactly the position that Lucille Miller's description of the accident would suggest, and the right rear wheel was dug in deep, as if it had been spun in place. It seemed curious to the detectives, too, that a sudden stop from 35 m.p.h. – the same jolt which was presumed to have knocked over a gasoline can in the back seat and somehow started the fire – should have left two milk cartons upright on the back floorboard, and the remains of a Polaroid camera box lying apparently undisturbed on the back seat.

No one, however, could be expected to give a precise account of what did and did not happen in a moment of terror, and none of these inconsistencies seemed in themselves incontrovertible evidence of criminal intent. But they did interest the Sheriff's Office, as did Gordon Miller's apparent unconsciousness at the time of the accident, and the length of time it had taken Lucille Miller to get help. Something, moreover, struck the investigators as wrong about Harold Lance's attitude when he came back to Banyan Street the third time and found the investigation by no means over. 'The way Lance was acting,' the prosecuting attorney said later, 'they thought maybe they'd hit a nerve.'

And so it was that on the morning of 8 October, even before the doctor had come to give Lucille Miller an injection to calm her, the San Bernardino County Sheriff's Office was trying to construct another version of what might have happened between 12.30 and 1.50 a.m. The hypothesis they would eventually present was based on the somewhat tortuous premise that Lucille Miller had undertaken a plan which failed: a plan to stop the car on the lonely road, spread gasoline over her presumably drugged husband, and, with a stick on the accelerator, gently 'walk' the Volkswagen over the embankment, where it would tumble four feet down the retaining wall into the lemon grove and almost certainly explode. If this happened, Lucille Miller might then have somehow negotiated the two miles up Carnelian to Bella Vista in time to be home when the accident was discovered. This plan went awry, according to the Sheriff's Office hypothesis, when the car would not go over the rise of the embankment. Lucille Miller might have panicked then – after she had killed the engine the third or fourth time, say, out there on the dark road with the gasoline already spread and the dogs baying and the wind blowing and the unspeakable apprehension that a pair of headlights would suddenly light up Banyan Street and expose her there – and set the fire herself.

Although this version accounted for some of the physical evidence – the car in low because it had been started from a dead stop, the parking lights on because she could not do what needed doing without some light, a rear wheel spun in repeated attempts to get the car over the embankment, the milk cartons upright because there had been no sudden stop – it did not seem on its own any more or less credible than Lucille Miller's own story. Moreover, some of the physical evidence did seem to support her story: a nail in a front tyre, a nine-pound rock found in the car, presumably the one with which she had broken the window in an attempt to save her husband. Within a few days an autopsy had established that Gordon Miller was alive when he burned, which did not particularly help the State's case, and that he had enough Nembutal and Sandoptal in his blood to put the average person to sleep, which did; on the other hand Gordon Miller habitually took both Nembutal and Fiorinal (a common headache prescription which contains Sandoptal), and had been ill besides.

It was a spotty case, and to make it work at all the State was going to have to find a motive. There was talk of unhappiness, talk of another man. That kind of motive, during the next few weeks, was what they set out to establish. They set out to find it in accountants' ledgers and double-indemnity clauses and motel registers, set out to determine what might move a woman who believed in all the promises of the middle class – a woman who had been chairman of the Heart Fund and who always knew a reasonable little dressmaker and who had come out of the bleak wild of prairie fundamentalism to find what she imagined to be the good life – what should drive such a woman to sit on a street called Bella Vista and look out her new picture window into the empty California sun and calculate how to burn her husband alive in a Volkswagen. They found the wedge they wanted closer at hand than they might have at first expected, for, as testimony would reveal later at the trial, it seemed that in December of 1963 Lucille Miller had begun an affair with the husband of one of her friends, a man whose daughter called her 'Auntie Lucille', a man who might have seemed to have the gift for people and money and the good life that Cork Miller so noticeably lacked. The man was Arthwell Hayton, a well-known San Bernardino attorney and at one time a member of the district attorney's staff.

In some ways it was the conventional clandestine affair in a place like San Bernardino, a place where little is bright or graceful, where it is routine to misplace the future and easy to start looking for it in bed. Over the seven weeks that it would take to try Lucille Miller for murder, Assistant District Attorney Don A. Turner and defence attorney Edward P. Foley would between them unfold a curiously predictable story. There were the falsified motel registrations. There were the lunch dates, the afternoon drives in Arthwell Hayton's red Cadillac convertible. There were the interminable discussions of the wronged partners. There were the confidantes ('I knew everything,' Sandy Slagle would insist fiercely later. 'I knew every time, places, everything') and there were the words remembered from bad magazine stories ('Don't kiss me, it will trigger things,' Lucille Miller remembered telling Arthwell Hayton in the parking lot of Harold's Club in Fontana after lunch one day) and there were the notes, the sweet exchanges: 'High Sweetie Pie! You are my cup of tea!! Happy Birthday – you don't look a day over 29!! Your baby, Arthwell.'

And, towards the end, there was the acrimony. It was 24 April 1964, when Arthwell Hayton's wife, Elaine, died suddenly, and nothing good happened after that. Arthwell Hayton had taken his cruiser, *Captain's Lady*, over to Catalina that weekend; he called home at nine o'clock Friday night, but did not talk to his wife because Lucille Miller answered the telephone and said that Elaine was showering. The next morning the Haytons' daughter found her mother in bed, dead. The newspapers reported the death as accidental, perhaps the result of an allergy to hair spray. When Arthwell Hayton flew home from Catalina that weekend, Lucille Miller met him at the airport, but the finish had already been written.

It was in the break-up that the affair ceased to be in the conventional mode and began to resemble instead the novels of James M. Cain, the movies of the late 1930s, all the dreams in which violence and threats and blackmail are made to seem commonplaces of middle-class life. What was most startling about the case that the State of California was preparing against Lucille Miller was something that had nothing to do with law at all, something that never appeared in the eight-column afternoon headlines but was always there between them: the revelation that the dream was teaching the dreamers how to live. Here is Lucille Miller talking to her lover sometime in the early summer of 1964, after he had indicated that, on the advice of his minister he did not intend to see her any more: 'First, I'm going to go to that dear pastor of yours and tell him a few things . . . When I do tell him that, you won't be in the Redlands Church any more . . . Look, Sonny Boy, if you think your reputation is going to be ruined, your life won't be worth two cents.' Here is Arthwell Hayton, to Lucille Miller: 'I'll go to Sheriff Frank Bland and tell him some things that I know about you until you'll wish you'd never heard of Arthwell Hayton.' For an affair between a Seventh-Day Adventist dentist's wife and a Seventh-Day Adventist personal-injury lawyer, it seems a curious kind of dialogue.

'Boy, I could get that little boy coming and going,' Lucille Miller later confided to Erwin Sprengle, a Riverside contractor who was a business partner of Arthwell Hayton's and a friend to both the lovers. (Friend or no, on this occasion he happened to have an induction coil attached to his telephone in order to tape Lucille Miller's call.) 'And he hasn't got one thing on me that he can prove. I mean, I've got concrete – he has nothing concrete.' In the same taped conversation with Erwin Sprengle, Lucille Miller mentioned a tape that she herself had surreptitiously made, months before, in Arthwell Hayton's car.

'I said to him, I said "Arthwell, I just feel like I'm being used" . . . He started sucking his thumb and he said "I love you . . . This isn't something that happened yesterday. I'd marry you tomorrow if I could. I don't love Elaine." He'd love to hear that played back, wouldn't he?'

'Yeah,' drawled Sprengle's voice on the tape. 'That would be just a little incriminating, wouldn't it?'

'Just a *little* incriminating,' Lucille Miller agreed. 'It really *is*.'

Later on the tape, Sprengle asked where Cork Miller was.

'He took the children down to the church.'

'You didn't go?'

'No.'

'You're naughty.'

It was all, moreover, in the name of 'love'; everyone involved placed a magical faith in the efficacy of the very word. There was the significance that Lucille Miller saw in Arthwell's saying that he 'loved' her, that he did not 'love' Elaine. There was Arthwell insisting, later, at the trial, that he had never said it, that he may have 'whispered sweet nothings in her ear' (as her defence hinted that he had whispered in many ears), but he did not remember bestowing upon her the special seal, saying the word, declaring 'love'. There was the summer evening when Lucille Miller and Sandy Slagle followed Arthwell Hayton down to his new boat in its mooring at Newport Beach and untied the lines with Arthwell aboard, Arthwell and a girl with whom he later testified he was drinking hot chocolate and watching television. 'I did that on purpose,' Lucille Miller told Erwin Sprengle later, 'to save myself from letting my heart do something crazy.'

11 January 1965, was a bright warm day in Southern California, the kind of day when Catalina floats on the Pacific horizon and the air smells of orange blossoms and it is a long way from the bleak and difficult East, a long way from the cold, a long way from the past. A woman in Hollywood staged an all-night sit-in on the hood of her car to prevent repossession by a finance company. A seventy-year-old pensioner drove his station wagon at five miles an hour past three Gardena poker parlours and emptied three pistols and a twelve-gauge shotgun through their windows, wounding twenty-nine people. 'Many young women become prostitutes just to have enough money to play cards,' he explained in a note. Mrs Nick Adams said that she was 'not surprised' to hear her husband announce his divorce plans on the Les Crane Show, and, farther north, a sixteen-year-old jumped off the Golden Gate Bridge and lived.

And, in the San Bernardino County Courthouse, the Miller trial opened. The crowds were so bad that the glass courtroom doors were shattered in the crush, and from then on identification discs were issued to the first forty-three spectators in line. The line began forming at 6 a.m., and college girls camped at the courthouse all night, with stores of graham crackers and No-Cal.

All they were doing was picking a jury, those first few days, but the sensational nature of the case had already suggested itself. Early in December there had been an abortive first trial, a trial at which no evidence was ever presented because on the day the jury was seated the San Bernardino *Sun-Telegram* ran an 'inside' story quoting Assistant District Attorney Don Turner, the prosecutor, as saying, 'We are looking into the circumstances of Mrs. Hayton's death. In view of the current trial concerning the death of Dr. Miller, I do not feel I should comment on Mrs. Hayton's death.' It seemed that there had been barbituates in Elaine Hayton's blood, and there had seemed some irregularity about the way she was dressed on that morning when she was found under the covers, dead. Any doubts about the death at the time, however, had never gotten as far as the Sheriff's Office. 'I guess somebody didn't want to rock the boat,' Turner said later. 'These were prominent people.'

Although all of that had not been in the *Sun-Telegram's* story, an immediate mistrial had been declared. Almost as immediately, there had been another development: Arthwell Hayton had asked newspapermen to an 11 a.m. Sunday morning press conference in his office. There had been television cameras, and flash bulbs popping. 'As you gentlemen may know,' Hayton had said, striking a note of stiff bonhomie, 'there are very often women who become amorous towards their doctor or lawyer. This does not mean on the physician's or lawyer's part that there is any romance towards the patient or client.'

'Would you deny that you were having an affair with Mrs. Miller?' a reporter had asked.

'I would deny that there was any romance on my part whatsoever.'

It was a distinction he would maintain through all the wearing weeks to come.

So they had come to see Arthwell, these crowds who now milled beneath the dusty palms outside the courthouse, and they had also come to see Lucille, who appeared as a slight, intermittently pretty woman, already pale from lack of sun, a woman who would turn thirty-five before the trial was over and whose tendency towards haggardness was beginning to show, a meticulous woman who insisted, against her lawyer's advice, on coming to court with her hair piled high and lacquered. 'I would've been happy if she'd come in with it hanging loose, but Lucille wouldn't do that,' her lawyer said. He was Edward P. Foley, a small, emotional Irish Catholic who several times wept in the courtroom. 'She has a great honesty, this woman,' he added, 'but this honesty about her appearance always worked against her.'

By the time the trial opened, Lucille Miller's appearance included maternity clothes, for an official examination on 18 December had revealed that she was then three and a half months pregnant, a fact which made picking a jury even more difficult than usual, for Turner was asking the death penalty. 'It's unfortunate but there it is,' he would say of the pregnancy to each juror in turn, and finally twelve were seated, seven of them women, the youngest forty-one, an assembly of the very peers – housewives, a machinist, a truck driver, a grocery-store manager, a filing clerk – above whom Lucille Miller had wanted so badly to rise.

That was the sin, more than the adultery, which tended to reinforce the one for which she was being tried. It was implicit in both the defence and the prosecution that Lucille Miller was an erring woman, a woman who perhaps wanted too much. But to the prosecution she was not merely a woman who would want a new house and want to go to parties and run up high telephone bills ($1,152 in ten months), but a woman who would go so far as to murder her husband for his $80,000 insurance, making it appear an accident in order to collect another $40,000 in double indemnity and straight accident policies. To Turner she was a woman who did not want simply her freedom and a reasonable alimony (she could have had that, the defence contended, by going through with her divorce suit), but wanted everything, a woman motivated by 'love and greed'. She was a 'manipulator'. She was a 'user of people'.

To Edward Foley, on the other hand, she was an impulsive woman who 'couldn't control her foolish little heart'. Where Turner skirted the pregnancy, Foley dwelt upon it, even calling the dead man's mother down from Washington to testify that her son had told her they were going to have another baby because Lucille felt that it would 'do much to weld our home again in the pleasant relations that we used to have'. Where the prosecution saw a 'calculator', the defence saw a 'blabbermouth', and in fact Lucille Miller did emerge as an ingenuous conversationalist. Just as, before her husband's death, she had confided in her friends about her love affair, so she chatted about it after his death, with the arresting sergeant. 'Of course Cork lived with it for years, you know,' her voice was heard to tell Sergeant Paterson on a tape made the morning after her arrest. 'After Elaine died, he pushed the panic button one night

and just asked me right out, and that, I think, was when he really –
the first time he really faced it.' When the sergeant asked why she
had agreed to talk to him, against the specific instructions of her
lawyers, Lucille Miller said airily, 'Oh, I've always been basically
quite an honest person . . . I mean I can put a hat in the cupboard
and say it cost ten dollars less, but basically I've always kind of just
lived my life the way I wanted to, and if you don't like it you can
take off.'

The prosecution hinted at men other than Arthwell, and even,
over Foley's objections, managed to name one. The defence called
Miller suicidal. The prosecution produced experts who said that the
Volkswagen fire could not have been accidental. Foley produced
witnesses who said that it could have been. Lucille's father, now
a junior-high-school teacher in Oregon, quoted Isaiah to reporters:
'*Every tongue that shall rise against thee in judgement thou shalt con-
demn.*' 'Lucille did wrong, her affair,' her mother said judiciously.
'With her it was love. But with some I guess it's just passion.' There
was Debbie, the Millers' fourteen-year-old, testifying in a steady
voice about how she and her mother had gone to a supermarket
to buy the gasoline can the week before the accident. There was
Sandy Slagle, in the courtroom every day, declaring that on at least
one occasion Lucille Miller had prevented her husband not only
from committing suicide but from committing suicide in such a way
that it would appear an accident and ensure the double-indemnity
payment. There was Wenche Berg, the pretty twenty-seven-year-old
Norwegian governess to Arthwell Hayton's children, testifying that
Arthwell had instructed her not to allow Lucille Miller to see or talk
to the children.

Two months dragged by, and the headlines never stopped.
Southern California's crime reporters were headquartered in San
Bernardino for the duration: Howard Hertel from the *Times*, Jim
Bennett and Eddy Jo Bernal from the *Herald-Examiner*. Two
months in which the Miller trial was pushed off the *Examiner*'s front page only by the Academy Award nominations and
Stan Laurel's death. And finally, on 2 March, after Turner had
reiterated that it was a case of 'love and greed', and Foley had
protested that his client was being tried for adultery, the case went
to the jury.

They brought in the verdict, guilty of murder in the first degree, at 4.50 p.m. on 5 March. 'She didn't do it,' Debbie Miller cried, jumping up from the spectator's section. 'She didn't *do* it.' Sandy Slagle collapsed in her seat and began to scream. 'Sandy, for God's sake please *don't*,' Lucille Miller said in a voice that carried across the courtroom, and Sandy Slagle was momentarily subdued. But as the jurors left the courtroom she screamed again: 'You're murderers . . . Every last one of you is a *murderer*.' Sheriff's deputies moved in then, each wearing a string tie that read '1965 SHERIFF'S RODEO', and Lucille Miller's father, that sad-faced junior-high-school teacher who believed in the word of Christ and the dangers of wanting to see the world, blew her a kiss off his fingertips.

The California Institution for Women at Frontera, where Lucille Miller is now, lies down where Euclid Avenue turns into country road, not too many miles from where she once lived and shopped and organized the Heart Fund Ball. Cattle graze across the road, and Rainbirds sprinkle the alfalfa. Frontera has a softball field and tennis courts, and looks as if it might be a California junior college, except that the trees are not yet high enough to conceal the concertina wire around the top of the Cyclone fence. On visitors' day there are big cars in the parking area, big Buicks and Pontiacs that belong to grandparents and sisters and fathers (not many of them belong to husbands), and some of them have bumper stickers that say 'SUPPORT YOUR LOCAL POLICE'.

A lot of California murderesses live here, a lot of girls who somehow misunderstood the promise. Don Turner put Sandra Garner here (and her husband in the gas chamber at San Quentin) after the 1959 desert killings known to crime reporters as 'the soda-pop murders'. Carole Tregoff is here, and has been ever since she was convicted of conspiring to murder Dr. Finch's wife in West Covina, which is not too far from San Bernardino. Carole Tregoff is in fact a nurse's aide in the prison hospital, and might have attended Lucille Miller had her baby been born at Frontera; Lucille Miller chose instead to have it outside, and paid for the guard who stood outside the delivery room in St. Bernardine's Hospital. Debbie Miller came to take the baby home from the hospital, in a white dress with pink ribbons, and Debbie was allowed to choose a name. She named the baby Kimi Kai. The children live with Harold and Joan Lance now, because Lucille Mller will probably spend ten years at Frontera. Don Turner waived his original request for the death penalty (it was generally agreed that he had demanded it only, in Edward Foley's words, 'to get anybody with the slightest trace of human kindness in their veins off the jury'), and settled for life imprisonment with the possibility of parole. Lucille Miller does not like it at Frontera, and has had trouble adjusting. 'She's going to have to learn humility,' Turner says. 'She's going to have to use her ability to charm, to manipulate.'

The new house is empty now, the house on the street with the sign that says

> PRIVATE ROAD
> BELLA VISTA
> DEAD END

The Millers never did get it landscaped, and weeds grow up around the fieldstone siding. The television aerial has toppled on the roof, and a trash can is stuffed with the debris of family life: a cheap suitcase, a child's game called 'Lie Detector'. There is a sign on what would have been the lawn, and the sign reads 'ESTATE SALE'. Edward Foley is trying to get Lucille Miller's case appealed, but there have been delays. 'A trial always comes down to a matter of sympathy,' Foley says wearily now. 'I couldn't create sympathy for her.' Everyone is a little weary now, weary and resigned, everyone except Sandy Slagle, whose bitterness is still raw. She lives in an apartment near the medical school in Loma Linda, and studies reports of the case in *True Police Cases* and *Official Detective Stories*. 'I'd much rather we not talk about the Hayton business too much,' she tells visitors, and she keeps a tape recorder running. 'I'd rather talk about Lucille and what a wonderful person she is and how her rights were violated.' Harold Lance does not talk to visitors at all. 'We don't want to give away what we can sell,' he explains pleasantly; an attempt was made to sell Lucille Miller's personal story to *Life*, but *Life* did not want to buy it. In the district attorney's offices they are prosecuting other murders now, and do not see why the Miller trial attracted so much attention. 'It wasn't a very interesting murder as murders go,' Don Turner says laconically. Elaine Hayton's death is no longer under investigation. 'We know everything we want to know,' Turner says.

Arthwell Hayton's office is directly below Edward Foley's. Some people around San Bernardino say that Arthwell Hayton suffered; others say that he did not suffer at all. Perhaps he did not, for time past is not believed to have any bearing upon time present or future, out in the golden land where every day the world is born anew. In any case, on 17 October 1965, Arthwell Hayton married again, married his children's pretty governess, Wenche Berg, at a service in the Chapel of the Roses at a retirement village near Riverside. Later the newlyweds were fêted at a reception for seventy-five in the dining-room of Rose Garden Village. The bridegroom was in black tie, with a white carnation in his button-hole. The bride wore a long white *peau de soie* dress and carried a shower bouquet of sweetheart roses with stephanotis streamers. A coronet of seed pearls held her illusion veil.

MARTIN AMIS

The Killings in
Atlanta

1 Murder in America

'It looked like a straight verbal mugging. The kid points the gun
and says: "Gimme all your money." The guy hands over $90, credit
cards, watch, links, everything. Then as the kid walks off he turns
around, real casual, and shoots him anyway. These days, man, it's
your money *and* your life.'

'Then the handyman flipped and laid into the old lady with an
ax . . . Then this transvestite took a monkey-wrench out of his
handbag . . . Buried her body under the . . . Sawed his head off
with a . . . Watch out for the Downtown Slasher . . . the Uptown
Strangler . . . the Midtown Mangler . . .'

Conversation about murder in America is as stoical and routine
as talk about the weather. A New Yorker will tell you about some
lurid atrocity in his own flatblock with no more animation than if
he were complaining about the rent. Terrible things happen all the
time. This is the terrible thing.

The outsider's view remains hazy, cinematic, exaggerated, formed
by cop-operas and a chaos of statistics. To the outsider, American
murder seems as vehement and anarchic as American free enterprise,
or American neurosis, or American profanity . . . But sometimes,
and far more worryingly in a way, shapes and bearings do emerge
from the turmoil, and portents are suddenly visible among all
the blood.

During the week that I was in Atlanta an eighteen-year-old boy
cut the throat of an elderly neighbour and stabbed her forty-two
times with a butcher's knife (over a trespass dispute); a schizophrenic

former jailer and preacher raped and sodomised one woman and then
shot both her and her friend in the head; a young crime reporter,
having been raped the year before by an escaped convict, was found
with thirty-five stab wounds in her chest (the convict was back inside
on another rape charge, so it couldn't have been *him*).

These are killings in Atlanta. But they are not the Killings in
Atlanta

2 The Killings in Atlanta

> Piano keys don't lock doors.
> Footballs don't have toes.
> And, of course, cabbage heads
> Don't have a mouth or a nose.
> And kids don't go with strangers.
> They never go with strangers.

But they do. In the last twenty months, twenty black children have
been murdered in Atlanta. No one has has any idea who is doing
this or why. District Attorney Lewis Slaton, in his creaking, leathery
office, leaned back in his chair and said, 'Oh, we got a lot of theories.
But we're not any nearer than we were when this thing started
happening. We got no motive, no witnesses, no murder scenes,
no hard clues at all. We ain't got lead one.' Only the compulsive
confessors, who monotonously turned themselves in at the station
houses, seem convinced of the identity of the culprit: 'Me. I did it,'
they say. 'I did them all.'

Kids don't go with strangers . . . The jingle comes from a local
rockabilly hit. Car-bumper stickers say the same thing. So do children's colouring books. There are curfews for minors, haphazardly
enforced. The Atlanta Falcons and the Westside Jaycees print
trading cards of their teams, with safety tips as captions. There
are teach-ins and pray-ins. There is great fear. But kids still go
with strangers, one every month.

The murders began in the summer of 1979. It took a long while
for any pattern to surface from the tide of Atlantan crime. Every
year five or six black kids meet violent deaths (three, perhaps four,
of the current cases are probably unconnected domestic killings: 'the
assailant was known to the victim' – this is code talk for murder

within the family). A year passed, and a dozen deaths, before anyone sensed the real scope of the disaster, the serial catastrophe, that was overtaking the city.

'Pretty early on I started to get a sick feeling about it,' said Camille Bell, who runs STOP, the Committee to Stop Children's Murders. The walls of her improvised office are covered with maps (coloured pins denote the site of the victims' disappearance and discovery), hand-painted uplift posters ('We are not about *Poverty*. Instead, we are about *Prosperity. Prosperity* of the *Heart* and *Soul* . . .') and information sheets from the Department of Public Safety.

Mrs. Bell has a holding device on her telephone. She dodged from call to call. 'Officer? There are two kids hanging around outside All Right Parking. Could you get 'em taken home?' 'Venus, you heard the latest? I'm getting $1,000 a lecture. Some joke, huh?' As Mrs. Bell talked, I scanned the public safety handout. There he was, number four:

YUSEF BELL, BLACK MALE, 9 YEARS OLD

Yusef Bell was last seen on October 21, 1979, en route to a grocery store on McDaniel Street. His body was found on November 8. The cause of death was strangulation.

Camille Bell is a public figure these days. There is a lot of glare in Atlanta now, and a lot of money, federal and commercial. Mrs. Bell has her critics. There is talk of cashing in, of joining the parade. I would be ashamed to question Mrs. Bell's motives; but these are poor people, and these things are inevitable in America. Camille Bell finished her call and said, 'The fear just grew, all through last year. I just knew it. Someone is stealing the kids off the streets.'

3 The Time Bomb in the Nursery

Atlanta, Georgia, is one of the model cities of the New South. The scene of many a crucial battle in the desegregation war, Atlanta has since dubbed itself 'the city too busy to hate'. The 600,000 population is predominantly black, as is the city administration. The airport, the world's largest, is designed by black architects, its concourses adorned with the work of black artists. Downtown, among the civic mansions and futuristic hotels, the streets are so clean that you expect to see ashtrays, standard lamps, Hoovers, on every corner.

It was the random nature of the killings which first persuaded Atlanta that the city's crisis was a racial one. Where else do you find any link or motive? This kid was shot, that one bludgeoned, that one stabbed. None of them had any money. There was no obvious sexual factor in the killings, except perhaps in the case of the two girls (Latonya Wilson was found four months after her death, her body partly eaten by dogs; Angel Lanier was found a week after her disappearance, sexually molested, tied to a tree). All the children were dumped, having been killed elsewhere. Some had been hidden, some had been laid out openly, in natural, relaxed postures. The victims have only three things in common: they were black, they were poor, and they were children.

'Sure we thought it was racial,' I was told. 'Or political anyway. Some movement might be doing this to force a situation. Might be extreme right or extreme left. And with us black folks squeezed in the middle.'

Racial disquiet climbed in the city all last year, until October. Then came the bomb in the nursery. An explosion in a day nursery killed three children and a teacher, all of them black. 'Now I am a mild man,' said an elderly negro. 'I don't hold with this vigilante stuff. But after that explosion, I was ready to go. I didn't think it was a bomb. I *knew* it was a bomb. And it was the Klan put it there.'

The day nursery is on a broad street, one marked by an air of colourful poverty, opposite a run-down school. It is not difficult to imagine the scene on that hot autumn day. Hoax calls forced five nearby schools to evacuate. There must have been a lot of fear and anger milling around on the street.

Mayor Maynard Jackson and Commissioner Lee Brown, the two prongs of the black administration, did what they had to do: they acted fast. Within hours black experts were on the scene, pronouncing the cause of the explosion: old boiler, faulty wiring. 'If that thing hadn't been open and shut the same day,' I was told, 'well, it could have been a bloody night in Atlanta.'

No one thinks the killings are primarily racial any more. No one thinks the killings are primarily anything any more. Fear and bafflement are very tiring, and Atlanta is a weary city by now. Twenty have died, but the effects of the trauma are incalculable.

In a sense, the bomb in the nursery is heard and felt every day. Children no longer play in the parks and streets. In the housing projects, council estates which combine urban decay with a tang of authentic suburban dread, children stand and talk in groups, and stare at the cars. There have been alarming increases in all symptoms of juvenile anxiety: bedwetting, refusal to sleep alone, fear of doors and windows. Reports go on about children having 'lost the capacity to trust people'. If the murderer or murderers, the leftist or rightist, the madman or madmen unknown are caught and convicted tomorrow, there won't be a black child in Atlanta whose life has not already been deformed by these killings.

4 Circus of the Supercops

Last November, Dorothy Allison, known as 'the vendetta psychic', came to town at the invitation of the Atlanta police. Dorothy had been fighting crime with her paranormal powers since 1967, when a dream led her to discover the body of a five-year-old boy, stuffed into a drainpipe. She worked on 100 cases, finding 38 bodies and solving 14 murders. But Dorothy drew a blank in Atlanta. Townspeople complain that she spent most of her time here promoting her autobiography on local radio shows. One mother said that the psychic never returned her only photograph of her murdered son.

The FBI were in Atlanta by this stage, and the Missing Persons Bureau (originally with a staff of four) had been belatedly expanded into a thirty-seven-member Task Force, working in the showrooms of the old Leader Lincoln-Mercury dealership in the centre of town. A reward of $100,000 was established. 'That ought to smoke them out' was the general view. 'That'll shake the trees.'

But it didn't. And then the supercops hit town: from Manhattan, Detective Charles Nanton, who worked on 'Son of Sam'; from Los Angeles, Captain Pierce Brooks, the man who caught the cop-killers in the 'Onion Field' case; and several other crack enforcers from all over the States. The supercops left Atlanta a fortnight later, quietly.

Epidemiologists from the Centre for Disease Control set up their computers. Advice was sought from the anti-terrorist training school in Powder Springs. The Guardian Angels from New York are the latest in a long line of fêted hopefuls. Two $10,000-apiece German Shepherd dogs, so high-powered that they respond only to German commands, contributed their hunting skills. Someone with tracking experience in Africa offered to . . .

'It made a lot of people mad,' said one old Atlantan. 'Hell, it was all PR. They all just wanted to *look* good.' Since the Killings in Atlanta are now world news, everyone wants to look good in the glow: George Bush, Burt Reynolds, Frank Sinatra, Ronald Reagan.

The supercop circus didn't find what it was looking for. But it found something else: more crime. Quotidian lawbreaking doesn't stop while massacres take the headlines; and the intense investigations in Atlanta were uncovering whole new layers of transgression and turpitude.

An officer searches an abandoned building for clues: in a stairwell he finds the skeleton of a forty-year-old man. A tracking dog returns to its master – with the skull of an adult female in its jaws. The weekly citizen area-sweeps routinely turn up caches of guns and stolen goods. Peaceable burglars panic at road-blocks.

Late last year three kids in their mid-teens were arrested for robbery. A health-check revealed that they had all contracted syphilis. Soon afterwards a forty-one-year-old man was arrested for sodomy; several other under-age boys were involved. A nine-year-old girl was picked up off the street by the police, for her own protection. She turned out to be an experienced prostitute. She had been giving 'head and hand' since she was five.

There is certainly a childish underworld lying beneath the surface of Atlanta life. But the murder victims did not belong to it. Several of the boys were street-wise; they hustled for work, for tips, for errands, but they were not delinquent. One boy, Aaron Jackson Jnr., aged nine, used to break into houses, but only for food and warmth. A woman woke up to find Aaron asleep on her sofa. The refrigerator had been raided. Little Aaron was last seen on

November 1, 1980, at the Moreland Avenue Shopping Center. His body was found the next day, under a bridge. The cause of death was asphyxiation.

5 The 'Invisible Man' Theory

'Theories – that's one thing we've got plenty of,' said the DA. 'Me, I still think it's sex'n'drugs.'

I mentioned that the bodies of the boys showed no sign of sexual interference.

'Don't *have* to be no sign of it. They get the kids, smoke a little marijuana, try some sex stuff. The kid might just be an onlooker . . . Or maybe some of the kids are pushing a little dope, and need teaching a lesson by the Man. Or maybe it's their *parents* who're being warned. Has to be money involved. Bottom line for a whole lotta stuff is money.'

On one of the early clue-sweeps, police entered a recently abandoned house. They found an axe, a hatchet, a shovel and some chldren's clothing. They also found two Bibles – nailed to the wall. The Bibles were open, one on Isaiah I:14 to 3:25, the other on Jeremiah 15:4 to 18:4. Back at the Atlanta America Hotel, I picked up the complimentary Gideon and read through the passages: *'Bring no more vain offerings . . . your hands are full of blood. Wash yourselves . . . /I have brought against the mothers of young men/a destroyer at noonday;/I have made anguish and terror/fall upon them suddenly.'*

After the discovery of the nailed Bibles the 'Cult' Theory gained currency for a while. The kids were being killed to satisfy the rituals of some voodoo brotherhood; several of the children had been carefully washed, after all, and laid out in stylised postures. For a short time in 1980, and again in the last three months, the monthly cycle of the killings encouraged the 'Disturbed Female' Theory. Perhaps a failed mother or a childless woman was acting out a complicated revenge on the living world.

Are the killers white or black? To begin with, of course, this was the crucial question. Several of the kids were picked up in areas where a white man would stick out like a pink elephant. The city population splits 60–40, but the street presence is much more one-sided than that. If the murderers and the victims turned out to be the same colour, the Killings in Atlanta would accord with the mainstream of American crime. Blacks make up an eighth of the US citizenry, and a half of its prison population. Most crime is still segregated. To a wildly disproportionate extent, violence in America is black on black.

Atlanta is a scattered city, surrounded by a lot of open and unfrequented country – lakes, wide plains, woodlands. The killers use all this space and are heavily reliant on their mobility. It sometimes seems that only a black could go to work with the unobtrusive speed and freedom that he needs.

In Chesterton's story, '*The Invisible Man*', the detective Father Brown orders four people, two of them policemen, to keep watch on the only entrance to the flat of a potential murder victim. The murder takes place, the four men claim that 'no one' went through the door. Oh yes he did, says Father Brown – and he walked past you all with the body in his arms. 'The Invisible Man?' someone asks. Correct, in a sense. The murderer was the postman, and he carried the victim in his sack.

A uniform confers facelessness, jurisdiction, and a degree of invisibility. 'Now that could be anyone,' said a local crime reporter, 'delivery man, bus driver, utility worker . . . or a cop.'

The switch from a white to a black administration has happened only over the last few years. A lot of people were edged out in that shift. Many white cops, in particular, got sacked or passed over for promotion (with accompanying scandals: exams were rigged to favour black candidates, and so on). Now, if the motive was to discredit and humiliate the black-run police force, then the 'Rogue Cop' Theory has life in it.

Perhaps, though, motive is the wrong thing, the irrelevant thing, to look for. It is possible that the twenty murders will break down into four or five weird clusters. What strikes you again and again is that the Killings in Atlanta have been so easy to do. Despite the propaganda, the campaigns, the fear, kids still go with strangers. Last month black and white plainclothes-policemen drove in unmarked cars round the housing projects, the vacant lots, the shanty houses with ripped car seats on their patios. There are no adults about, there is no authority,there is not even a memory of the survival instincts of the old ghetto. 'Hey, kid,' the decoys would call to the children they found, 'you want to earn ten bucks?' Hop in.' They got a rider *every time*.

6 *The View from Peachtree Plaza*

The Peachtree Plaza Hotel is the centrepiece of downtown Atlanta. It is a billion-dollar masterpiece of American efficiency, luxury and robotic good manners. 'Mm-hm. Mm-hm,' everyone says five times a minute as they glide across its fountained halls.

Among its other accomplishments, the Peachtree is the tallest hotel in the world. If it's essence of vertigo you want, take the scenic elevator to the seventy-second floor and enjoy a Cloud Buster ('a refreshing blend of coconut milk, pineapple juice and vodka served in a souvenir replica of the Hotel' – $7.95. 'Thank you.' 'Mm-hm') in the revolving Sundial Lounge.

There you will see the scalextric of the city, with its flyovers and chicanes, the dwarfed high-rise car-parks, the windshields blazing in the malls, the elevated trains, EQUITABLE, OMNI, LIFE OF GEORGIA, thruways, glistening like canals . . . and the acres of toytown prefabs on the criss-crossed suburban streets, where a person or persons unknown is still stealing the kids off the streets.

To the south-east lies Miami. Last May, four white policemen were acquitted there after the fatal beating of a black suspect, Arthur McDuffie. It happened on the street, after a chase. The medical examiner said that McDuffie's injuries were consistent with 'falling four storeys and landing between your eyes'. When the acquittal was announced there were three days of rioting: 16 dead, 400 injured, $100 million worth of damage.

In Buffalo, New York, last September, four random blacks were shot in the head by the same white man. A fortnight later, two black cabbies were found with their hearts ripped out. In Oklahoma City, a black man and a white woman were shot to death in a parking lot. In Fort Wayne, Indiana, black leader Vernon Jordan was shot in the back while climbing out of a white woman's car. In Johnstown, Philadelphia, a mixed couple were murdered as they walked across the street. In Salt Lake

City, Utah, two black men were shot while out jogging with white women.

In Birmingham, Alabama, there is a Ku Klux Klan military training camp, called My Lai in honour of the war criminal William Calley. In Greensboro, North Carolina, last November, an all-white jury acquitted six Klansmen and Nazis of the murder of five black and white Communists. In Chattanooga, Tennessee, acquittals and dropped charges have released five Klansmen accused of killing five black women on the streets.

Are these things connected? Are the Killings in Atlanta connected, to these killings or to each other? It is very tempting to see patterns here, or simply a change in the emphasis of murder in America.

Atlanta looks peaceful enough in the mild winter light. Atlanta in August will be a different proposition from Atlanta in January. The killings will not have been solved; and by then, too, President Reagan's passive attitude to pro-black legislation will have begun to hurt. Anyway, the summer is the time for racial anger and despair. In summer, the ghettos always heat up. They will expand and swell in the sun. Some will burst.

Observer 1981

★   ★   ★

Postscript Early in 1982, an irregularly employed black disc-jockey called Wayne Williams was convicted of two of the Atlanta child murders and, by implication, some or all of the remaining twenty-seven. There was much that was unsatisfactory about the trial. The evidence for the prosecution centred on the (circumstantial but compelling) fact that 'fibres' found on the victims matched the Williams family carpet. Williams's defence was agreed to be feeble verging on incompetent. The trial raised all sorts of questions about the exertion of public – and media – pressure to effect a palliative outcome. It seemed to me weirdly character-istic that the first thing Williams did, on his arrest, was call a press conference. Meanwhile, serving his life sentence, Williams ponders the legal options, his hand occasionally strengthened by such things as Abby Mann's five-hour drama-documentary for CBS, *The Atlanta Child Murders*, which was very partial, very anti-establishment and very pro-Williams (the killer, Mann implies, was probably white). Have the murders come to an end? The violent death of poor American blacks, unless given urgency by politics, has never much exercised the American judiciary; and some observers suggest, most depressingly, that the Atlanta murders continue, as they always have and always will. Perhaps, then, the Killings in Atlanta are over, while the killings in Atlanta go on.

The Miscarriage of Justice

ANN JONES

Alice Crimmins

When the police arrived at the apartment in Kew Gardens, Queens, they found Edmund Crimmins, a husky aircraft mechanic thickened by too much beer-drinking, and his twenty-six-year-old wife, Alice. Eddie, separated from his wife, had been summoned by her frantic 9.00 a.m. phone call: the children, five-year-old Eddie and four-year-old Alice Marie, called Missy, had disappeared from their bedroom. Detective Gerard Piering, in the absence of senior detectives, fell into command of his first major case; and according to all reports, he took one look at Alice Crimmins and disliked her. Alice Crimmins was what the newspapers called a 'shapely' woman in toreador pants, her strawberry blonde hair carefully teased and lacquered, her makeup perfectly applied. She cast herself in the same mold as Candy Mossler and Lana Turner, but she was a working-class housewife. To Jerry Piering, Catholic father of six, she did not look like 'Mother'. When he gave orders to question Eddie and Alice Crimmins separately, he announced to his partner, 'I'll take the bitch.' That afternoon he took Alice Crimmins to a vacant lot half a mile away to look at her dead daughter. Missy was lying on her side in the sun, her pajama top knotted around her neck, her body swarming with flies. Alice Crimmins staggered, swooned, and fell into the arms of a detective; but she didn't cry. To Piering her reaction was too theatrical – not like a real mother; he was sure he had his murderer. That evening when reporter Kenneth Gross went on assignment to the Crimmins apartment, other reporters and photographers popping flash-bulbs in Alice Crimmins's face told him what the police had told them: 'The bitch killed her kids.'

The police continued to question Eddie Crimmins and to check out tips on prowlers and known sex offenders, but they focused on Alice Crimmins. They tapped her telephone and bugged the new apartment that she and Eddie, temporarily reconciled by crisis, shared; but in three years of listening in on the life of Alice Crimmins, they found no bit of incriminating evidence to use against her. Perhaps that's why they turned nasty and began to harass her in other ways. When she went to bed with another man in her apartment, the listening police phoned Eddie and told him to go home. Whenever she got a new job under her maiden name – she was an executive secretary and reportedly an excellent one – the police visited her employer and told him who she was. They leaked word to the press that although their bugging tapes wouldn't be admissible in court, they proved that Alice had killed her children. Soon it was 'common knowledge' among the police and the press that Alice Crimmins was guilty of murder, though so far there wasn't any evidence to prove it. There was plenty of evidence, however, on the tapes and off, that Alice Crimmins had had sexual relations with several different men. What's more, she never denied it, never was ashamed of it, and even when she knew the police were watching her constantly, she never made the slightest effort to change her ways. 'If she were my wife,' said Detective Piering, 'I'd kill her.' Instead, on September 13, 1967, he arrested Alice Crimmins for the murder of her daughter. She was tried and convicted of manslaughter.

During the trial there was scarcely a fact that was not in dispute. A good deal of what should have constituted the physical evidence in this case existed only in the memory of Detective Piering. Whether the children could have been taken or enticed through the bedroom window and whether they had eaten veal or manicotti for supper became issues of crucial significance, but only Piering had seen the layer of dust on the bureau under the window and the manicotti carton in the trash. He had made no note at the time, no photographic record. He just remembered. The testimony of the star witnesses for the prosecution, Joseph Rorech and Sophie Earomirski, was equally problematical. Rorech, once a high-rolling contractor rapidly going bankrupt and an ex-boyfriend of Alice Crimmins, testified that she had confessed killing Missy in anger, and through the help of another boyfriend, summoned a hit man to silence little Eddie, who had witnessed the killing. Alice screamed that Rorech was lying.

There was no incontrovertible proof on either side; everything depended on whose word was believed. Could one believe the testimony of star witness Sophie Earomirski, the middle-aged housewife who came forward eighteen months after the children's disappearance to say that at 2.00 a.m. on July 14, 1965, she had seen Alice Crimmins, a little boy, a dog, and a big man throwing a bundle into the back of a car? The defense pointed out that Sophie Earomirski had filed a workman's compensation claim for brain damage – she had jumped and struck her head at work when a 'yellow mouse' ran up her arm – had attempted suicide with an overdose of tranquilizers, and had once been found with her head in the oven. (She was checking on dinner, she said.) Sophie Earomirski marched into court like a soldier, and after telling her improbable tale, she marched out again with her fist raised in triumph while the appreciative courtroom crowd cheered her on. She was photographed like that – the moment's hero – for all the papers. Nothing made it quite so clear that what was going on was not a search for justice but a war on Alice Crimmins.

Crimmins reacted accordingly: scornful, unashamed, hurt, and defiant. Outside the courtroom she masked the grief she refused to share with the public behind a desperate, brittle gaiety. Inside the courtroom, she was angry; and when she took the stand her cold anger told against her. Later she told reporter Gross that when she reread her own testimony she thought she sounded like a bitch. 'But the thing is,' she explained, 'I was angry. I just wanted to get to the point. That man, the prosecutor, he kept asking me those questions about sex. I wanted to get to the point. He only wanted to know about sex.' Her own attorneys wanted her to change her hairdo, her dress, her style; they wanted her to break down and cry for the jury, but she would not. The prosecution took her angry composure for hardness and worse.

To the press she was a sexy swinger. The pulp *Front Page Detective* featured the story of 'Sexpot on Trial', calling her an 'erring wife, a Circe, an amoral woman whose many affairs appeared symptomatic of America's Sex Revolution'. The New York *Daily News* called her 'the Queens housewife with hamster morals'. Her name was rarely mentioned without some descriptive swipe: curvy, comely, shapely, flame-haired, blonde. And always she was identified by an occupation she had filled for only six months: the ex-cocktail waitress – a term used pejoratively to sneer at Alice Crimmins and a whole category of women workers at once. Before long the terms lost their meaning and became merely slurs so that on a single page of a newspaper she might be identified as a 'sllekly [*sic*] attractive redhead' in one column and a 'shapely blonde' in the next. But they all added up to bitch and the capacity to kill. A Queens housewife who attended several sessions of the trial told *New York Times* reporter Lacey Fosburgh that she found it hard to believe that any woman could kill her children, but 'a woman like that . . . well . . . it makes it easier to understand.' One of the jurors agreed: 'A tramp like that is capable of anything.' There was no question that Alice Crimmins was a woman 'like that'; her own attorney said she was 'amoral' and acknowledged that the jury had been forced to listen to a lot of 'filth'.

But Alice Crimmins, who thought the prosecution never did get to the point, got a new defense team and fought back. In May 1968 the Appellate Division reversed her conviction and ordered a new trial because three of the jurors admitted visiting the scene without permission. The prosecution retaliated by carrying the case before a second grand jury which, in July 1970, returned indictments charging Alice Crimmins with manslaughter in the death of her daughter and murder in the death of her son. (Indicting her a second time for murder in her daughter's death would have constituted double jeopardy.) On March 15, 1971, she went on trial again.

The court heard the same conflicting, inconclusive evidence that had filled the newspapers before; and a few additional witnesses added to the confusion. The alleged hit man identified by Crimmins's ex-boyfriend Joseph Rorech took the stand for the defense; Vincent Colabella, serving a twenty-year sentence in Atlanta penitentiary on drug charges, testified that he had never seen Alice Crimmins before but that a former Queens assistant district attorney had offered to let him "go home free" if he would say that he had gone to the Crimmins apartment and found both children already dead. A woman testified that she had seen the same group – woman, boy, dog, and man with bundle – that Sophie Earomirski claimed to have spotted from her window. Marvin Weinstein testified that he and his family, leaving a friend's Kew Gardens apartment at

2.00 a.m., may well have been the group that Earomirski saw. The friend, Anthony King, said the Weinstein family hadn't been at his house. Mrs. Weinstein came in to court to say that they had so; and another of King's acquaintances testified that King was a notorious liar.

So it went, back and forth, until Dr. Milton Helpern, New York City's chief medical examiner and undoubtedly the world's most famous 'coroner', testified unequivocally that Missy Crimmins had died within two hours of eating her last meal, which consisted in part of 'macaroni'. Somehow, in that snarl of charge and countercharge, Helpern's testimony seemed a decisive scientific fact that pinned the murder on Alice Crimmins and the vanished manicotti carton – despite her own insistence that she had fed the children veal at 7.30 and seen them alive at midnight. Meanwhile, the press raked over Alice Crimmins's sex life again, and there was nothing to prevent twelve graying, middle-aged male jurors, who were never sequestered, from taking it all in. The judge instructed them to use their common sense, and on April 23, 1971, they announced their verdict: guilty of murder in the first degree – the most severe judgement they could have reached. Crimmins was sentenced to life imprisonment on the murder charge and five to twenty years for manslaughter; bail was denied as attorney Herbert Lyon, who always maintained that she had been tried for her morals and not for murder, began the complicated legal battle to free her.

Two years later, on May 7, 1973, the Appellate Division overturned both convictions because of various 'errors and improprieties' by the prosecution prejudicial to the defendant. The court threw out the murder conviction altogether and ordered that Crimmins be retried on the manslaughter charge. Having served two years in prison, Crimmins was released, but in February 1975 the State Court of Appeals reversed the decision of the Appellate Court. (The Appeals Court did agree to throw out the murder conviction because the state could not prove beyond reasonable doubt that little Eddie Crimmins, found five days after his disappearance and too badly decomposed for autopsy, had in fact been murdered.) But it upheld the manslaughter conviction – although in order to do so it had to establish a new interpretation of the law. Formerly errors in trial procedure had been considered prejudicial to the defendant if there was a 'rational possibility' that the jury would have acquitted the defendant if the error had not occurred. The Appeals Court now maintained that an error was prejudicial only if there was 'significant probability' that without it the case would have gone the other way. Two dissenting justices argued that by accepting the new standard the court was 'dangerously diluting the time-honored standard of proof beyond a reasonable doubt, cornerstone of Anglo-Saxon criminal jurisprudence', but the majority bounced the case back to the Appellate Division judges with orders that they look at it again; and, in light of the new standard applied by the higher court, the Appellate Division reversed its own reversal and declared that Alice Crimmins was indeed guilty of manslaughter. On May 16, 1975, she was returned to prison to continue serving out her five-to-twenty-year term; and in December the Court of Appeals ruled that she could not appeal any further. It took a succession of district attorneys, a flock of underlings, thousands of police man-hours, three grand juries, two trials, a reinterpretation of appellate law, and ten years, but at last Alice Crimmins was put away.

Perhaps Alice Crimmins was guilty. Perhaps not. Certainly the fragmentary evidence did not prove her guilt beyond a reasonable doubt; but she was granted no presumption of innocence. It is not that anyone deliberately set out to convict an innocent woman, but that so many people – beginning with Detective Piering – almost immediately assumed she was guilty because she was 'like that'. That assumption skewed the initial investigation – the police had hours of tape recordings of Alice Crimmins in bed and no photographs of the window through which her children may have been abducted – and that assumption, picked up by an almost all-male press corps, colored everything that followed. Alice Crimmins touched a raw nerve not just in Detective Piering but in troubled society just beginning to recoil from too much domestic togetherness. Even if Crimmins hadn't killed her children, said one reporter, she had plenty to feel guilty about. '*IF* she had been a faithful wife – and mother – whose primary concern was her home, her husband, and her children, there probably would have been no estrangement from her husband. *IF* there had been no estrangement, her husband would very likely have bean at home on that fateful night. . . . *IF* her husband had been at home that night, the children might never have been abducted, might never have been murdered.' But as they had in the twenties, women seemed to be seizing sexual prerogatives reserved for men. If Alice Crimmins had been the only nice Catholic housewife 'sleeping around' in Queens, there would have been no need to make her a public example. But of course she was not.

Prosecutors, reporters, police, and jurors alike condemned her morals and never questioned those of the married men who were her partners in sex. Nor did they seem to find anything particularly odd in the behavior of husband Eddie Crimmins, who during their separation tapped Alice's phone, went to her apartment when she was away just to be around her 'things,' hid in the basement under her bedroom to listen to her have sex with other men, and by his own admission, exposed himself to little girls in the park. To women, Alice Crimmins was a home wrecker – a threatening woman freer that those traditional wives who clung, whether happily or not, to the security of house and husband. And to mothers – 'good' and 'bad' – she was sinister. Following up the prosecution theory that Crimmins had strangled Missy in momentary anger, the press asked over and over: 'What kind of woman could do a thing like that?' A high school classmate said Alice couldn't have done it because she was "no different from the rest of us." But the press quickly found an answer in 'that kind' of woman: a bleached blonde, a promiscuous ex-cocktail waitress – a woman totally unlike 'the rest of us'. Yet any mother, isolated day after day with her children, would know – if she could bear to think about it – that maybe, just maybe, she could do it too. Several more years passed before the statistics began to appear regularly in the newspapers: the figures on how many children had been beaten, burned, scalded, strangled, broken, and killed by mothers and fathers behind closed doors. But there were then thousands of women and men who did not need the statistics to know.

Only the New York Radical Feminists offered to support Alice Crimmins, and their offer was turned down by her attorneys. Crimmins was already under attack precisely because she was under no man's control or protection. Sexually, at least, she was a free agent, a threat to society. The last thing the Crimmins defense attorneys wanted was to have her identified with equally

subversive feminists, although paradoxically the anxiety that provoked the war on Alice Crimmins was undoubtedly riled by the
renewed women's movement. Reporter Gross concluded: 'The
Alice Crimmins case . . . was perceived as frightening because
the women's movement was just coming into existence when the
case broke, and the implications – a housewife grown rebellious and
out of control – terrified those who felt a stake in maintaining the
status quo.' Certainly Crimmins herslef was no feminist. 'Oh, I'm
for equal pay for equal work,' she said in 1971. 'But not for all the
far-out things. I don't hate men. I believe that women are put on
this earth to serve men. A man should be dominant. I believe in
women's liberation, but not at the price of my femininity.' Only the
Radical Feminists with their simple slogan, 'Free Alice Crimmins',
suggested the real problem: that 'feminine' Alice Crimmins was, in
effect, a prisoner of sexual politics.

In January 1976 Alice Crimmins became eligible for a work-release
program and began work in a secretarial job. In March 1977 she
became eligible for parole, but her application was denied because
'taking into account the extreme seriousness of the offense', the
parole board feared that 'release at this time could promote dis-
respect for the law.' In addition, the board doubted that she could
'live and remain at liberty without violating the law.' Then in August
1977 the New York *Post* in a front-page photo story broke the news
that Alice Crimmins had spent Sunday – 'as she has spent many
balmy summer Sundays of her prison term – on a luxury cruiser
at City Island'. Crimmins, it seemed, like other prisoners in the
work-release program, had every other weekend to herself; and
she had been spending many of those weekends with Anthony
Grace, a wealthy sixty-six-year-old contractor, the boyfriend who
allegedly had sent her Colabella, the hit man. Grace testified for
the defense at both trials, visited Crimmins regularly during her
imprisonment, and as the *Post* soon discovered, married her in July
1977 – with the requisite permission of correction officials. In a full
page of telephoto shots of Crimmins in bikini and T-shirt 'looking
remarkably attractive for her 37 years,' the *Post* tried to rake up
the public anger that had sold so many papers over the years. The
Post followed up the next day with a front-page story headlining the
opinion of Queens District Attorney John Santucci: ALICE SHOULD

BE BEHIND BARS. Beside a picture of Crimmins (now officially Mrs. Grace) about to enter her husband's white Cadillac, the paper quoted a juror who had helped convict her. 'They should lock her up and throw away the key.' Santucci announced his opposition to Crimmins's parole request, claiming that 'this defendant has not served adequate time for the crime of which she was convicted'. Over at the *Daily News*, columnist Pete Hamill denounced that 'smarmy' little story and jeered: 'Santucci is running for reelection; he knows a great irrelevant issue when he sees one.'

Then, at last, the newspapers gave it up. For the Alice Crimmins case, dredged up and recycled, was an embarrassment of history. Even the *Post* knew that the issue was no longer sex but class. Nobody cared anymore about Crimmins's bed partners; she was attacked not for sleeping with Anthony Grace (who cared whether they were married or not?) but for driving in a Cadillac, relaxing on board a 'yacht'. The Crimmins case had gone on too long. After twelve years even the most faithful tabloid reader began to ask: 'Why do they keep picking on her?'

So, on September 7, 1977, Alice Crimmins Grace was paroled. The board delayed it as long as they could. They sent her for a psychiatric examination. Then they 'exercised a seldom used option' and sent her for another psychiatric examination. Then, on September 9, 1977, they had to let her go. District Attorney Santucci tried to block the parole; a Queens assemblyman, who had been one of the prosecutors at the second Crimmins trial, blasted the decision. But it was perfectly legal; Crimmins, after thirty months in prison and nine months in the work-release facility, was free. Ironically, if she had never appealed her first conviction, she would have been eligible for parole six years earlier.

Alice Crimmins still wanted vindication, but her petition for a new trial was denied on November 1, 1977. So she remains a woman smashed in a society's shifting gears – too far ahead of her time for people to think her innocent, then too far behind for people to care if she were guilty. Many men made a lesson of her, and when they found (like John Santucci) that continuing the war on Alice Crimmins wouldn't win votes or promotions, they gave it up. But Alice Crimmins, unlike Ruth Snyder, never gave up; and she never lost track of what it had all been about. Before she was sentenced at her second trial she turned to the two prosecuting attorneys and said, 'Anything you people have done to me in the past . . . anything you are doing to me now . . . and anything you may do to me in the future can't be worse than what was done to me six years ago when my children were taken from me and killed. And I just hope and pray the world will see all your lying and scheming against me. And I just hope and pray to have the chance to put you all down some day for what you are. . .'

MARY HIGGINS CLARK

Edgar Smith –
The Human Copperhead

On Tuesday evening, March 4, 1957, my husband and I were in the den of our new home in New Jersey watching 'Sergeant Bilko' on television. It was a raw night with the incipient chill peculiar to March, a good night to be snugly at home with our four young children. When the program went off at 8.30, we began to chat about how glad we were that we'd made the move to New Jersey. Native New Yorkers, we'd loved apartment living in Manhattan, but the city wasn't the same anymore. Crime was on the increase there. How much better, we agreed, to have decided to raise our family in one of the small safe hamlets in northern New Jersey.

Even as we talked, a few miles away teenager Vickie Zielinski was saying good-bye to her friend, Barbara Nixon. They'd been doing their homework together. Small and slender, Vickie was a cheerleader at Ramsey High School. Her shoulder-length brown hair falling over her school jacket, her thick white bobby socks stuffed into penny loafers, her purse and school books in her arms, Vickie started the ten-minute walk home. Her fourteen-year-old sister, Myrna, was to meet her halfway.

Concentrating on her own homework, Myrna had to be reminded at twenty of nine that she was supposed to meet her sister. She ventured as far as the Nixons' house but nowhere along the way did she see her sister. Confirming with the Nixons that Vickie had left at 8.30, Myrna returned home. Her mother was annoyed but not alarmed. Maybe Vickie had met another girlfriend and gone off with her. Anthony Zielinski, a laborer, exhausted from his day's work, was already asleep. At 12.30, his panic-stricken wife finally roused him. Their daughter Vickie was missing.

The next day, the *Bergen Record*, northern New Jersey's largest newspaper carried the shocking headline, 'Girl Murdered in Mahwah'. The story began: 'Murder overtook a fifteen-year-old girl walking home on a Mahwah road last night. Her mother and father found her body near Fardale School this morning.'

So savagely had she been beaten that the Zielinskis thought they were staring down at the back of her head where hair had been pulled from her scalp. Instead they were looking at what had been the face of their pretty second child.

Two young men from the Mahwah area discussed the crime. Twenty-one-year-old Donald Hommell had dated Vickie. Twenty-three-year-old Edgar Smith, an ex-Marine, married and the father of an infant, knew her too. Occasionally he'd given her a ride home when he saw her walking. Donald said, 'When they get this guy, they'll probably hang him.'

'No,' Smith replied. 'He'll plead insanity.'

The Bergen County Prosecutor's office began asking about Vickie's friends. Their queries led them directly to Edgar Smith. At 11.30 the night of March 5, he was brought in for questioning. The following morning, he admitted the crime.

The confession. Smith's bloodstained shoes and pants. The bloodstains in the borrowed car he was driving. The blood-stained baseball bat that had been in the car and was found in the sandpit. The evidence was overwhelming. It appeared that the trial would be merely a formality: an open-and-shut case. There were few of us who did not expect Edgar Smith to be found guilty of first-degree murder. In 1957 in New Jersey that verdict could mean death in the electric chair.

Smith's speedy apprehension tended to quell our fears that a killer was loose in our area. But even so, for parents like us it could never be the same. The myth that by moving to the suburbs we could offer our children the quality of life we had enjoyed at their age was shattered forever. As the *Record* pointed out: 'There are very few women and girls on the streets after the sun goes down. The residents of the communities are not outspokenly angry at Edgar Smith. Rather they are deeply resentful that he has destroyed the bond of faith and trust that people of small towns place in one another.'

The Vickie Zielinski-Edgar Smith case compelled me from the first bulletin. The incredible viciousness of the crime haunted me. Suppose, someday, someone capable of that kind of evil stalked one of my daughters? The wanton selection of the victim. Edgar Smith had no plans to meet Vickie. She simply had had the incredible misfortune to leave her friend's home at the exact moment he cruised down the block. I was interested in knowing more about the mind of the man who was capable of such a monstrous act.

I had just begun my writing career. I could not conceive then how drastically it was to be influenced by the Edgar Smiths of this world.

From the first, the case attracted nationwide attention. Capital crimes often did and this one promised all the elements of drama; the violence of the murder . . . the young girl victim . . . the ex-Marine defendant. Their pictures ran side by side in newspapers all over the country; Victoria, smiling and vibrant in a short skirt and turtleneck sweater, her iceskates over her shoulder; Smith's mug shot portraying a sneering ne'er-do-well. He might have been impersonating a young Burt Lancaster, typecast as the villain.

But when he was led into Court, Smith's outward appearance had been altered to fit the image he would portray for the next twenty years. One reporter wrote: 'With his dark-rimmed glasses, sports jacket and slacks, he looks like a night school or college student listening to a lecture.'

His twenty-year-old wife, Patricia, attended every session. It was the era of the billowing skirt, the tiny hat, the spike heels. Pat Smith, demurely pretty, looked as though she had dressed for church as she came in carrying her infant daughter, Patti Ann, and took her seat in the first row.

Bergen County Prosecutor, Guy Calissi, tried the case. A former assistant prosecutor, John E. Selser, was retained for the defense. Widely respected County Judge Arthur J. O'Dea presided.

The jury selection was a long and tedious affair. The prosecution challenged any juror who did not believe in capital punishment, a usual procedure in a first-degree murder trial. Later journalists, William F. Buckley, Jr., among others, would scornfully suggest that Smith's rights had been violated by *not* including jurors opposed to capital punishment.

Today advocates of capital punishment are fighting to have it
restored in many states including New Jersey. Twenty years ago,
studying the pretrial publicity, I was struck by the 'will he get
the chair?' aspect of the headlines. Even then, long before I began
intensive research into crime, I decided that the death penalty
glamorized a murder case. Later in my research I came across a
statement of Supreme Court Justice Jackson. 'The death penalty,'
he said, 'completely bitches up the criminal law. It ties up the
judicial process with endless appeals and trials. It sentimentalizes
the judicial process. It sensationalizes justice.'

Nowhere were those words to be more clearly proven than in the
Edgar Smith case.

The trial began on May 15, 1957. In his opening statement,
Prosecutor Calissi told of Victoria leaving her friend's home:

> Smith passed her going in the opposite way. He noticed Victoria and she
> noticed him. He pulled down a short distance, backed into a drive-way
> and came back and picked her up and proceeded down Wyckoff Avenue
> toward the home of Victoria Zielinski, but instead of going all the way
> down, Smith turned onto Crescent Avenue Young Road and went down
> to what is called the sandpit. In the sandpit he pulled right into . . . he
> went right into the sandpit. They talked. Victoria talked about school but
> the defendant, Edgar Smith, didn't have school problems on his mind.
> He molested this girl immediately. He ripped up her sweater and he fon-
> dled her breast, this fifteen-year-old girl, and he bit her right breast. She
> refused his advances and she tried to get out of the car. He grabbed her
> by the wrist but she still released herself and started running. He finally
> caught up with her down on Fardale Avenue and he struck her with a
> blunt instrument. . . . He got her back into the sandpit and crushed her
> skull with a very heavy implement which we will offer in evidence. Her
> brains were spattered on the sand. In the sandpit he took that body, that
> mutilated body, he took it to the top of the knoll and dumped it down at
> the bottom of the knoll and then he proceeded to get into his car. . .

By the time the opening statement had been completed, the
atmosphere in the crowded courtroom was saddened and subdued.
Spectators sitting in the squeaky visitors' seats stared at Edgar Smith
who listened attentively to every word or cast furtive glances back
at the victim's mother who sat in stony-faced silence in the rear of
the room. Everyone wondered what Defense Attorney Selser could
possibly say to soften the horror of what they had just heard.

Selser readily admitted that Smith had picked up Victoria and driven her to the sandpit. He explained that Smith became outraged when Victoria told him that his wife was running around with another man. In his fury, he'd slapped her and she ran from the car. According to Selser, Vicky went up the road; another car came along with its lights off and Smith heard a commotion. Afraid that Vickie had been met by her father, he grabbed the baseball bat from the car to protect himself. But it was his friend, Donald Hommell, who returned with a badly bleeding Vicky. Selser continued:

> Smith dropped the bat on the ground and said to Hommell, 'What happened?' And Hommell said, 'She fell and struck her head.' Smith looked at her head . . . and it was bleeding badly and Smith said, 'Get in the car and I will take you to the doctor.' . . . And she got into the car and laid her head back on the back of the seat of the car . . . Don Hommell then grabbed her by the sleeve of the jacket she was wearing and yanked her out of the car and she fell to the ground head first with her feet still in the automobile and as she fell, her head bleeding as it was, went upon the right foot and trouser bottom of Smith's trousers and it became saturated with blood. The girl pulls herself up from the ground and Smith and Don Hommell helped her to her feet and Smith said to Hommell, 'She should go to a doctor,' and Hommell said, 'I'll take care of it; I'll take care of her, you go on.' Smith then got in his automobile and drove from the scene of the offense and drove on home to his trailer camp. . .

This was the defense. Edgar Smith, claiming that he had left a bleeding Vickie with an angry Donald Hommell in the sandpit where she met her death, had figured out a better defense than insanity, one that later the prosecutor would label 'the foulest, dirtiest legal trick that was ever pulled by a defendant'.

The trial lasted two weeks. The spectators heard Mary and Anthony Zielinski describe their search for their missing daughter, their finding of one of Vickie's loafers and her kerchief. Anthony Zielinski told his wife to phone for the police while he continued to search. Joined by a police captain they walked further into the sandpit and found Victoria's red gloves. They came across her broken locket. Then Anthony Zielinski looked down over the bank and cried, 'Mother dear, come here. I found her.'

The penny loafers, the gloves, the jacket, the tee-shirt, the saddlebag, the scarf, were placed side by side in the courtroom. The judge looked down at the saddlebag. It was exactly like the one his own fifteen-year-old daughter carried.

But Edgar Smith protested his innocence. He claimed his confession was a lie told because, 'I was afraid for my wife, afraid for my child and therefore I gave that statement.'

Donald Hommell was called a psychopathic liar by the defense.

Selser: 'You had been out with Vickie, had you not?'
Hommell: 'Casually, that is all.'
Selser: 'Do you remember saying to Smith on the drive from Ridgewood to the trailer court, "Don't forget, you have a baby"?'
Hommell: 'Definitely not, sir.'
Selser: 'Do you remember saying to him, "It would be unwise to mention my name"?'
Hommell: 'Definitely not, sir.'

John Selser, an attorney with a fine reputation, passionately believed in the innocence of his client. State Prosecutor Calissi passionately believed in Smith's guilt. But as he later commented, he not only had to convince the jury that Edgar Smith was guilty, he had to prove that Donald Hommell was innocent.

On May 28, 1957, the case went to the jury. It took the twelve men and women one hour and fifteen minutes to return a guilty verdict with no recommendation of mercy. When Judge O'Dea dismissed the jury he said, 'I first want to commend you on your verdict. If it had been the Court's decision without a jury I would have found the same as you do. . .'

On June 4, 1957, Edgar Smith was sentenced to 'the punishment and judgment of death at the hand of the Principal Keeper of the New Jersey State Prison at Trenton, New Jersey, during the week commencing Monday, July 15, 1957'.

The case was over. But in effect it had only begun. The death sentence was to gain for Smith notoriety and controversy that made him a cause célèbre. If there had not been a death penalty he would have vanished into the obscurity of prison and his many appeals would have gone unpublicized. But the carnival atmosphere that is engendered by the race to see if a man will beat the chair kept Smith front-page news. For the next fourteen years he lived on Death Row, as appeal after appeal was rejected. Excerpts from the endless file of headlines tell the story:

June 5, 1958: *Death House Visit on Wedding Date*
June 25, 1958: *Smith Murder Conviction Upheld by New Jersey Supreme Court*

August 22, 1958:   *Smith Case Will Return to State Supreme Court*
April 8, 1959:   *Selser Pleads for Murderer – Court Is Cool.* Chief Justice
  declares case is as complete as any he's seen.
May 4, 1959:   *Smith to Try Federal Court*
November 3, 1959:   *Smith Is Notified of Execution Date*
May 5, 1961:   *New Petition Filed by Smith's Lawyers*
June 5, 1961:   *Smith to Get Reply in Fall*

A few days later an editorial appeared. It pointed out that 'the
reluctance to execute speaks for itself.'

Significantly the last paragraph read: 'Legislation to abolish capital
punishment dies year after year in committee. Evidently we are not
yet quite ready to formalize our now fully developed horror. We do
the next best thing which is to defer our grisly ignominy and hope
the judges or at length the Governor can find a way to spare us. In
our hesitancy we have let our heart speak for our head. Perhaps the
day will come when we shall let our head return that compliment.'

March 5, 1964:   *Smith Awaits Execution for Murder Seven Years Ago*
March 17, 1964:   *Execution of Smith Set for Next Month*
April 18, 1964:   *Doomed Murderer Will Appeal Again*
June 3, 1964:   *Court Hears New Smith Appeal*

A December 26, 1964, editorial commented: 'Now Great Britain
has all but abolished the death penalty, perhaps by way of showing
that among the civilized nations of the world, she is still the serene
sovereign. . . The United States is still thinking in 19th century
terms on capital punishment.'

March 29, 1965:   *Smith's Time Running Out – Killer of Girl to go to Chair
  April 27th*
April 17, 1965:   *Execution Stay Granted Smith*
July 20, 1965:   *Smith Files Seventh Death Stay Petition*

In 1965 William F. Buckley, Jr., conservative candidate for mayor
of New York City, author, editor and television personality, learned
that Edgar Smith subscribed to his magazine, *The National Review*,
and began corresponding with him. Eventually Buckley became
Smith's champion and actively fought to win for him a new trial.

December 25, 1968:   *Smith's Tenth Christmas in Death House*

During his years in prison Smith had taken correspondence
courses, worked on his own defense, and now had written a book
entitled *Brief Against Death* which became a best-seller. Filled with

distorted facts and outright lies it arrogantly ridiculed the New
Jersey courts but did manage to implant some doubt in many
more minds of his guilt. In the book Smith again claimed that
Donald Hommell had been with Vickie in the sandpit when Smith
drove away.

December 29, 1970   *New Twist in Hearing for Smith*
'Unlike all of Smith's previous appeals, 18 in the last 12 years, this
hearing will require appearances by some of the witnesses who figured
in the case more than a decade ago. Earlier appeals had been decided
based on transcripts of Smith's original trial.'
September 12, 1971:   *The United States Supreme Court Agreed to Consider
Smith's Request for a New Trial . . .*
October 12, 1971:   *High Court Boosts Smith Over Hurdle*
February 4, 1971:   *Court Says No to Plea of Coercion*
February 10, 1971:   *He Couldn't Take It Anymore, Smith Says of Police
Tactics*
May 14, 1971:   *Smith Granted a New Trial*
October 15, 1971:   *Smith Will Be Tried in Bergen*
December 1, 1971:   *Kugler Blasts Uproar Over Smith*
'State Attorney General George F. Kugler says there is enough
evidence to convict Edgar H. Smith again of a murder committed
fourteen years ago.

'In a stinging response to the uproar over the case, Kugler told a
press conference in Trenton, "He just happens to be a clever guy
who knows how to get publicity." '

December 3, 1971:   *Man Smith Accused Loses Alibi Witness*
'A strange quirk of fate has killed an alibi witness for the man Edgar
Smith says murdered Victoria Zielinski. . . . Hommell testified at
Smith's first trial that at the approximate time the fifteen-year-old girl
was killed, he was drinking at Pelzer's Tavern in Mahwah. Hommell
said he was seen there by a friend, Charles R. Rockefeller of Ramsey.
Rockefeller, who corroborated Hommell's alibi, was killed November
21 in Middletown, New York, by a man later charged with drunken
driving and manslaughter. Ironically the man who helped send Edgar
Smith to Death Row was killed by a man named Smith – Thomas F.
Smith of Warwick, N.Y.'

Then on

December 12, 1971:   *Edgar Smith's 'I Did'*
'Edgar Smith rather than go on trial again for first degree murder
confessed to the killing of Victoria Zielinski. Judge Morris Pashman
asked: "Did you and you alone kill Victoria Zielinski?" Without pause,
in a barely audible voice, Smith answered, "I did." '

Resentenced to the time he had already served, Edgar Smith left the courtroom a free man. Outside the courthouse he entered the limousine of his patron, William Buckley, and was whisked to a television studio where on Buckley's program 'Firing Line' he repudiated the confession he had made under oath. 'What you saw wasn't justice, it was theater,' he said, smilingly, and then piously explained that the only reason he'd confessed was that his wife, Pat, was now remarried, his teenage daughter believed her stepfather was her natural father and he would not want to shatter the privacy of the family by bringing Pat back to New Jersey to testify at a new trial.

When he repudiated his original confession, he'd claimed that he feared Hommell would harm his wife and child if he involved him. Now, having confessed to the crime, he was once again using Pat and Patti Ann to muddy the truth.

Once free, Smith was treated with the same acclaim usually reserved for a war hero fresh out of the clutches of the enemy.

One headline read: *A Life Without Bars Awaits.*

One television reporter followed him down the streets of Manhattan, recording his comments on the sights, sounds, and smells of New York.

A year and a half later Edgar Smith wrote a book called *Getting Out* in which he ridiculed the Chief Judge of County Court, the Prosecutor, and members of the Prosecutor's staff. A reviewer from the *Washington Post* scathingly dismissed the book as 'rubbish'.

Through it all, the nineteen appeals, the plea bargaining, the follow-up, I stayed doggedly with the case. And reading over and over the details of that desperate uneven struggle in the sandpit, I wondered how Victoria's family could bear to have that scene vividly recreated every few months in newspaper headlines.

I wondered how Don Hommell could live a normal life with that accusing finger constantly pointing him out.

I had begun my own research into sex crimes and was appalled to learn how frequently the sex offender is highly intelligent, a pathological liar, persuasive, capable of deluding even the most astute psychiatrist, and a recidivist.

Edgar Smith seemed to fit that profile. He'd been arrested when he was fourteen for molesting a ten-year-old girl, another crime he'd always denied, claiming the girl was hysterical and – to quote him – 'had in the past accused other boys of the same offense, each time relating an essentially similar tale which had always proved to be untrue'.

I wondered if we had heard the last of Edgar Smith.

We had not. After his release from prison, Smith enjoyed brief fame as an author and college lecturer, basking in the attention.

But it didn't last. His third book was not well received. The writing assignments dwindled. His desirability as a lecturer faded. He married Paige Hiemer, a twenty-two-year-old girl from Ridgefield, New Jersey, and they moved to San Diego. Once again Smith began bouncing from job to job. He sold advertising copy and did the housework while Paige supported them by working as a bank teller.

Smith began to brood and on October 1, 1976, he drove to a deserted parking lot in Chula Vista, a town not far from San Diego, and waited for a woman to come along. A thirty-two-year-old housewife, Lefterlya Ozbun, finished work and came out to the parking lot where her husband was to pick her up. Wielding a six-inch knife, Smith forced her into his car. Struggling with the woman during a frantic fifteen-minute drive on the freeway, he stabbed her below the breast. She still managed to open the door and throw herself from the car.

Apprehended two weeks later, Smith admitted that he had often visited the Chula Vista sandpit to sit and think about raping a woman. He had once stalked a doctor's receptionist but did not approach her. Finally, as he waited in the parking lot Mrs. Ozbun came along.

Smith pleaded guilty to the California abduction. At his sentencing he also admitted unequivocally that he had killed Victoria Zielinski and that, yes, when he was fourteen, he had molested a ten-year-old girl in Oakland, New Jersey.

It was over. For Edgar Smith the possibility of parole seems unlikely ever. No doubt he will now sink into the obscurity of the convicted long-term or life prisoner who cannot be let loose in society again.

But I hope he has served one purpose. As advocates for capital punishment plead their case in the legislatures of nearly every state, his lesson is one that should be studied. Nineteen appeals . . . endless expense . . . endless burdens on the court . . . endless anguish for the families of his victims.

This is what we're letting ourselves in for again with the reinstituion of capital punishment. We are hoping by reviving it that it will be a deterrent to murder. In 1972 Edgar Smith was asked if he thought it was a deterrent. 'I don't think it makes much difference either way,' was his answer.

What if Smith, wily and clever as he was, had managed to convince people that Donald Hommell had been the real murderer of Victoria Zielinski? What if Donald Hommell had been found guilty of that crime while the death penalty was in effect?

The Edgar Smiths of this world need to be swiftly apprehended, swiftly tried and sentenced to long prison terms that stick. Proven recidivists like Edgar Smith should never be released to prey on society again. Victoria Zielinski's father is now sixty-five years old. Since Smith got out of jail in New Jersey in 1973, Anthony Zielinski had prayed that he would make some mistake, commit some crime that would put him behind bars again. After the sentencing in California, he said, 'A rattler will give you a warning when it's going to strike again. But a copperhead snake will never warn you. It'll strike a second and third time if you let it. Smith is a human copperhead.'

I agree. It is now more than twenty years since that evening when my interest in the Smith case led me into crime writing. Now with whatever influence I can exercise as a writer, I intend to protest the reinstatement of the death penalty. I've just completed a new novel. It's about a psychopathic killer who stalks young women. And it's about a nineteen-year-old boy who is going to die in the electric chair for a crime he did not commit.

CHRISTIANNA BRAND

Into a Thrilling Silence

What happens to a gallows when it is not in use? In Glasgow, at any rate, a hundred years ago, it was dismantled and packed away tidily in the prison, to be brought out and erected in Jail Square when occasion demanded. And tremendous occasions these public hangings were, with gay family parties gathering together for a day out, the great square crowded, side-shows, liquor stalls and a splendid time being had by one and all.

It could be on the fringe of such a crowd that we first meet the two protagonists in this case – an old man of somewhere round eighty, very spry for his years, and a young woman of twenty-six – a frail creature, rather pretty, with a lovely figure and a gentle, slightly plaintive manner. She is respectful but she evidently knows him well. They part and go their different ways. He may well push on towards the central scene; she will certainly hurry away from it.

And yet it is under these revolting circumstances that she herself may be hanged one day in the as yet undreamed of future – either he or she, for her defence will be that it was he who committed the murder of which she is accused: the brutal murder of her dearest friend.

The background was Glasgow – that lovely old city of sepia and smokey-blue-black with the brown waters of the Clyde running through its heart. Here, overlooking the river in the district known as the Broomielaw, Jessie M'Lachlan lived with her husband who was a sailor – his pay was thirty shillings a week – in a second floor 'house', two rooms and a kitchen. Then, as now, the city was seething with interest and vitality: for those were the days of the change-over from wood to iron, from sailing ships to steam.

The evening of Friday, 4th July, and 'a bonny clear night'. Her husband was away at sea and Jessie was putting her baby boy to bed. Her lodger, Mrs. Campbell, would keep an eye on him while she called to her friend Jess, up in Sandyford Place, Sauchiehall Street. Before her marriage, they had worked together as servants there, to a family called Fleming. Jess's full name was Jessie M'Pherson; she was about thirty-eight at this time, a big, brawny, good-looking woman. They were as warmly devoted as two affectionate sisters.

Jessie left her visit till late – in the hope that Grandpa would have gone to bed. The Fleming family consisted of John Fleming, a prosperous accountant, his sister, a son of twenty and two daughters – and Grandpa. Grandpa was the plague of Jess's life, a nasty, prying, lecherous old man who had, not very long ago, been obliged to confess to his kirk the sin of fornication and nowadays would not leave Jess unmolested. Now she was alone in the house with him, the family being away at their holiday place by the sea.

It was ten o'clock, therefore, before Jessie set out, walking part of the way with a friend. She wore a velvet bonnet, and a grey cloak over a brown Coberg dress; poor as she was, and she was so poor that many of her possessions spent most of their time in pawn, she still had a great fondness for pretty clothes.

Within a week, this brown Coberg dress had become one of the two main talking points in Scotland – and at last in the whole of the British Isles. The other was a dress also: a cinnamon-coloured dress trimmed with blue velvet. The second one had belonged to poor, murdered Jess.

Beneath the tall masts of the sailing ships walked Jessie with her friend, along the cobbles of the Broomielaw: parting from her at last and going on alone – going on alone in the twilight of a summer's evening, into a blackness of horror and mystery as dark and deep as the night was bright and fair.

An hour later, Mr. Littlejohn, who kept a liquor store in North Street close to the house in Sandyford Place, shut up his shop and went off to bed. At the same moment, two gossiping women observed a woman in a grey cloak coming out of the narrow lane that ran behind the houses in Sandyford Place; she disappeared into North Street and shortly re-appeared again and went back down the lane. At just the same time, another woman, a Miss M'Intyre, overheard a group of people close to 17, Sandyford Place, talking about moans which they thought they had heard coming from the basement there; and herself heard someone cry out, 'a moaning, doleful sound which rather frightened me', as she passed by the house. A couple mooning down Sandyford Place remarked that one of the servants must be 'catching it' down there. And in the early hours of the morning, three jolly sisters, rolling home from a wedding, noticed that in the dining-room of No. 17, the gasolier was alight. At about the same time, Mrs. M'Lachlan's lodger heard the child crying and went in and comforted him. His mother was not there; and since the lock was defective and the front door could not be opened from the outside, she could not have been back and gone out again.

At twenty to eight in the morning, the milkboy ran up the steps of No. 17 and rang the bell. After some delay, he heard the rattle of the chain coming off the door, and old Mr. Fleming poked out his head and said that 'they were for nae milk that day'. He appeared to be fully dressed. The boy and his master were astonished. No. 17 was never 'for nae milk' and the old man had never before answered the door; it would always be Jess, the maid, whom they knew well.

At nine o'clock Mrs. Campbell opened the door of the house in the Broomielaw to her landlady. Mrs. M'Lachlan made no comment, simply murmured her thanks and went down the corridor to her own room.

She was carrying a large bundle; and now she wore, not a brown Coberg dress but a cinnamon-coloured merino, trimmed with blue.

Saturday passed and Sunday and Monday. Old Mr. Fleming toddled about on his rounds – he had a little job rent-collecting for his son – and on Sunday went twice to the kirk. Several people called at the house in Sandyford Place, including a young man who came twice, asking to see Jess. She was out, said Mr. Fleming to all comers; he had no idea when she would be back. He showed a marked reluctance to let anyone down to the basement.

And Jessie meanwhile was spending a busy Saturday. Long over-due rent was suddenly paid up in full. A shaded poplin dress was brought out of the pawn-shop and replaced the cinnamon brown;

the cinnamon was taken in to be dyed, together with the grey cloak. And a black japanned box was purchased and later sent off to Ayr station 'to lie till called for'. A further small trunk was packed up and sealed and a little girl was paid a shilling to lug it up to the station and despatch it to Hamilton, also 'to lie till called for'. And a quantity of silver was pawned, all marked with an 'F'; and suddenly all over Glasgow, other pawn-shops yielded up their long-hoarded pledges at the chink of coin. That evening Jessie showed to Mrs. Campbell a little bonnet which she had bought for her boy.

On Monday afternoon at half past four, Mr. John Fleming and his son came home. They had left the rest of the family at their house by the sea.

On the way Mr. Fleming stopped to order some meat, young John going on ahead of him. The meat was delivered with such despatch that it arrived before young John did. His grandfather was at the door taking it in. John said, surprised: 'Where's Jess?'

'She's awa', she's cut,' said the old man, 'and the door of her bedroom's locked.' She must be away, he suggested, seeing friends. Young John knew jolly well that she was not away seeing friends; she was far too good and reliable to have gone off in that way. He began to feel 'very queer'.

Mr. Fleming arrived and together they all went down to the basement. In the kitchen, the fire was cheerfully burning but there was no sign of the servant and her door was indeed locked. The bedroom window giving on the area, was barred, but Mr. Fleming remembered – what the old man also knew quite well – that the pantry key fitted that door. He opened it and they all crowded in.

She lay on the floor, poor Jess! – her clothes pulled up over her head, as though she had been dragged along by the legs, concealing the terrible sight of no less than forty wounds on her face, head and hands, caused by some such sharp instrument as a cleaver. The room was in horrid confusion. The bed looked as though it had been slept in, the sheets and pillows damp, and marked, though not heavily, with blood. A clothes chest stood almost empty; the few things left in it looked 'as though they had been racked through with a bloody hand'.

Old Mr. Fleming lifted up horrified hands. 'All this time she's been lying here: and me in the house!'

One of the gossiping women who on the Friday night had seen the woman come out of Sandyford Lane and return there, was a Mrs. Walker; and into Mrs. Walker's shop now came running a policeman, needing a candle, for 'one of the servants had been got dead at Fleming's'. Mrs. Walker, though heavily pregnant, thoughtfully snatched up a box of matches and ran after him, in case they should need those too.

She found quite a little crowd assembled in the hall, listening in amazement to old Fleming's story of how, though the maid had been missing since the Saturday morning, he had thought nothing of it, told no one, instituted no search. 'Did you hear no noise that night?' asked Mrs. Walker.

'Oh, ay,' said the old gentleman. 'I heard some squeals.' He had risen on his elbow, he added, and looked at his watch and it had been just four o'clock.

Astonishment! 'When you were upon your elbow,' cried Mrs. Walker, 'could you no' have got up and cried down what was the matter?'

But Mr. Fleming said he hadna thocht of that.

Mrs. Walker – it was all no business of hers, whatsoever – made a little tour of the basement. And here something very strange was observable. In the kitchen, part of the stone floor had been washed – so recently as to be still damp. And something had been dragged from the kitchen to the bedroom and the marks had been washed away – and here too it was still quite damp. Within the mercifully closed door of the bedroom, a patch of the floor also had been washed, though this was perfectly dry. Outside the washed area, there were three footprints.

The prints in blood of a woman's naked foot.

On the following day, the Tuesday, the first news of the murder appeared briefly in the papers; and on that day Jessie M'Lachlan went by train to Hamilton. She reclaimed from the station the small trunk which the child had sent off, and from it took a large bundle. It was a hot, dusty day but she wandered away with it into the fields beyond the town. When she came wearily back, she was carrying no bundle.

On the following morning, old Fleming was taken into custody on suspicion of murder. That night, Jessie's husband, James, came home from sea.

Now whispering began and there grew to be an atmosphere of unease and fear in the home in the Broomielaw. Policemen drifted in and out making casual enquiries. Had not Jessie been a friend of the dead woman? Was it not true that she'd been intending to visit her that night? Could she help with descriptions of her dead friend's possessions? – all her best clothes, it seemed, were missing from her clothes chest – including a cinnamon-coloured merino, trimmed with blue. She held an anxious confabulation with her husband. Jess, she told him, had recently sent her some clothes to get altered and when she'd heard of the murder, she'd been afraid to be found with them in her possession. She had packed them into a japanned tin box and sent them to Ayr station 'to lie till called for'. Could James get them back from there and take them somewhere safer? He had a sister in Greenock – she would keep the box for him.

James got the box back and sent it to his sister's; but now a pawnbroker came forward, handed in to the police the silver marked with an 'F' which had been pawned on the morning after the murder at Mr. Fleming's house; described the woman who had pawned it. 'That's unco' like you,' said James to his wife. 'It's ower like me,' said poor Jessie. Terrified, he hurried back to his sister's house; the box was opened and one by one on the bed were laid the clothes missing from Jess M'Pherson's room. We can imagine the frantic discussion between him and his large family of somewhat over-powering sisters. It ended in defeat for Jessie; next morning the box was packed up again and re-addressed – in care of the police.

On the Sunday, a cab arrived at the Broomielaw; and Jessie and her husband, both, were driven away, charged with theft and murder.

So now she was a prisoner – caged up, helpless, this gentle, frail and charming creature – no one was ever found to say a word against her – charged with having brutally murdered her beloved friend for, almost literally, a handful of silver, and a few worn clothes;

and far and wide the country became divided, for or against her, for or against the old man. The Press took violently partisan sides, friendships were broken, families rent with civil war between the Flemingites and the M'Lachlanites. For many, many months the mystery was to remain a *cause celèbre*.

James M'Lachlan was questioned and immediately released; he had been with his ship during all the relevant time. She, faced with relentless and provocative questioning, made one wild statement after another, packed with evasions and lies. But the burden of it all was clear. She had not killed poor Jess, had been nowhere near the house that night; and anyway, had nothing to worry about really, for 'old Fleming will surely clear me'. She knew the old man well, having worked so long with Jess in the house in Sandyford Place.

But old Mr. Fleming repudiated her utterly; and, still hale and hearty, entirely unmoved by his invidious position – nine days after his first incarceration was suddenly set free.

Now three new protagonists appear upon the scene: three young lawyers charged with Jessie M'Lachlan's defence. Of the three, Mr Dixon was to acquire through it at last a somewhat dubious fame; but at the outset they all believed privately that their client was guilty and her hopes of escaping justice, exceedingly low. It was a fearful bore when she sent yet again for one of them to visit her in prison. In view of Mr. Fleming's release, her message said, she would like to make a new statement.

Mr. Dixon went off reluctantly to see her. When he got back, the whole fantastic business had suddenly taken on a new interest, was lit with enthusiasm and hope. In their frowsty offices, they burned the midnight oil, into the early hours of the morning paced the empty streets, still in talk and argument, canvassing the opinion of legal friends, planning the defence. The splendid young barrister, Mr. Rutherford Clark, was briefed and had soon caught fire from the enthusiasm of the three in their championship of Jessie. They pored over every line of her statement – it was true, it must be true! And yet. . . . She had made four different statements already to the police, none of which, by her own present admission, *could* be true; if she failed to prove this one, it would go very hard with her. They compromised at last: the defence should be that she had not been near the house that night – for surely there was no prove-able evidence to show that she had? Should this fail, then, when she was asked if she had anything to say before sentence was pronounced – she could fall back upon this statement. It was taking a chance, a very big chance; but this chance they would have to take.

This may be the place to say that the verdict when it came was unequivocal: there was no question of collusion, nor any recourse to the invidious Scottish evasion of Not Proven. Guilty – or Not Guilty. The nation held its breath.

In a packed courtroom, with a vast mob battling and surging in the square outside, deathly pale but controlled and quiet, Jessie M'Lachlan, in September, 1862, for three and a half days, stood her trial; each day lasting, with brief intervals, eleven hours. She wore a straw bonnet trimmed with white ribbons, and a lilac gown.

The trial was remarkable – almost unique – for this: that the defence was that the crime had in fact been committed by the principal witness for the prosecution – namely Old Fleming.

The case built up against him: that his advances to Jess had been, as usual, repelled, that she had threatened to inform against him, that in a struggle he had killed her; that he had faked a robbery and taken the silver to Jessie M'Lachlan, with an excuse, asking her to pawn it. (This would account for her possession of money on the day following the murder.) But no robbery had in fact taken place, for the back door had been locked and the milk boy had heard the rattle as the chain was taken down from the front door. . .

The old gentleman bore his cross-examination with fortitude – secure, no doubt, in the unbounded partisanship of the judge. Lord Deas was a great judge; but his conduct of this case was biased beyond belief and it was now that he acquired the nickname of Lord Death.

In the witness box, Mr. Fleming's age shot up suddenly from seventy-eight to eighty-seven, and he had as suddenly grown very deaf and short-sighted: too frail a figure, altogether, in fact, to have made so appalling an attack as had been suggested, upon a big, brawny young woman. Faced with facts, he went off into garrulities and non sequitors which soon had Counsel as much muddled up as he appeared to be himself. He had – he hadn't – he had – he hadn't

– opened the door to the milkboy that morning; he had – he hadn't –
he had – he hadn't – been fully dressed at the time. 'She didna come
up that morning and I was surprised she didna come. I wearied very
much for her. I lay still till nine o'clock, then I raise and put on ma
claes. I forget whether I washed masel before I went down; but I
gaed to her door and gied three chaps that way. . . .' He knocked
three times with his knuckles on the ledge of the witness box. But
he could not explain how he had failed to observe marks of blood
all about the house, nor why blood-stained floors should have been
washed so recently that on the Monday morning they were not yet
dry; nor why, had Jessie been the murderer she should have gone
to the trouble and risk of staying to wash them. Nor why, during
the three days of Jess's absence he had mentioned it to no one; and
been anxious to prevent anyone from going down to the basement.

Nor how it had come about that the injuries to the dead woman
appeared to have been inflicted in two stages; nor why at some time
the face and neck should have been bathed. . .

In 1862, of course, the accused could not go into the witness box
in her own defence. Mr. Rutherford Clark must battle for his client
unaided: the intended visit to Jess, the return next morning, having
been out all night, and wearing a dress that had belonged to Jess;
the disposal of the contents of the clothes-chest from Jess's room;
the discovery, hidden about the fields outside Hamilton which she
had visited soon after the murder, of three petticoats, one of which
had belonged to Jess, the other two being her own; and a brown
Coberg dress – all blood-stained and torn into shreds. All, all to be
somehow explained away; and one fact made credible, which fact
certainly was not true – that she had been nowhere near Sandyford
Place that night.

Three days and a half of trial: almost forty hours of standing there
in the dock. . . . The jury took just fifteen minutes to make up their
minds. Verdict unanimous: Guilty.

'The deathly pallor of her countenance seemed to increase,' says
a contemporary record, 'but the same strength of will she had
heretofore displayed was again shown . . .' Her advisers went over
to her, placed a paper before her. She took it up as though to start
reading, but her courage failed her. She gave it back to Mr Clark
and raised her white face to the judge. 'My lord, I desire to have

it read.' And she cried out, distinct and clear: 'I am as innocent as my child who is only three years old at this date.'

Mr. Rutherford Clark took the paper from her and, standing there, one arm propped on the high ledge of the dock, 'into a thrilling silence' read out the statement she had made to her young solicitor in her prison cell two months ago.

The truth was, said the statement, that she *had* gone to Sandyford Place that night. The old man was still up, sitting in the kitchen with Jess. He asked her to go for half a mutchkin of whisky and she put on her cloak and went; but the shop was closed.

When she got back she found to her horror her friend Jess, lying moaning dreadfully on the floor of her bedroom, with three terrible wounds across her face. She bathed the injuries and got her on to her bed. She would have gone for a doctor but Jess would not be left. And the old man refused to go. If a doctor came all would be known; and he fetched a Bible and with many promises of benefits to come, made them both swear never to tell what had happened that night. He brought water and a cloth and began crawling about the floor washing out the marks of blood; but he slipped and the water was tipped all over Jessie's feet; she took off her boots to dry and so, doubtless, made the blood-stained footprints later found on the unwashed part of the floor. Jess whispered to her that the old man was afraid that she would complain of him to his son; he had arrived home one night 'gie 'en tipsy' and later come to her bed and tried to 'use liberties with her'. But she would never really have told; she would have been too much ashamed.

Jessie sat with her quietly by the bedside; but at two o'clock she complained of being cold and wanted to go and sit by the fire. They got her into the kitchen and arranged a bed of cushions for her in front of the grate; but she grew steadily worse and at last Jessie insisted upon going to get help. Her skirts were still wet and bedraggled where the water had been spilt and she took down Jessie's cinnamon merino from its hook and slipped it on over her own dress; she was a great deal smaller than Jess. The old man tried to prevent her but she ran off up the stairs to the front door.

The door was locked and the key had been removed; and as she stood uncertain, she heard a sound that brought her flying down again. She stood paralysed with terror at the foot of the stairs: and saw through the kitchen door the terrible rise and fall of the cleaver – silencing Jess for ever.

Petrified with fear, she turned to escape up the stairs again; but he came out and with his bloody hands grasped at her skirts. Jess had been going to die anyway, he said; and now they were both in it together. If she told, he would deny it all and charge her with the crime. They must stand by one another and the best thing to do would to make it appear a burglary. She sat stunned and terrified in the kitchen while he dragged the poor corpse through into the bedroom, collected silver and clothes, explained to her how to dispose of them: gave her money to buy boxes, make journeys. In fear of her life, she swore silence, promised obedience; still sitting there in the kitchen as the hours went by, too sick and shocked, frightened and dazed to move. She was still there when, at twenty to eight, the milkboy rang the bell.

At half past eight, creeping by round-about ways, she dragged herself home. She was still wearing the cinnamon merino dress.

Every word of this statement, fits in with the facts; and many of the facts, much of the case being built up against her, could not have been known to Jessie when she made it. The two gossiping women who had seen a woman in a grey cloak go round the corner to North Street – just at eleven o'clock when the spirits store had closed – and return again. The light seen in the dining-room at the time she had said the old man was up there collecting silver; the fact that he had been up and fully dressed when the milkboy called. The two separate attacks, the bathing of the wounds between the two attacks; the marks of blood on the bed, consistent with the minor injuries to the face, the washing of the floors: the floor in the bedroom dry by the Monday morning, those outside it washed long after the murder and still damp; the naked footprints in the room. These and many, many minor points; but above all a fact which did not appear in court, was not known till after the trial, which she could have known nothing of: a surely conclusive fact which, however, has never till now been observed. Moans were heard coming from the basement bedroom at the time that Jessie was out on her errand to North Street. If it be accepted as inconceivable that she should have left Jess lying on the floor of her room, half killed and noisily moaning, while she popped out around the corner for a dram – then her story must be true; it was while she was absent that the first attack was made.

The jury had taken fifteen minutes to find her guilty. The judge took just thirty seconds to consider her defence. Such a tarradiddle of wicked nonsense he had never heard in his life. He picked up the triangle of material that is called the Black Cap and, in the Scottish manner, held it above his head; and so holding it, pronounced the terrible Scottish sentence of death which ends with the words 'which is pronounced for Doom'. He added the traditional prayer that God Almighty have mercy on her soul. She whispered into the stunned silence of the Court: 'Mercy! Aye, He'll hae mercy: for I'm innocent.'

A tremendous upheaval of public indignation ensued, though Old Fleming still had his large following of equally fervid supporters. He was having a difficult time, hooted and stoned in the streets, but he bore it with his usual affable equanimity and apparently rather enjoyed his notoriety. On either side, activity was frantic for though he could not now be brought to trial, any alteration in the verdict against Jessie M'Lachlan must tacitly accuse him of the murder. An enquiry was set up into the facts presented by the statement, a stay of execution granted for a limited period. . . .

With that period expiring and just five days to go before her public hanging, Mrs. M'Lachlan was visited in the comdemned cell by her Champion of Champions, Mr. Dixon. He had unearthed some evidence that Old Fleming had been seen at the front door of No. 17 in the early hours of the morning. Could that be true?

Jessie looked him limpidly in the face; she said no, it couldn't possibly be true. 'I may just as weel tell ye – the auld man wasna' there at a'.'

'Wasn't *there*?' said Mr Dixon. 'What do you mean?'

What she meant, said Jessie, was that she had not seen Mr. Fleming at all that night. 'He'd be awa' in his bed.'

And she launched out into a brand new story; the last story of Jessie M'Lachlan as to the events of that fatal night.

The fact was, she said, that she and Jess had taken too much to drink; and Jess, who was a great one for laudanum had given her some. The next thing she remembered was Jess crying out, 'Jessie, Jessie, what are you doing?' and then she was crawling about on her hands and knees in the darkness, but where she was or what she was doing she did not know. . .

Mr. Dixon crept away from the prison a defeated man. At a dozen points her new story fails to hold water, but it convinced him at least and from that moment he went over to the enemy. She was 'a damnable woman who all that night was ranging the house for what answered her'. The old man was innocent; the famous statment was all a lie.

The Home Secretary evidently did not entirely agree; a few days later his decision was made known. Jessie M'Lachlan was innocent of the murder but had been a constrained witness of its commission and must be given justice accordingly.

In other words her story was true.

His idea of justice under these circumstances – while the murderer went free – was penal servitude for life.

Down the years comes ringing Jessie's terrible cry: 'And I'm tae be kept in jail a' my days?'

And so she lived out her long tragedy, her child in the care of relatives, her husband emigrated and gone away, leaving her there alone – a model prisoner, quiet, reserved, mixing not at all with her terrible fellow inmates – 'caged tigresses' they were called by a prison officer of the day; throughout it all steadily protecting her innocence.

A 'bonny clear summer's night' in Glasgow, a hundred years ago – and a harmless, good-natured woman done violently to death.

Did the senile admirer strike her down for fear of what she would tell? Did the gentle friend turn to ferocious murder for love of what she possessed?

Anyone Could
do it . . .

PAMELA SMITH

Perfect Murderers

Every three days in Britain a woman dies at the hands of her husband, cohabitee or lover, or a man with whom she's had such a relationship. Most of these cases of murder or manslaughter don't make news, largely because they often seem to be provoked by the day-to-day pressures of living and the men who commit the crimes are, at first sight, quite unremarkable. They are usually what the world describes as 'model husbands' – quiet, solicitous, even retiring, men.

Eight years ago, Graham, a well-respected teacher, killed his wife and her lover. He says that he had never been violent before: 'It is not raving maniacs that kill, it is people who are inadequate to the stresses of life and finally crumple in an awful, destructive way.'

Graham is quite typical of the great majority of men who kill their spouses. Only about one in five are psychopaths or violent men. Inevitably, of course, a man who is persistently beating his wife, or children, will sometimes kill them, but, the majority of people who actually kill have no history of aggressive behaviour.

Tony Black, formerly the chief psychologist at Broadmoor Hospital, spent much of his career working with domestic killers. He explains that the typical killer is most likely to be a quiet, retiring person, who wants to be accepted socially and may have difficulty expressing or identifying emotions. 'Many have never felt able to lose their temper and when they kill it is a disastrous attempt to express their feelings after a long period of pressure.'

But why do these people kill in circumstances where many others wouldn't? Tony Black describes it as rather like mixing gunpowder. We all have the same elements which give us the potential to kill,

239

but just as the elements of gunpowder have to be mixed in the right – or wrong – proportions before it will explode, so the mix of elements and circumstances in people's lives must attain a critical match. This, in fact, applies equally to men and women, although the mixture of elements in women seems to make them less likely to kill. Women are also less likely to be able to kill with their bare hands; one critical element is to have an effective weapon to hand.

I have interviewed 18 people who have killed – 14 men and four women. When I began meeting them, I was sceptical about Tony Black's theory that killers were non-aggressive and over-controlled, but with one frightening exception, they were all, regardless of their class or gender, polite, introverted, 'gentle' people.

The men were from a broad social spectrum: two had university degrees, three were farmers, six had been in manual work and two were professional. One killed during an armed robbery, but only one of the others had ever been violent before. They were all guarded about expressing their opinions and particularly their emotions.

Six had strangled their victims, two battered them to death, four shot them, one stabbed them and one set fire to them. One of them had cut up his wife after he killed her and distributed her around London. With an ironic similarity to the statistical pattern, two of them I believed to be psychopathic; the others were, on the whole, sad people with broken lives.

Two of them – Graham and Peter – best exemplified most of the elements common to them all and were better able to articulate their feelings.

Graham was 31 when he killed. He and his wife had been married for a period of five years: 'I couldn't have in my wildest dreams imagined that I was capable of killing anyone and the way I see it happening was a whole chain of events that ran out of control, an effect where $1+1+1+1$ doesn't equal four, but maybe 20 or 50, it wasn't additive, it was like building a house of cards and the final card causing the whole house of cards to collapse.

Peter was 61 when he killed his wife after they had been married for 42 years. He had a career of caring jobs, he had been a mental nurse and a fireman. In 1976, he was awarded the 'Mr Perfect' title by the local paper for the way he looked after his family. 'I can honestly say I have never been violent in my life. I've never struck anybody. I just don't like violence.'

What was it that caused these two well-respected, law-abiding men to commit murder? In some senses it is a very British condition. The socially admired stereotype of man who is always seen to cope, who is never seen to be over-emotional, can for some people be an inappropriate way of life.

I first met Graham three years ago, not long after he had left the secure hospital. He was then 36 and said he felt like a tree that had lost its leaves and was waiting for spring. He is classically good-looking, tall and dark, and he'd obviously been an attractive, thoughtful and charismatic person. But he was then pale and unable to look anyone in the eye. He is now stronger; he's taken an MSc course and has had two significant relationships with women, but his life is still not workable. At the centre he still feels frozen in time, aware that he and others can only see him for what he's done, not for who he is.

Graham grew up in a middle-class family where his father was prone to violent outbursts. After studying agriculture at university, Graham went into teaching in the third world. He had no shortage of girl-friends. In 1975, he met his wife Ellie at a party and married her within a couple of weeks. She was French and Graham found her 'fey, and light-hearted, and good fun to be with. She was very beautiful to look at'.

After five happy years a disastrous chain of events began at Christmas 1979. Graham's father discovered he had a brain tumour and Graham gave up a good job to help nurse him. After his father died, they moved temporarily to Spain and lost their house through letting it to people who failed to pay the rent. Graham then took a demanding housemaster's post at a residential school in Yorkshire and Ellie, who took a job at the local pub, discovered a lump in her breast. Graham was stressed from the previous year's traumas and very busy at the school. He found it difficult to spend time with her.

Ellie met a local farmer, who was older, settled and supportive and they decided to live together. Graham was devastated. He went to see all his family trying to sort himself out. A few days before the killings he even called into a psychiatric hospital and said he felt out of control. They suggested admitting him, but instead he tried once more to persuade Ellie to come back.

She was absolutely determined to stay with David. Graham locked himself in his room so no one could see the state he was in. After three sleepless nights he took the remains of a bottle of sleeping pills which simply induced a trance-like state. He decided he would kill himself in Ellie and David's house to make them feel guilty. He broke in when they were out and went into the bedroom – on the bed were two frogs that he and Ellie had had in their bedroom. Graham had been called 'froggy' at school because he was a high jumper and Ellie had been his little frog because she was French. The frogs were in a copulating position.

At that point Graham's house of cards collapsed. There was a crucial switch from wanting to kill himself to wanting to kill them. He waited until they got back and when Ellie came home alone he stabbed her with a knife from the kitchen. When David came home he shot him with David's own gun.

Graham's verdict in court was manslaughter on the grounds of provocation. He was on remand for a year and, surprisingly, given the verdict was provocation, finally sentenced to be confined to a secure hospital for an indeterminate period. He spent some time in a regional secure unit and was finally transferred to Park Lane Hospital in Liverpool where he was given support and help from the staff who felt he was fit to be conditionally released after three years there. In all he served four years.

Does Graham have any insight into why he killed? 'If people don't regard themselves as loveable, if they are without a network of friends for support, if they grit their teeth and don't reveal when they're struggling, they are brittle and vulnerable to breaking. That would have described me.'

There are rarely common circumstances, or motives behind domestic killings, but one personality thread which seems to emerge is an inability to deal with pressure. Tony Black: 'They seem to ignore the situation around them. Most normally adjusted and coping people would deal non-aggressively with moderate levels of provocation, but respond aggressively to higher levels of provocation. Because these people tend to repress or inhibit moderate reaction, when they finally react, their response is extreme and uncharacteristic.'

When I met Peter I was struck by how much his story fitted Tony Black's analysis. He is now 65, charming and articulate, and lives alone in an immaculate flat in central London. He is socially aware and an important factor in deciding to talk publicly was his sense of social duty.

Born in 1924, Peter grew up in an army family and lied about his age to get into the army. He was just 19 when he met his wife, Maureen. He had left the army and they were both nursing. Despite being an ex-soldier he hadn't had much experience of girls. Maureen became pregnant. She was Irish, both were devout Catholics and they automatically married. Not long after, Maureen gave birth to twins prematurely.

One of the twins was born with spina bifida. From the age of 19 Maureen and Peter were having to deal with the financial pressures of an instant family and the constant treatment for spina bifida. Eight years later, after their third child was born, Maureen developed a cancerous lump above her knee and within a week her right leg was amputated. She had been an active person and back in Ireland she had been a ballroom dancing champion. It was heartbreaking for her not to be able to dance.

Peter was left to run the home and cope with more than one job. He had three heart attacks in ten years. The strain was also telling on Maureen. In 1972, after the children had left home and Peter's second heart attack, she started drinking heavily. She had always had a fiery temperament, but Peter found it difficult to deal with the combination of the two.

Throughout, Peter never admitted to the outside world that they weren't coping. It was four years after Maureen started drinking heavily that the local paper awarded him 'Mr Perfect' for the way he had 'overcome the family difficulties'. But Peter wasn't coping: 'I had to get up in the morning, put on an outside face with a smile on it and go out to work again, all the time worrying what I was going to walk into when I walked back into the house again at night.'

Christmas 1981, Peter claims, was no more stressful than any other week for the previous 40 years. They were staying with their daughter in her pub in the country. Peter was working as a theatre fireman and had to be back in London for work on Boxing Day. Maureen was staying behind. So on Christmas day he left the party and went to bed.

At three o'clock in the morning Maureen woke him. The party had deteriorated into a drunken row and she insisted on leaving. Peter loaded the car: 'Coming back on the North Circular road, the most horrible thing happened to me. I ran over a cat . . . I love animals and cats especially and it shook me up a little.'

Peter didn't sleep that night and went straight on duty. He didn't talk about the home situation with anyone. That evening Maureen was subdued, and they decided to go for a drive the next day.

'She'd been as good as gold while we were out, no arguments, no fighting, but suddenly as we were coming to within half a mile of home she started raving at me, hitting me while I was driving. I said, "Oh you must stop this."

'I got her home and she started on and on raving and accused me of assaulting her and doing all sorts of things . . . and she picks up the phone, just smashes it down on the glass topped table and then insists I get it fixed . . . and she was raving on at me, calling me all the names under the sun, accusing me of going with women – and men – of all things. I get to the door and she comes up, I'm coming with you. I thought, God, and outside . . . just in the doorway there she started yelling out to the neighbours, telling them all about me and . . . saying all the most foul things of what I was doing with these men up at the theatre and it really upset me because I'm so heterosexual you wouldn't believe it and I think it really did upset me . . . and that's when it happened . . . I strangled her.'

Peter turned out the lights on the Christmas tree, had a drink of water and went to the police station to tell them he'd killed his wife.

When the case came to court people who had known Peter wrote giving him character references. He was given a verdict of provocation and a one year prison sentence, suspended for two years.

Does he understand why it happened? 'It comes back to the old question about straws that break camels' backs. I suffered a stressful situation for a long, long period. Forty-two years it took for that final break to come and maybe with other people it may have come much earlier, I don't know, it may not have happened at all.'

Both Peter and Graham, in common with all the others I met, had been brought up to believe that getting upset was a sign of weakness. The fact that women find it easier to accept they are vulnerable may be another factor to explain why less of them get to the pitch where they can kill. Interestingly, all the four women I spoke to had been brought up in the stiff-upper lip tradition.

Can a true punishment be defined? For Peter and Graham private torment far outweighs public retribution. Peter: 'The law thought that I didn't need to pay for it by imprisonment and I was released, but my punishment will last me all my life because I've got a cross that I'll bear to the day I die.' 'Hanging would have been the easier option,' says Graham.

One third of murder suspects commit suicide before they come to trial or soon after.

Sources and Acknowledgements

Kurt Vonnegut, 'There's a Maniac Out There,'. from *Wampeters, Foma and Grandfalloons* (Delta, 1975), copyright © 1965 by Kurt Vonnegut. Reprinted by permission of Bantam/Doubleday/Dell Publishing Group, Inc.

Truman Capote, 'Then It All Came Down'. from *Music For Chameleons* (Hamish Hamilton, 1981), copyright © 1975 by Truman Capote. Reprinted by permission of Random House, Inc.

Colin Wilson, 'Dennis Nilsen', from *The Encyclopaedia of Modern Murder* by Colin Wilson and Donald Seaman (Pan, 1983), copyright © 1983 by Colin Wilson and Donald Seaman. Reprinted by permission of David Bolt Associates.

Joe Eszterhas, 'Charlie Simpson's Apocalypse', from *Rolling Stone*, collected in *The New Journalism*, ed. Tom Wolfe and E. W. Johnson (Picador, 1975), copyright © 1972 by Joe Eszterhas. Reprinted by permission of Picador/Pan Books Ltd.

Amanda Mitchison, 'In the Grip of Murder', and Matrick Marnham, 'The Devils of Nancy', from *The Independent Magazine*. Reprinted by permission of The Independent Newspaper Publishing PLC.

Brian Masters, 'Fiona Jones', from *The Evening Standard*. Reprinted by permission of The Evening Standard Ltd.

Martin Amis, 'The Case of Claus Von Bulow' and 'The Killings in Atlanta', from *The Observer Magazine*, collected in *The Moronic Inferno* (Cape, 1986), copyright © 1981, 1983 by Martin Amis. Reprinted by permission of Random Century Group.

Clancy Sigal, 'Brando—A Family Affair' from *The Observer Magazine*, copyright © 1990 by *The Observer*. Reprinted by permission of The Observer Ltd.

Robert Rand, 'Nightmare on Elm Drive', from *The Guardian*, copyright © 1990 by *The Guardian*. Reprinted by permission of Guardian News Service Ltd.

Jay Robert Nash, 'A "Wronged" Woman's Fury', from *Murder Among The Mighty* (Delacorte, 1983), copyright © 1983 by Jay Robert Nash. Reprinted by permission of Bantam/Doubleday/Dell Publishing Group, Inc.

Joan Didion, 'Some Dreamers of the Golden Dream', from *The Saturday Evening Post*, collected in *Slouching Towards Bethlehem* (Deutsch, 1973) copyright © 1971 by Joan Didion. Reprinted by permission of André Deutsch Ltd and William Morris Agency, Inc.

Ann Jones, 'Alice Crimmins', from *Women Who Kill* (Ballantine, 1980), copyright © 1980 by Ann Jones. Reprinted by permission of Henry Holt and Company, Inc.

Mary Higgins Clarke, 'Edgar Smith, the Human Copperhead', from *I, Witness*, ed. Brian Garfield (Times Books, 1978), copyright © 1978 by Mary Higgins Clarke. Reprinted by permission of McIntosh and Otis, Inc.

Christianna Brand, 'Into a Thrilling Silence', from *Blood On My Mind*, ed. H. R. F. Keating (Macmillan, 1972), copyright © 1972 by Christianna Brand. Reprinted by permission of A. M. Heath & Co., Ltd.

Pamela Smith, 'Perfect Murderers', from *The New Statesman*, copyright © 1989 by Pamela Smith. Reprinted by permission of The Observer Cover Stories.